VISITING UTOPIAN COMMUNITIES

VISITING UTOPIAN COMMUNITIES

A Guide to the Shakers, Moravians, and Others

Gerald and Patricia Gutek

University of South Carolina Press

Published in Columbia, South Carolina, by the
University of South Carolina Press

Manufactured in the United States of America

02 01 00 99 98   5 4 3 2 1

Library of Congress Cataloging-in-Publication Data

Gutek, Gerald Lee.
  America's historic utopian communities : a travel guide /
Gerald and Patricia Gutek.
    p. cm.
  Includes index.
  ISBN 1-57003-210-6
  1. Utopian socialism—United States—History. 2. Utopias—
United States—History. 3. Communitarianism—United States—
History. I. Gutek, Patricia, 1941–   . II. Title
  HX653.G87   1998
  335'.973—dc21   97-4635

CONTENTS

INTRODUCTION

In the nineteenth century, a number of communities were organized by Americans who believed that they could create perfect places in which to live—utopias. Some people were utopian idealists who thought that they could actually create a heaven on earth. They would not accept the imperfection of human society and sought to construct their own version of utopia. Others were members of religious societies who wished to create sacred cities of holy people who would, with eager anticipation, await the imminent Second Coming of Jesus Christ.

The word utopia, from Thomas More's book *Utopia* (1516), refers to an ideal world that is to be found nowhere. In American history, "utopia" needs to be expanded to include the concept of communitarianism, a societal arrangement in which property is owned jointly by a group rather than by individuals.

American communitarianism has had two broad currents—one secular and the other religious. Both strands of communitarians created social environments, towns, in which members lived according to a shared set of beliefs about human nature and society and had a communal economy without ownership of private property. Historically, communities established by religious communitarians endured longer than did those of secular groups.

Utopian communities were instituted by religious communitarian societies—the Shakers, the Harmonists, the Separatists at Zoar, and the Inspirationists at Amana—whose members, as true believers, considered themselves to be a separate and consecrated people who were to live apart from a sinful world. As a chosen people, they were to build a city of God and await the Second Coming of Jesus Christ, which would usher in the thousand-year millennium of harmony, peace, and holiness.

Religious communitarians were children of the Protestant Reformation, especially its Anabaptist wing. For them, human nature was a product of Divine Creation, a given, as stated in Genesis, and not something to be refashioned by man-made ideology. Human beings were sinful by nature, but certain elect persons might be redeemed and perfected by faith and divine election.

Religious communitarians established socially isolated but economically self-sufficient communities governed by specific scripturally based rules. Sepa-

1

ration, a most important requirement of communitarian life, would not only protect community members from persecution but also from enticements to deviate from the founder's prescriptions for following the true ways of life. Their lifestyle, social and economic organization, and educational practices were heavily influenced by the theology of an originating and often charismatic founder, such as Mother Ann Lee of the Shakers, George Rapp of the Harmonists, Erik Jansson of the Janssonists, and John Humphrey Noyes of the Oneida Perfectionists.

The religiously based community was a total social and economic communal milieu. Life in a Shaker colony, at Bishop Hill, or in the Amanas was a totally formative experience that involved the mutually reinforcing elements of prayer, work, and learning. Living in these communities involved a high degree of social, economic, and religious integration but also profound social control that erased individuality. The importance of work both to economic production and religious indoctrination was a key element of community life. Religious communities were to create a spiritual "we-feeling" among the church membership and build into their psyches a willing conformity to the religious practices and lifestyle prescribed by the society's founder.

Another goal of the religious communitarians was developing profitable agricultural and handicraft products that would contribute to economic prosperity. They characteristically maintained a profitable economic connection with the larger society. The Shakers, Rappites, Zoarites, Janssonists, and Inspirationists established self-sufficient, financially viable "little city states" that produced a surplus for sale to the larger society. Land, intensively cultivated, produced bountiful crops of corn, wheat, oats, hay, and potatoes. The Shakers were noted for their seeds, herbal medicines, and craft items, which found a profitable market outside of their communities.

Based on economic functionalism, each colony often had a cabinetmaker's shop, general store, bakery, winery, and sawmill. Production was made efficient by means of a planned division of labor. Industriousness often made these religious communities into centers of handicraft production.

The religious communitarians' social attitudes and behaviors were shaped by the particular group's beliefs about marriage and family. Shakers, following Mother Ann Lee's doctrines, and Harmonists, followers of George Rapp, were celibate. Children enrolled in their schools were the offspring of original "charter members," new converts, or orphans entrusted to the community's charitable care. Noncelibate religious communitarians such as the Inspirationists established and maintained community schools for their children in the traditional sense of schooling designed to transmit the cultural heritage from adults to children to perpetuate the group's cultural ethos and identity.

As community builders, the religious communitarians were functionalists who deliberately created communal agencies that would efficiently perform needed services. For example, communal child care centers, kitchens, dining rooms, and laundries were used to free women to perform other economic functions in the

Introduction

community rather than for intellectual or aesthetic liberation as was the case with secular communitarians such as the Owenites, Fourierists, and Icarians.

In contrast to the religious communitarians, secular communitarians often rejected religion and scriptural authority. They wished to establish perfect cities based on sociological and economic theories. The impetus for the secular communitarians derived from the Enlightenment doctrine that it was possible, and indeed desirable, to use science to discover nature's laws and then apply these laws to creating a new society—a new world order.

For secular communitarians such as Robert Owen, the overriding goal was to do no less than create a new man and woman by reshaping human nature itself. Owen, who saw human nature as completely malleable, believed it was possible to shape any kind of character. The key to creating the new personality type was found in controlling the social and economic environment.

Both the religious and secular communitarians of the nineteenth century shared common characteristics. They formed voluntary societies whose alternative lifestyles differed from that of the larger mainstream society. While both followed prescriptive and proscriptive codes for leading the common life, religious communitarians differed from their secular counterparts in that their practices followed the theological doctrines and scriptural interpretations of a charismatic founder as contrasted with the more philosophical or ideological orientation of secular communitarians.

Because they differed in their basic purpose, secular and religious communitarians also differed in their orientation and relationship to the larger society. Secular communitarians such as the Transcendentalists at Fruitlands and Brook Farm and the Owenites at New Harmony believed they were constructing exemplary communities that could serve as models for the larger society. These communitarians were not seeking self-isolation but rather wanted to influence and reshape the larger external society and create a worldly heaven, a utopia, on earth.

Social control and education were used to create the new society. Persuasive ideological polemics were used to attract converts to the secular creed. Once the community was established, education of all the members of the community, young and adult, ensured that they followed the ideological prescriptions of common life. Then secular communitarianism resumed its outward ideological mission to convert the larger society, but now, appended to the initial polemic would be a narrative of the community's success. In historical reality, however, the secular communitarians' experiments were short-lived, often torn by internal factions, dissent and inept administrators.

The chapters that follow will introduce you to what can be called America's utopian heritage, much of which was communal. Many of these fascinating secular and religious communities have been restored as historic sites that recapture an important but often overlooked dimension of America's past. These museum villages can be visited, toured, and enjoyed today.

THE ORGANIZATION OF THE BOOK AND YOUR SITE VISIT

As we researched this book, we soon came to realize that leadership was a key factor in establishing a society and keeping it together. The founder's personality was crucial in attracting people and making converts. Many of the religious founders, such as Ann Lee of the Shakers, George Rapp of the Harmonists, and John Humphrey Noyes of the Perfectionists, were charismatic personalities who through power of personality exercised leadership and control. The book includes biographical sketches of these strong characters who ruled by incorporating personal charisma, a distinctive religious doctrine, and social control and conformity. We discovered that religious communitarian leaders maintained a greater and longer lasting control over their followers than did the secular leaders.

The portrayal of the founding leader is followed by a description of a particular community founded by that person. Often the leader believed he or she was creating a "holy city" where the chosen people could dwell until Christ's Second Coming. The design and architecture of the communities often reflected their impressions of how such a city should be organized. For example, the Shaker buildings were designed to incorporate the practice of celibacy and the separation of women from men. An important feature is a description of the lifestyle at each community.

USING THE BOOK

In this, as in our other books on museum villages, we have included only those sites where there are extant remains of the historic community, usually buildings that you can visit. We define a museum village as a setting, a place, in which a collection of historic buildings have been either restored or recreated to illustrate a particular people's way of life—the community, society, religion, architecture, industry and occupations, furniture, and art—at a particular period in history.

Each historical site begins with a **Brief Description** that provides the name of the utopian or communal group, the name of the historic site, its address, telephone, location, dates and hours when it is open, admission fees, restaurants, shops, and facilities. (Please note that we have tried to provide current admission fees at the time of publication, but they are subject to change.) "NR" indicates that the site is listed on the *National Register of Historic Places*, "NHL" indicates that the site is a National Historic Landmark, and "HABS" indicates that buildings on this site are included in *Historic American Buildings Survey*.

Next, an **Overview** section provides a capsule description of the site's founder, people, history, features, and significance. This feature of the book gives you a quick glance at the museum village so that you can determine if it is of interest to you.

The **History** narrative that follows provides a biography of the founder or leader of the group, its principal religious or ideological beliefs, and the community's form of social, economic, and educational organization. This section describes how the particular group was established, the major events in its history, and what happened to it.

Finally, a **Tour** section identifies the buildings, describes their features, and comments on the industries, crafts, and artifacts associated with the site.

VISITING THE SITE

Most of the historic utopian or communal sites in this book have a visitor's center, which is the first place that you should stop. Spend some time in the center, where you may see an orientation film or audiovisual program that explains the group and the site. There may also be a display of photographs or illustrations about the site and a collection of artifacts. Often brochures or maps of the site are available.

Reading the section in this book on the particular site should provide the background that will help you appreciate the group's history, organization, and artifacts.

After getting an overall general orientation to the group that lived at the site, begin your tour. Some of the sites provide guided tours while others have self-guided tours. See the village in terms of its founders, people, their beliefs, their society, and their work.

Each traveler has her or his own special interests. For the person interested in religious history, the Shaker, Harmonist, Inspirationist, Janssonist, and Perfectionist sites provide insights into small, often overlooked, but fascinating religious sects. For the student of architecture, the buildings at the sites are physical remnants of each group's ethos and its impact on the dwellings for the city of God. The very large Shaker, Harmonist, and Zoarite buildings give evidence of a functional tendency to make work a group rather than an individual effort. This was based on a desire to make life and work efficient so that more time could be given to God. The person interested in decorative arts and antiques will find many of these artifacts displayed in their original settings. For example, the Shaker buildings with their chairs hanging on wooden pegs from the walls create a distinctive impression of utility, practicality, and orderliness.

That the communitarian sites were comprehensive communities is evidenced by the location of the buildings, gardens, and fields. For the person interested in gardens, many of the sites are planted with historic varieties of flowers and herbs that were common at the time. We have enjoyed walking through the carefully planted gardens at Old Economy, where one can see a great variety of columbines and dahlias. Whatever your particular interest, we hope that your visit to utopia will be a pleasant, entertaining, and rewarding journey into our country's past.

Conrad Beissel's Ephratans

The 1743 Sisters' House, also called the saron, is the three-story medieval-German wooden structure that contained the tiny sleeping cells, kitchens, and workrooms of the single sisters. Photograph by Patricia A. Gutek.

EPHRATA CLOISTER

1732–1796, Ephrata, Pennsylvania

NR, NHL, HABS

ADDRESS: 632 West Main Street, Ephrata, PA 17522
TELEPHONE: (717) 733-6600, (717) 733-4811
LOCATION: In southeastern Pennsylvania, in Lancaster County, 5 miles south of PA Turnpike Exit 21, 12 miles northeast of Lancaster.
OPEN: Monday–Saturday, 9:00 a.m.–5:00 p.m.; Sunday, noon–5:00 p.m.; closed Thanksgiving, Christmas, New Year's Day, Easter, Columbus Day, Veteran's Day, Martin Luther King Day, and President's Day.
ADMISSION: Adults, $5; groups and senior citizens, $4; children 6–17, $3.
RESTAURANTS: No.
SHOPS: Museum Store.
FACILITIES: Restored eighteenth-century buildings; Visitor Center with orientation slide show; guided tours; craft demonstrations; special events; picnic area.

OVERVIEW

Ephrata Cloister, site of an unusual and fascinating communal society in colonial America, is located in the rolling green hills of Lancaster County, Pennsylvania.

The Ephratans were a mystical Christian Pietist German group founded in pre–Revolutionary America by a German immigrant named Conrad Beissel (1691–1768). In 1720, he arrived in Pennsylvania, where thousands of German people had already immigrated. Ephrata was located in William Penn's colony, which was known to insure freedom of religion.

At Ephrata Cloister, men and women lived communally in what they described as holy poverty. Inhabitants of the cloister included two celibate orders of brothers and sisters who dressed in long white hooded robes. They lived in large, multistory wooden European-style medieval structures built in the first half of the eighteenth century and slept in austere cells. Their daily lives revolved around prayer, meditation, music, work, and fasting. In addition to the monastic orders, there were married Ephratans, called householders, who lived in the vicinity.

The religious group, which eventually disintegrated, left a rich cultural heritage, including rare architecture, a body of original religious music, and many beautifully hand-illuminated manuscripts decorated with *Frakturschriften*, the medieval style of ornate lettering. They had the most complete printing and publishing establishment in America and produced religious books and hymnals in both German and English.

Today, a visit to Ephrata, with its carefully restored buildings in a pastoral setting, presents an idyllic picture. A little imagination is required to recall the ascetic self-denial and discipline Ephratans practiced in their effort to achieve personal union with God.

Ephrata Cloister

HISTORY

Conrad Beissel was the founder and original leader of the mystical Pietist group called the Ephratans. Like so many other leaders of communal groups, Beissel had charisma, that indefinable quality that attracts followers eager to embrace their leader's beliefs. Beginning in his youth, Beissel's magnetic personality began drawing people, particularly women.

Johann Conrad Beissel was born March 1, 1691, in Eberach, in what was then the Palatinate, Germany. He was the son of Matthias Beissel, a baker who died a couple of months before his son's birth, and Anna Beissel. The family was very poor, and the widowed Anna was left with the overwhelming task of providing for her many children alone. She died when Conrad was eight or nine years old, and he was subsequently raised by a variety of siblings. Said to be a small man, it is speculated that Beissel suffered from malnutrition throughout his childhood.

As a young man, Conrad was apprenticed to a baker in Eberhard, and lived with his master's family. The master taught his young charge to play the violin, and the two frequently entertained at weddings and parties.

Around the same time, Beissel became involved in the Pietist movement in Germany. Pietism developed as a reaction against the institutionalized formalism of the Lutheran Church. Based in part on the writings of Philipp Jakob Spener, Pietism stressed participation by layman, Bible study, and a return to the simplicity of early Christianity. Conventicles, small groups of Pietist believers who met in their homes, were banned by both church and state and forced to meet in secret.

At the end of his apprenticeship, Beissel was promoted to journeyman baker by his local guild. Before becoming a master baker, he was required to work in other towns specified by his guild and to acquire the commendation of their guilds. One of these towns was Strasbourg, where, in addition to working as a baker, Beissel encountered several mystical religious sects, including radical Pietism, Inspirationism, and the Society of Philadelphians. The beliefs of these sects were grounded in the writings of the mystical philosopher Jakob Boehme.

In Heidelberg, another stop on his travels, Beissel baked a new highly acclaimed bread that made his reputation as a master baker. As required by Jewish and Muslim tradition, the bread was made with oil rather than pork lard. His success led Conrad to be appointed treasurer of Heidelberg's bakers' guild.

Beissel was active in the underground religious movement in Heidelberg, meeting with radical Pietists some of whom belonged to the Brotherhood of the Rosy Cross or Rosicrucians, an ancient mystical sect. Meetings were frequently held in the forests at night. While in Heidelberg, Beissel decided to stop attending church services thus severing permanently his ties with the Lutheran Church.

In his role as bakers' guild treasurer, Beissel attended the social functions of the guild. He earned the displeasure of fellow members when he criticized their wild, disorderly behavior at banquets. In retaliation, they informed the authorities of Beissel's nonattendance at church and membership in banned religious sects, serious civil charges because there was no separation of church and state. Twenty-five-year-old Beissel was arrested, jailed, and tried. He was banished from the Palatinate, and his *Wanderbuch*, the official record of his journeyman's experience as a baker, was confiscated.

Without his baker's license, Beissel could no longer earn a living. A homeless vagrant, he contracted tuberculosis. His wanderings eventually led him to Schwarzenau, where he joined a group of Pietists who in 1708 had founded the Brotherhood at Schwarzenau. The Brotherhood, heavily based on the beliefs of Ernst Christoph Hochmann von Hohenau, originally had been communal and celibate.

In 1715, a branch of the Brotherhood lived at Krefeld, located west of the Rhine. They were called Dunkers because their baptism required total immersion three times. After being persecuted repeatedly, the sect, led by Peter Becker, migrated to America in 1719 and settled at Germantown, Pennsylvania, where they were later known as the German Baptist Brethren.

Around 1717, Beissel became active in the Community of True Inspiration (see Amana Colonies). Although he was an assistant of Johann Friedrich Rock, Beissel did not join the community.

Clearly, Beissel was searching for a separatist religion that he could wholeheartedly embrace. A sect that greatly attracted him was a spiritual hermitage under the leadership of Johannes Kelpius in Pennsylvania. A desire to explore joining that group prompted Beissel to go to America.

Beissel, George Stieffel, Simon Konig, Jacob Stuntz, and Heinrich van Bebber sailed to America in 1720, traveling to the city of brotherly love founded by William Penn. Beissel intended to join Johannes Kelpius and his band of celibate hermits, known as the Society of the Woman in the Wilderness, living communally on 175 acres on the west bank of the Wissahickton near Germantown. By the time Beissel arrived, Kelpius had been dead for a dozen years, and most of the hermits had dispersed.

Disappointed and lacking alternative plans, Beissel accepted an invitation to live in Germantown with Peter Becker whose Schwarzenau Brotherhood had scattered. Beissel spent a year as Becker's weaving apprentice.

Conrad Matthai, a follower of Kelpius still at Wissahickton, urged Conrad Beissel to seek solitude on the western frontier, in the Conestoga Valley. Accompanied by shipmate Jacob Stuntz, in 1721 Beissel traveled to the Conestoga forest, where the men built a cabin on the banks of the Muhlbach. Three miles from the cabin, a large group of Swiss Mennonites led by Hans Herr lived on a 10,000-acre site.

Isaac van Bebber, a nephew of Heinrich van Bebber, who had traveled to America with Beissel, joined the two men at Conestoga. Van Bebber convinced Beissel to accompany him to Maryland to visit his father and another uncle. Van

Ephrata Cloister

Bebber's relatives were German Mennonites who in 1704 joined the Labadist commune, which had been established in 1683 at Bohemia Manor, Maryland.

The Labadists were followers of Jean de Labadie (1610–74), a French ex-Jesuit who advocated a return to the teachings of the early church, a monastic lifestyle, and communalism. Labadie and his followers established communes in Amsterdam and Friesland, North Holland.

A branch of the Labadists was established in 1683 on 3,750 acres of land at the head of the Chesapeake. This colony of approximately 100 people from Holland and northern Germany led by Bishop Peter Sluyter lived an ascetic, spartan, communal life based on early Christianity. Most were celibate, though marriage was tolerated. Members lived in unheated cells in communal dwellings, ate scant meals, and labored long days in the fields.

Beissel was deeply impressed by the life of holy poverty he observed at Bohemia Manor in 1722. On his return, he began preaching. His magnetic personality generated a religious revival on the frontier.

After his cabin mates dispersed and sold the cabin in 1723, Beissel moved into the forest and built a small log cabin beside a spring with the intention of leading a hermit's life. This was not to be, as his followers wanted to be near him. In late 1724, Becker and some of his brethren settled nearby. Becker baptized Beissel November 12, 1724, in Pequea Creek.

A congregation of a dozen people with ties to the Germantown brethren was formally organized at Conestoga on November 26, 1724, with Beissel as its leader. Saturday was designated as their Sabbath as in Judaism. Most of the people were celibate, and they were referred to as solitaries. Married couples were called householders. A lifestyle of holy poverty was adopted. Beissel began baptizing additional converts in May 1725; many of them erected cabins close to that of their spiritual leader. In 1728, Beissel's community and Becker's Germantown congregation severed their connection.

Beissel wrote religious tracts including a treatise on Sabbatarianism in German. Michael Wohlfahrt, a follower, wrote the English translation. Other works by Beissel in this period include a volume of orthodox moral proverbs, hymn-poems, and a book against matrimony, printed by Benjamin Franklin.[1]

In May 1729, Lancaster County was established. It included the region of the Conestoga Valley where Beissel and his followers lived. Many of them had built cabins on lands owned by the London Company and were regarded as squatters. In 1730, notices were posted that warned squatters to vacate company land or face legal action. Beissel's community began contemplating relocation. Another problem revolved around the Sabbath. According to law, Sunday was the Sabbath, and members of Beissel's community who observed a Saturday Sabbath were arrested for working on Sunday.

Beissel, who sought to live the life of a hermit, had become the leader of a group of people. Preaching and administrative duties kept him busy. In February 1732, Beissel announced his resignation as leader, appointed two male elders and one female matron, and moved to a cabin eight miles north. The cabin was located on a stream that the Indians called Hoch-Halekung or Achgookwalico, which meant "snake hole" or "den of serpents," because the area was infested with snakes. Beissel spent much of his time there writing hymn-poems.

Beissel's attempt to live a hermit's life failed. He was wrong in assuming none of his disciples would join him at his new home on the Cocalico Creek, as it was called in English. As more and more people followed their spiritual leader, another community was established that included single solitary of both sexes and married householders. Thus, in 1732, the society that came to be called Ephrata was established on the shore of Cocalico Creek in Lancaster County. Beissel dispatched two men to Philadelphia to ask permission of Thomas Penn to form a communal settlement, and Penn gave his consent.

The Beissel community's use of the name Ephrata can be traced to at least 1736 when it was listed at the end of the preface to a hymnbook printed by Benjamin Franklin. In the Old Testament, Ephrata was the pre-Israelite name for Bethlehem. Why Beissel chose the name is unclear.

The Ephratan communalists lived an austere, strict life of intentional poverty, work, prayer, spirituality, and subjugation of physical drives like hunger and sex. Personal property was rejected. Initially, members wore plain garments based on the garb of early Quakers. In the mid-1730s, they adopted habits based on the style of Capuchin monks made of unbleached linen in summer and wool in winter. Members usually ate only one sparse vegetarian meal a day and lived in 20-by-25-foot cabins, which they built themselves.

Although they were not always regarded benevolently by their neighbors, the community extended kindness and charity to them. They operated a school for the children of indigent German settlers. They built a large brick bake oven and distributed bread to residents in the region and frequently constructed cabins for new settlers.

Beissel's missionary activities among the German settlements in Pennsylvania met with much success. Others in Germany and Switzerland heard about Beissel's community and traveled to America to join it. Members, who were referred to as brothers and sisters, replaced their family names with monastic names. Beissel was known as Father Gottrecht Friedsam.

As the community grew, larger structures were constructed. They included the 1734 Berghaus, where meetings and love feasts were held, and the 1735 Kedar, which was a three-story wooden building with cells for brothers on the first floor, cells for sisters on the third floor, and large rooms for meetings and love feasts on the second floor. Shortly, the Kedar developed into a convent for the sisters, who formed the Order of Spiritual Virgins. Next, a large Bethaus or house of prayer featuring a large hall or Saal was completed in 1737. The Zion Saal, a three-story chapterhouse for the Zion Brotherhood was built in 1738. By 1740, Ephrata's population was over 200.

Administratively, Beissel was the spiritual leader. Samuel Eckerling was in charge of the community's economy. Beissel and Eckerling, who was one of four Eckerling brothers in the community, had extremely different economic philosophies. Beissel advocated holy poverty. Ephrata was not to be operated for profit but should only generate enough income for internal sustenance and charitable works.

The Eckerling brothers were good business managers who pursued every avenue of generating income. In the early 1740s, Ephrata became a thriving agricultural and handicraft colonial community. A diversified agricultural plan included the production of wheat, flax, hemp, and millet. Cattle were raised. Water rights on the south side of Cocalico Creek enabled the society to operate two gristmills, a sawmill, a linseed oil mill, a fulling mill, and a paper mill. Orchards and a vineyard were planted. A large tannery was the basis for a shoemaking business and a bookbindery. Abundant produce was grown in society gardens.

To engender a successful economy, brothers and sisters worked long hours under the supervision of foremen. Outside laborers were hired as work demands expanded. The Eckerlings began trading in flour. They bought grain at low harvest, stored it in their granaries, then milled the flour and sold it for high prices in Philadelphia. Although Ephratans opposed both human and animal slavery so that even plows were pulled by men, the Eckerlings bought horses and wagons so they could market Ephrata's products in a wider area.

Disputes over economic policies resulted in a power struggle between the Eckerlings and Beissel in which Beissel emerged as the victor. The Eckerlings left the community in September 1745, and Ephrata returned to being a religious hermitage. The mills were closed to outside trade with the exception of the paper mill and the printery. Outside workers were dismissed. The horses and wagons were sold. Even the Zion Brotherhood, which had been created by the Eckerling brothers, was dismantled, and the male solitary became the Brotherhood of Bethania.

The community's return to holy poverty received unexpected help when, a short time later, unknown persons uprooted their 1,000–tree orchard. Also, in December 1747, a fire destroyed the gristmill and its stored food and grain, the fulling mill, and the oil mill.

Instead of economic priorities, the community concentrated on spiritual and cultural concerns including literature, education, publishing, and *Fraktur*, but most especially music. Their unique style of singing, unaccompanied by musical instruments, was described as ethereal and brought them fame both in the American colonies and in Europe. Beissel as well as other members composed music and songs, which were performed during religious services.

Beissel became the choir leader after choir members balked at his original appointee. With little musical background other than learning the violin while a baker's apprentice and studying the notes of Ludwig Blum, the first choir master, Beissel claimed that through divine inspiration, he had learned "harmony and composition."[2] He wrote over a thousand sacred songs, set in four, five, six, or seven parts for a mixed choir of soprano, alto, female tenor, and male bass voices. Some anthems were of his poetry while others were Bible

Conrad Beissel's Ephratans

chapters. He composed hymns and anthems in simple harmony. He published a book of original music.[3] Artistically, the Ephratans are known for their illuminated music writing, called *Fraktur*. This baroque art, which originated in Switzerland and the Rhine country, was similar to the script in medieval illuminated manuscripts.[4]

Beissel wrote many religious tracts, some of which were printed at Benjamin Franklin's printing house in Philadelphia. Franklin was suspicious of the religious German immigrants and demanded payment in advance. Beissel's writings were later printed on the community's printing press, purchased in 1743. The Ephratans also printed works for others. From 1745 to 1748, fifteen Ephratans devoted themselves to the publication of the *Martyrer-Spiegel* (*Martyrs' Mirror*) for the Mennonites. After translating it from Dutch to German, the manuscript was edited, typeset, printed, and bound. The paper and the ink used in the 1,300 copies of the 1,512-page book were produced at Ephrata. This book, the largest volume published in America before 1800, is considered as the premier example of colonial bookmaking.

Features of Ephrata's religious practices were the love feast, singing, night watches, and open confession. Open confession was introduced for the male solitary in 1736. On Friday, the day before the Sabbath, each solitary wrote a report on his spiritual condition. During the Sabbath service, Beissel read the reports to the congregation. Night watches, introduced around 1735, were undertaken by the solitary and initially lasted four hours but were soon cut to two hours. These penitential meetings were held at midnight because that was the time Beissel felt that the Judgment would occur. Habit-clad brothers marched, prayed, and sang. Within the male solitary was a secret mystical society called the Zion Brotherhood, whose rituals were extremely demanding on both body and mind.

Beissel died July 6, 1768, in Ephrata, Pennsylvania. More than 700 people attended his funeral. In 1775, seven years after his death, a memorial stone was placed on his grave; it read "Friedsam. Here rests an offspring of the Love of God."

Peter Miller succeeded Beissel as leader of the Ephrata community. A history of the Baptist religion by Morgan Edwards in 1770 records the names of the remaining Ephratans. According to Edwards, there were fourteen solitary brothers, forty-two Roses of Sharon, and ninety-nine people in the secular congregation. Most of the members in the monastic orders were aged.

Into this cloistered pacifist world intruded the long- simmering American Revolution. Later, the Ephratans, though wishing to remain neutral, found themselves dragged into the hostilities generated by the colonists' attempts to achieve independence from Britain.

The Provincial Council of Pennsylvania's Revolutionary colonial leaders contracted with the Ephrata press on December 4, 1775, to translate into German and print 400 copies of "Rules and Regulations and Articles of Association" for the many German residents of the colony. Peter Miller, Ephrata's leader, translated the new government's official diplomatic correspondence.

The Battle of the Brandywine, fought September 11, 1777, near Chadds Ford, seventy miles from Ephrata, resulted in large losses for the Revolutionary army, including 300 dead and 600 wounded. General George Washington ordered the wounded taken to Ephrata Cloister, a difficult three-day journey away. Two large buildings were converted into hospitals and the brothers and sisters valiantly nursed the suffering troops. About 150 soldiers died that winter. Camp fever, typhus, and scarlet fever epidemics ravaged both the military and the Ephratans. Food and blanket reserves were depleted. After the soldiers' departure, the Ephratans burned the buildings used as military hospitals to prevent the reemergence of disease. The loss of their largest buildings was a tremendous misfortune for the community.

General George Washington commandeered Ephrata's supply of paper, as the army was in dire need of paper for shot wadding. Two wagons full of paper were taken, including unsold copies of the magnificent *Martyrs' Mirror*.

Many of America's religious communal groups were nonviolent pacifists who refused to bear arms and sought exemptions from active military service. In times of war, these pacifists were held in suspicion and considered nonpatriotic. For example, the Shakers during the Civil War and the Amana Inspirationists during World War I were adversely affected by war. Despite their opposition to war, these good people, who attempted to live separately from the larger society, gave generously of their food and facilities and willingly nursed injured soldiers. Their facilities were sometimes looted by troops and their buildings commandeered as hospitals.

Already aging and declining in productivity before the war, the community was left with little strength and vitality after the Revolution. Of the twenty sisters who remained at Ephrata during the 1780s, most were in their sixties and seventies, as were the few remaining brothers. The most significant event of those years was the publication of the *Chronicon Ephratense*, the history of Ephrata, printed in German by the Ephrata press in 1786. This work is believed to have been based primarily on the diary of Jacob Gast, also known as Brother Jethro, and on the reminiscences of Peter Miller.

According to a visitor's report in 1794, only thirteen sisters and six brothers remained at Ephrata. Peter Miller died September 25, 1796, and no leader replaced him. Now that the solitary orders were almost completely depleted, the lay congregation assumed authority. In 1814, Pennsylvania's General Assembly incorporated "The Society of Seventh Day Baptists of Ephrata" with four trustees appointed by the lay congregation as administrators of the lands and buildings. By 1823, there were only fifty lay members of the Ephratan Church.

A small offshoot community of Ephrata called Snow Hill endured for almost a century. Its name derived from a member family named Schneeberger which means snow hill. Their name was later anglicized to Snowberger. Peter Miller appointed Peter Lehman, a hermit, as its leader in 1788. This small group also was monastic and communal and lasted until 1889.

Over time, the abandoned property at Ephrata deteriorated. Around 1912, Bethania, the Brothers' House, was declared unsafe and torn down. In 1940, the property, known as Ephrata Cloisters Park, was placed in the care of the Pennsylvania Historical Commission. G. Edwin Brumbaugh was hired as the restoration architect in 1941 and the careful restoration of the site continued until 1968.

The community at Ephrata Cloister shared some characteristics with other pietistic European groups while differing in other respects. Like the Community of True Inspirations, Ephratans were German radical Christian Pietists whose religious beliefs included strong elements of mysticism. In the case of Inspirationism, the community originated in Germany and was brought to America by its leader Christian Metz to obtain freedom to practice their religion. Erik Jansson, leader of the Swedish group, also relocated an established religious community to America to escape religious persecution. The founder of Ephrata, Conrad Beissel, was a German who came to America to join an already existing religious community. Finding that group disbanded, Beissel eventually founded his own community.

Although Ephrata's religious beliefs originated in Germany, the Ephrata community was founded before the American Revolution in colonial Pennsylvania, one of the earliest utopian settlements in the United States.

TOUR

Guides explain the history and customs of this unique community as they lead you through the saron, saal, and cabin. The rest of the tour is self-guided.

Purchase your admission tickets at the **Visitor Center,** and begin your tour there with the slide show and museum displays of printing and *Frakturschriften,* including a copy of *Martyr's Mirror.* There is also a wooden Communion service, thought to be a gift from George Washington for the cloister's care of soldiers wounded in the Battle of Brandywine.

Howard Pyle, an American writer and artist, described Ephratan architecture in "A Peculiar People: A Tale of the Ephrata Cloister" in the October 1889 issue of *Harper's Magazine.* Pyle describes the village as "a curious pile of buildings of quaint, old-fashioned architecture. The larger are weather-boarded with planks or shingle; the smaller, which have something of a foreign look— half Swiss, half German—are built of stone. . . . The buildings . . . are great steep-roofed houses, several stories in height, spotted by many very small windows twinkling in the sunlight. The flooring beams of good sound poplar pierce through the walls and are pinned upon the outside."

The 1743 **Sisters' House,** also called the **saron,** is an outstanding example of medieval German architecture. A three-story building, it was originally occupied by married householders. In 1745, it was remodeled to accommodate the celibate sisterhood. Each floor is designed with a central kitchen joined on either side by a common workroom and sleeping cells. The cells are small, provided only with wooden plank beds and wooden block pillows. Meals were eaten in the refectory, which is furnished with simple tables and benches. A room in which the sisters practiced the art of *Frakturschriften* contains a display of that work. The interior is very plain, with white walls, wooden plank floors, narrow halls, and low doorways.

Sisters led an austere life, dividing their time between work and prayer: private prayer, from 5:00 to 6:00 a.m., work from 6:00 to 9:00 a.m., prayer from 9:00 to 10:00 a.m., work from 10:00 a.m. until noon, a church service from noon to 1:00 p.m., work from 1:00 to 5:00 p.m., private prayer from 5:00 to 6:00 p.m., a vegetarian meal at 6:00 p.m., singing or *Frakturschriften* school from 7:00 to 9:00 p.m., sleep from 9:00 p.m. to midnight, service from 12:00 midnight to 2:00 a.m., and sleep from 2:00 to 5:00 a.m.

The **Meetinghouse**, or **saal**, which adjoins the saron, was built in 1741. Church services were held on the lower floor of this two-story building; singing and writing schools were upstairs. There are four original benches and some original candlesticks inside. Framed *Frakturschriften* hang on the walls.

In Ephrata, the Sabbath was on the seventh day, Saturday. The service was an informal meeting consisting of singing and extemporaneous discourses. Beissel, who wrote many of the hymns, prescribed a unique method of choral singing; visitors commented that its falsetto intonation created an otherworldly effect. No other instruments were used. The service also included Communion and sometimes foot washing.

The meetinghouse refectory was used for love feasts. Normally vegetarians, the Ephratans would eat lamb stew and bread at a feast. Any member could initiate a love feast at any time by inviting other members to this meal. Everyone ate out of the same bowl.

The small community **Bakehouse**, erected prior to the founding of the cloister, is probably the oldest building at Ephrata. Bread baked here was distributed free to the needy. The building is now the site of a candle-making demonstration.

Adjoining the old bakehouse is the **Beissel Cabin**, a small clapboard-sheathed log house built in 1748. This hermit's cabin is sparsely furnished with benches and tables made at Ephrata and is heated by a 1756 five-plate stove. Beissel was a hermit for part of his life. Even after founding the cloister, he spent a great deal of time alone.

The 1735 **Almonry** (a place where alms were given out) is a large three-story stone building where male travelers or the homeless could find free shelter. Women in need of shelter would spend the night in the Sisters' House. This tradition of hospitality was common in European convents. The squirrel-tail ovens, located to the side and rear of the almonry's large fireplace, were used for baking bread.

A mid-eighteenth-century two-story frame cabin has been furnished as a typical **Householders Cabin**; however, most of the householders would have lived away from the cloister. The cabin has been restored to look as it would have

Conrad Beissel's Ephratans

The tombstone of Peter Miller, the leader who succeeded Conrad Beissel, Ephrata Cloister's founder. Miller died September 25, 1796, and is buried in the Ephrata graveyard. Photograph by Patricia A. Gutek.

around 1800; the furnishings are simple but not as stark as those in the saron.

The **Craft House**, built around 1750, is architecturally interesting because it is one of the few remaining colonial, half-timbered structures. The construction consists of a pegged timber framework chinked with stone. The interior walls are mud- plastered, and the outside is clapboarded. The ceiling beams, which extend to the outside of the building, are particularly unusual.

The **Printshop** contains a press built in Philadelphia and brought to Ephrata in 1804. It is the oldest American-made press still in operation.

The **Solitary House** is a mid-eighteenth-century cabin. It shows the domestic life of a celibate member of the cloister society who chose to live as a hermit.

A rebuilt stonewall surrounds the **Graveyard**. Many of the graves are aboveground. Conrad Beissel and Peter Miller are buried here. Here is a translation of the German inscription on Beissel's gravestone:

> Here rests an offspring of the love of God. [Friedsam Beissel was known as Father Gottrecht Friedsam at the cloister], A Solitary. But later became leader, guardian and teacher of Solitary and of the congregation in Christ in and about Ephrata. Born at Eberach in the Palatinate. Called Conrad Beissel. Fell asleep July 6th Anno 1768. Aged according to his spiritual age, 52 years, but according to his natural 77 years and 4 months.

After visiting the cemetery, walk over to the **Academy**. This building dates from 1837, new by Ephrata standards. The church operated a private academy until the time of the Civil War, when it was leased to the township and used as an elementary school until 1926. The two-story building with a belfry displays schoolroom furniture of the 1840s.

There is a Christmas candlelight tour in December.

Moravians or Unitas Fratrum or Church of the Brethren

The half-timbered brick-and-stone Single Brothers' House was built in 1769; an addition was added in 1786. It was a residence for the unmarried men and also contained the shops of the master craftsmen. Photograph by Patricia A. Gutek.

OLD SALEM
1766–1856, Winston-Salem, North Carolina
NR, NHL

ADDRESS: Box F, Winston-Salem, NC 27108
TELEPHONE: (910) 721-7300
LOCATION: Winston-Salem is in northwest North Carolina; Old Salem is near the intersection of I-40 and US 52.
OPEN: Monday–Saturday, 9:30 a.m.–4:30 p.m.; Sunday, 1:30 p.m.–4:30 p.m.; closed Thanksgiving, Christmas Eve, and Christmas.
ADMISSION: Old Salem: adults, $10; children 6–14, $5. Old Salem and Museum of Early Southern Decorative Arts: adults, $13; children 6–14, $6.
RESTAURANTS: Old Salem Tavern; Mayberry's.
SHOPS: T. Bagge Merchant; Salem Gift and Book Store; Winkler Bakery.
FACILITIES: Visitor Center with orientation film; special events; Museum of Early Southern Decorative Arts.

OVERVIEW

The Unitas Fratrum, commonly known as the Church of the Brethren or Moravians, was a German-speaking religious group, some members of whom lived in communal church societies in eighteenth-century America. The Church of the Brethren was a pietistic Protestant denomination whose roots dated from fourteenth-century Bohemia and which later flourished in Germany. Some Moravians, who immigrated to America in 1736, established a short-lived settlement in Georgia. In the 1740s, Moravian communities were founded at Bethlehem, Pennsylvania, and Wachovia, North Carolina.

In 1766, before the American Revolution, Moravians founded a planned town in North Carolina. Old Salem's nine museum buildings are within a sixteen-block area of Moravian-built eighteenth- and nineteenth-century structures.

Salem was a congregational community, strictly planned by Moravian Church leaders. The site for Salem ("peace" in Hebrew) was chosen because of its good water supply, proper drainage, and southern exposure. Not an agricultural center, Salem was conceived as a trading center for artisans and craftsmen.

Today, the busy city of Winston-Salem has grown up around the colonial town of Salem so that it is a historic eighteenth-century area in a modern twentieth-century city. To ensure an authentic appearance in the historic area, more than a hundred nonconforming structures within the congregation town limits were demolished when restoration began. As at Williamsburg, many buildings in the historic area are privately owned, but their exteriors have been restored.

The combination of original European-style historic structures, the interesting group that lived in Salem, the beautiful gardens, and the high-quality restoration makes Old Salem a fine museum village. While admission is charged to enter museum buildings, you are free to stroll along the brick paths through the restored area at any time, eat at the Old Salem Tavern or shop in museum stores.

HISTORY

Moravians trace their origins to John Hus (also known as Jan Huss), a fifteenth-century Roman Catholic priest in Prague who called for reforms of the clergy and the church 100 years before Luther launched the Protestant Reformation. His belief that the Bible was the highest principle of authority was in disagreement with Catholic Church doctrine. This Bohemian reformer, who thought that the Bible should be read by all believers, had the Bible printed in the vernacular in addition to the traditional Latin.

Hus was declared a heretic for his beliefs by the Council of Constance and was burned at the stake on July 6, 1415. His followers, called Hussites, were fiercely persecuted for the next thirty years.

In 1457, when the persecutions had greatly diminished, Hussites regathered at Kunvald, east of Prague, in the Barony of Lititz, to organize a church. They were a pietistic sect whose religious practices can be traced to the Bible study groups, called *Collegia Pietatis*, or societies of piety, formed by Philipp Jakob Spener, a German Lutheran pastor, as well as to Hus's original teachings. Spener's movement spread throughout Germany, Scandinavia, and England.

In 1467, these Moravians, known as Unitas Fratrum or Brethren, formally seceded from the Church of Rome and established their own ministry. They accepted converts, opened churches and schools, and had over 100,000 members in Bohemia by the onset of the Protestant Reformation.[1] In the early seventeenth century, more than half of the Protestants of Bohemia and Moravia were members of the Church of the Brethren.[2] However, these Bohemian Protestants were nearly decimated after their defeat at the Battle of White Mountain in 1620 during the Thirty Years War. The Lutheranism that entered Bohemia during this war was radically different from Moravian Pietism, which considered the Bible the ultimate authority and de-emphasized doctrine and creed.

The remaining Moravian Brethren who still surreptitiously practiced their faith were inspired by the writings of the distinguished educator and Moravian bishop Jan Amos Komensky (1592–1670), also known by his Latin name, John Amos Comenius. Comenius called those who secretly worshipped "The Hidden Seed," and he collected funds for their support.

In 1722, these Brethren faced a choice of renouncing their faith or leaving their homeland. Count Nikolaus Ludwig von Zinzendorf of Saxony, a devout Lutheran who believed that religious sects should not feud but coexist without rivalry, offered them a part of his land. Scores of Brethren fled across the northern borders of Moravia and Bohemia into Saxony, where they were given refuge on the Upper Lusatia estate of Count Zinzendorf.

The exiles named their settlement on Zinzendorf's estate "Herrnhut," "expressing the prayer that . . . a city might rise which should not only be unter des Herrn Hut (under the Lord's watch care) but also auf des Herrn Hut (on watch for the Lord)."[3] In 1725, ninety Moravian refugees were living at Herrnhut. Two years later, with the addition of German and Polish followers, the population had reached 300.

Zinzendorf saw Herrnhut as a Christian society within the general framework of the Lutheran Church. Some Herrnhutters wanted to join the Lutheran Church, but most of the exiles from Moravia favored reestablishing a separate church patterned on primitive Christian practices.

Ferment within the community led Zinzendorf to seek a solution. After hearing all opinions and concerns, he proposed a set of rules that the community would live by in the future called "Brotherly Agreement of the Brethren from Bohemia and Moravia and others, bidding them to walk according to the Apostolic rule." On May 12, 1727, the Herrnhutters accepted forty-two statutes. Twelve elders were chosen to oversee compliance with the rules that governed daily life. Shortly after the regulations were adopted, Zinzendorf discovered a copy of Comenius's *Ratio Disciplinae* and noticed a great similarity between the discipline of the Unitas Fratrum and the rules now governing Herrnhut.

Religiously, Zinzendorf's compromise sought to satisfy the Moravians' desire to create a separate church, which was forbidden by state law, while remaining within the Lutheran Church. It required them to remain members of the Lutheran Church at Berthelsdorf but allowed them to manage their spiritual affairs as a distinct Christian society within the Lutheran Church.[4]

Zinzendorf's influence on the development of the renewed Moravian Church was enormous. He stressed religious feeling and experience over dogma and doctrine. Beliefs centered around Christ and his sufferings on the cross. Religion was also regarded as a social experience binding the faithful together in brotherly love but apart from others.

When he was a student, Zinzendorf had established a religious society, "The Order of the Grain of Mustard Seed." Its members pledged "To be kind to all" people, "be true to Christ," and preach "the Gospel to the heathen."[5] Following these principles, the Moravians became known for their missionary zeal. Moravian Brethren believed that the spirit of love should be constantly manifested toward all the children of God, regardless of race or creed. In the late 1730s, missionaries were sent to the West Indies to convert enslaved Africans and to Greenland to work among the Eskimos. Other missions were established in the 1700s at Surinam (Dutch Guiana), Labrador, Ceylon, Cairo, Jerusalem, Constantinople, and Baghdad.

The Moravians established their church in America both as a refuge where their faith could be freely practiced if they were forced to leave Saxony and for missionary work among the Indians. First attempts at an American settlement were in Georgia in 1735, where a small group of Brethren led by August Gottlieb Spangenberg obtained a grant of land. When war broke out between England

and Spain in 1740, the Moravians abandoned their Georgian community rather than bear arms.

The next Moravian settlements were in Pennsylvania, in the villages of Bethlehem, Nazareth, and Lititz, and in North Carolina. In response to an invitation from Lord Granville, holder of a large North Carolina land grant, a party of Moravians from Pennsylvania led by Spangenberg selected a tract of land they named Wachovia. On August 7, 1753, Earl Granville conveyed the Wachovia lands—a total of 98,985 acres—to the Moravians.[6]

In Herrnhut, Bethlehem, and Wachovia, a communal lifestyle prevailed. American Moravian communities adopted a common economy out of necessity, as most immigrants had little personal property in contrast to some of the aristocrats at Herrnhut. Pooling resources and working for the benefit of the group rather than the individual were solutions to the problems associated with creating self-supporting villages on the frontier and providing for the missionaries and their families who could not contribute financially.

Under the communitarian system, Moravians did not separate church and state. The business of running the town and enforcing the rules of the congregation was vested in three main boards or committees. The duties of the *Aufseher Collegium* (board of overseers) were to superintend trade, enforce zoning laws and building codes, discipline wayward apprentices and masters, control community accounts, and allocate funds for capital-improvement projects. Matters of a strictly spiritual nature were referred to the Elders Conference, while the Congregation Council dealt with issues involving all members.

Moravian community members were required to give their labor and time to the church. There were no private enterprises; all businesses belonged to the church. The church owned all real estate, and the central board assigned work duties. In return for their labor, the Brethren received a home and were provided with food and clothing but did not receive wages.

The Moravians had a unique method of social organization called the choir system, which developed out of "bands" formed in 1727 at Herrnhut at Zinzendorf's suggestion. Bands consisted of people of the same sex, age, and marital circumstances who joined together for prayer, song, and liturgical services for mutual spiritual enrichment. The voluntary bands evolved into the choir system, which was mandatory by the late 1730s.

Choirs fostered greater spiritual fellowship than was possible in the larger settlement and facilitated meeting individual needs through more intimate social relationships. By providing members with a common residence, choirs offered members more extensive religious and social participation in religious activities "than had been possible in the weekly or even biweekly meetings of the bands."[7]

Although the number of choirs varied with the size of the community, they usually included the single sisters, the single brothers, the widowers, the widows, the married, the youths, the big girls, the little boys, the little girls, and the infants in arms. Members ate, slept, prayed, and worked within the choir organization. They lived in large houses rather than in family units. A typical choir house was a large, multistory building with dining halls, sleeping rooms, and craft shops. The income generated by each choir was turned over to the central administration. Choir members were not permitted to work outside of the community.

Another purpose of the choirs was to segregate unmarried people by gender. This was a primary concern of Count Zinzendorf, who feared that during religious excitement, "sensual relationships, with their attendant evil consequences, may develop all too easily."[8] Sexual relationships were governed by a rule adopted at Herrnhut that stated: "Familiar or intimate relations between single men and women are to be positively forbidden; moreover the Elders have the power to prohibit social intercourse as soon as they have even the slightest suspicion, no matter how worthy its purported goal."

Moravians did not practice celibacy, and married couples were allowed to meet privately once a week. However, the choir system, not the family, was the primary economic and social unit in the Moravian community. Married couples did not usually live together. Husbands lived in the Married Men's Choir, and wives lived in the Married Women's Choir.

Children were raised communally, with religious and secular training begun early. Moravians stressed education, and founded schools throughout the world. Their curricula included Latin, Greek, Hebrew, French, German, English, Mohawk, reading, writing, arithmetic, sewing, knitting, spinning, music, drawing, geography, history, and, of course, a great emphasis on religion.

Initially, all decisions in Moravian villages were based on community goals. Individual wishes were not considered important. Commitment to community goals was so strong that a person would marry when and whomever the leadership directed, would agree to live communally rather than with their spouse, would allow their children to be raised by others, would perform the kind of work needed by the community, and would contribute the profits from their work to the general coffers. Moravians were allowed to use alcohol and tobacco in moderation, but dress codes were severe, particularly for women. Each sister wore an ankle-length dress and, at church service, a traditional *Haube* (head covering).

Missionary work, which had been an extremely high priority among the Moravians under Zinzendorf's leadership at Herrnhut, was transplanted to America. Although their intention was to spread the message of Christ, they were not necessarily looking for converts to Moravianism. Christian Henry Rauch launched missionary work among Native Americans in 1740 at the village of Shekomeko in New York. He then made converts in neighboring Indian villages.

Colonial antagonism to the Moravian missionaries' work among Native Americans resulted in the Assembly of New York requiring them to swear an oath of allegiance to King George. Refusing to swear oaths on religious grounds, Moravian missionaries faced imprisonment and fines. They moved their Indian missions to Pennsylvania and founded a mission named Gnadenhutten, now in Ohio, on the Mahoning River. On November 24, unfriendly Indians attacked Gnadenhutten and burned the mission house, killing eleven missionaries, and then burned the entire village. The Christian Indians who had lived at Gnadenhutten fled to Bethlehem, and, in 1756, built another village, called Nain, a mile west of Bethlehem.

Hard-working Moravian colonists who strove to achieve financial self-sufficiency supported the Missionary work. The first settlement in North Carolina, named Bethabara, had a mill, smithy, cooperage, tool house, brick kiln, pottery, tannery, washhouse, tailor's shop, Gemeindehaus (meetinghouse), Single Brothers' House, and two bridges.

The Moravian beliefs combined pietistic religious behavior with a zeal for commerce. A person's work and its profit were considered essential to spiritual growth. Whether a candlemaker or a tinsmith, a Moravian craftsman was obligated to fully develop his skills to glorify the divine taskmaster.

The guild system was the way that the Brethren accomplished their many objectives. Salem youth began their apprenticeship under master craftsmen at age fourteen and, with rare exceptions, remained apprentices for a full seven years. Apprentices lived and worked in the Single Brothers' House. After achieving journeyman status, they continued to live with the single Brethren until they married.

Religion was well integrated into the life of every Moravian. Their day began with collective morning prayers followed by a noon liturgy. In the evening, the Moravians sang their favorite hymns at a *Singstunde*. On the Sabbath, celebrated on Saturday, the Moravian routine varied. They worked half a day, holding afternoon services. A Communion service was conducted every fourth Saturday.[9]

Distinctive Moravian religious practices were their use of the lot, great love of music, and love feasts. The lot was a method of determining God's will when a decision needed to be made. A question was put to the Lord, and then yes, no, and blank ballots were drawn blindly from a box. All important decisions were submitted to the lot, including marriage partners, choice of church leaders and missionaries, locations of towns, and acceptance of new members into the community. Both secular and religious decisions were made using the lot. If a proposal received a negative response, it was not implemented. However, the proposal could be resubmitted at another time and implemented when it received a favorable response.

A love feast was a meal eaten in common by the whole community to celebrate an event. Frequently, love feasts were intertwined with economic pursuits, like the completion of a building or the harvesting of a crop. They were joyful occasions that included hymn singing. Large cooking facilities were needed to prepare the food required, and the restored Moravian community site at Old Salem, has a remarkable eighteenth-century quantity kitchen.

Gradually, the Moravian commitment to communal living and choir organizational pattern began to weaken. Possibly, their social interaction with non-Moravians was a factor. Although living in closed communities, Moravians had business dealings with outsiders and even provided hotels for visitors. At Bethabara, a palisade was built around the village in 1755 to protect its residents from attacks by hostile Indian tribes. Non- Moravians in the area sought and were given refuge inside the palisade. Gradually the two groups became friendlier and less suspicious of each other. There were also some married couples at Bethabara who wished to live in nuclear family units. In 1759, those people along with many of the non-Moravian refugees sought and received permission to start their own community, named Bethania.

The general economy ended in 1762 in Bethlehem. The end of the communal economy did not cause the immediate break up of the Moravian societies. In fact, Bethlehem remained a closed church community until 1844. All real estate was still owned by the Moravian Church, which leased it to individuals. If a person was not considered desirable, the lease would be denied, thus effectively forcing the individual out of the community. In 1844, the policy of exclusiveness ceased when the church ended the lease system and land could be sold to Moravians and non-Moravians alike.

Although there was also discontent with the general economy in Bethabara, church leaders did not consider any changes until the original plan to build Salem, a manufacturing and trade center near Bethabara, had been implemented. Salem was a town where economic development and architectural details would be regulated as strictly as people's lives.

Construction at Salem began in 1766, and by the spring of 1772, most of the major buildings had been completed; early settlers and the government of Wachovia proceeded to move into the new town. By the time the buildings of Salem were completed, some married couples had requested separate houses for their families. So in addition to the large choir houses for single brothers and sisters, family homes were constructed.

Another change at Salem was that the general economy was modified so that men could profit from their work. Although they were allowed to take apprentices, the hiring or firing of an apprentice was still subject to church approval.

Under the church's leasehold system, the Brethren were free to live in their own homes. However, the church retained a right to the land on which their houses stood and could choose building styles.

As the area surrounding Wachovia grew more populous, the highly regimented congregation system of Salem lost much of its appeal. Gradually, the old rules were either relaxed or abandoned; and by the middle of the nineteenth century, Salem no longer functioned as a congregation town. In 1856, the lease system ended at Salem and non-Moravians were allowed to live there. Today, only the church, an active Protestant denomination, remains as a Moravian entity.

Although the original Salem ceased to exist, many of its buildings remained standing. The founding of a new town, Winston, on its northern borders in

Old Salem

1849, the growth of Winston's tobacco and textile industries, the merger of Winston and Salem in 1913, and the gradual spreading of the city until it all but engulfed the old Moravian town led to its deterioration and near extinction.

In the spring of 1950, a broad-based, nonprofit organization known as Old Salem, Inc., brought together Moravians and non-Moravians in an effort to preserve the historic town. More than fifty buildings have now been restored or reconstructed on their original sites, recreating another era in the heart of a bustling metropolis.

TOUR

Salem's large eighteenth and early ninteenth-century buildings show strong European influence. Houses sit flush with the sidewalks and have half-timbered walls, tile roofs, central chimneys, and symmetrically placed windows. The principal structures, which included houses for the single brothers, single sisters, a community store, and a tavern, were built around an open square.

After viewing the slide show at the **Visitor Center**, begin your tour at the **Town Square**, which was originally farmland but eventually came to resemble a New England commons. The reconstructed **Market Fire House** contains an exhibit of early fire-fighting equipment.

The **Single Brothers' House** is a long, two-story structure with a high basement and two attics. The northern, half-timbered portion dates from 1769; the southern, brick portion was added in 1786. Because lime, needed for mortar, was scarce in Wachovia, oak timbering was used in 1769 to reinforce the house's brickwork. By 1786, when the addition was built, lime was more plentiful, and the community used brick in all its building projects.

The Single Brothers' House was not only a residence but also contained the shops of the master craftsmen. The restored building contains craft shops stocked with appropriate tools, and craftspeople demonstrate and explain their work. Shops include a tin shop, gun shop, dye shop, weaver's room, tailor's shop, potter's shop, cooper's shop, and joiner's shop.

The **Boys' School**, a brick building facing Salem's square, was built in 1794 by master builder Johannes Gottlob Krause. It is noteworthy for the artistry that appears in the pattern of the brick masonry on the west gable, the coved cornices, and the belt course of brick on the east gable. The school was attended by boys aged six to fourteen until 1896, when it became the home of the Wachovia Historical Society. Collections of artifacts acquired by Moravian missionaries were displayed here until the 1950s, when Old Salem, Inc., restored the building and assumed management of the collection. Exhibits in the **Wachovia Museum** now relate directly to the history of Wachovia: Moravian pottery, church history, Moravian music, ironwork, lighting devices, and a restored classroom. Moravians placed great emphasis on education, and the boys' curriculum included geometry, Latin and English grammar, geography, history, penmanship, and German.

Moravians

North of the square is the **Miksch Tobacco Shop**. This 1771 building was the first privately owned house in Salem. Matthew Miksch not only lived in but also operated a tobacco business from this house. The house was built of logs, but because the Brethren disapproved of plain log houses on their Main Street, it (like others) was covered with clapboards. Originally, the house had two rooms, but Miksch added a third room at the back and a loft.

The **Winkler Bakery** was built in 1800 for a baker named Thomas Buttner. In 1808, Christian Winkler acquired the shop. Bread is still being baked in the wood-fired domed brick bake oven attached to the south side of the building. Eighteenth-century baking processes are used to produce European-style breads, cakes, and cookies. The aroma of fresh-baked bread permeates the restored area.

South of the square is the **John Vogler House**, which was built in 1819. This house has many Federal characteristics and thus represents a departure from Salem's Germanic architectural tradition. Vogler was an accomplished silversmith who also dabbled in clock making, gunsmithing, jewelry making, and silhouette making. Seventy percent of the furniture in the house belonged to the Vogler family. One room is used as a Vogler family museum, with their silver, guns, and artwork exhibited. Another room houses Vogler's silversmithing shop, displaying his spoons, ladles, and snuffboxes.

The **Schultz Shoemaker Shop** was built in 1827. Samuel Schultz originally operated his business from his 1819 home but decided to construct a separate building adjacent to it. The shop displays the tools and products of early-nineteenth-century shoemaking.

The **Vierling House,** built in 1802, was the last and largest masterwork of Johannes Krause. Unique features of this brick Georgian house are the exposed stone foundation and the herringbone gable patterns. Krause was commissioned to build the house by Dr. Samuel Benjamin Vierling, the most renowned of Salem's early physicians. It was in this house that Vierling practiced the professions of physician, surgeon, and apothecary. He is said to have performed mastectomies, skull trepans, and other major operations in his apothecary.

The **Salem Tavern Museum,** a plain three-story brick building with a veranda, was built in 1784. George Washington spent two days in 1791 at this tavern, which had a fine reputation for its food and drink. The first floor has a **Publick Room,** where the ordinary (a standard meal at a fixed price) was served each day on long tables with benches. Across the hall is a **Gentlemen's Room** for the more elite clientele, furnished with private tables and Windsor chairs. Cooking was done in the twin fireplaces of the large kitchen. There are several sleeping rooms in addition to the innkeeper's bedroom.

Old Salem Tavern, where today's visitors can stop for a meal, was originally a boardinghouse built in 1816 as an adjunct to the main tavern building. The outside is restored to its 1816 appearance, while the inside has been adapted for dining in a tavern atmosphere.

Gardens were part of the early congregational town plan. Each family maintained its own garden to supply vegetables for the table. Gardens that have been restored to various time periods include the **Treibel** and **Miksch Gardens**, 1759–61; **Eberhardt Garden**, 1814; **Levering Garden**, 1820; **Leinbach Garden**, 1822; **Cape Fear Bank Garden**, 1847; and **Anna Catharina Garden**, 1772. There is also an arboretum of native trees near the Museum of Early Southern Decorative Arts.

Operated by Old Salem, Inc., the **Museum of Early Southern Decorative Arts** was founded in 1965 by Frank L. Horton, Old Salem's first director of restoration, who also donated a large part of the collection. Nineteen rooms representative of the early South have been removed from their original locations and reassembled in the museum. They are decorated with furniture, paintings, metalwork, pottery, and glasswork produced by southern craftsmen. The museum emphasizes the products of craftspeople used between 1640 and 1820 in the three principal cultural regions of the Old South: the Chesapeake, the Carolina low country, and the back settlements.

God's Acre, founded in 1779, is the graveyard for Salem's Moravian congregation. Long rows of identical gravestones attest to the sect's belief in equality. People were buried with their fellow choir members rather than with their families. A large square is provided for each choir: married women and widows, married men and widowers, single men and boys, and single women and girls.

Salem Academy and College, a four-year liberal arts college for women, is an outgrowth of the girls' boarding school operated by the Moravians. The first building for the school was erected in 1805; it has been restored to its 1837 appearance and now serves as a dormitory. College buildings are not open to tourists.

The **Home Moravian Church** was built in 1800. Although it has undergone many interior renovations, its exterior looks much as it did originally. This church has been occupied continuously by the Moravian congregation since 1800.

Two shops are operated at Old Salem. One is in the southern half of the restored 1775 **T. Bagge Community Store,** and the other, the **Salem Gift and Book Store**, is in an 1850 addition to the 1810 **Inspector's House.**

At Old Salem, classes or lectures are given on weaving, wool dyeing, candle making, vegetable and flower gardening, nineteenth-century architecture, rug hooking, beehive-oven baking, and ice cream of the colonial period. Concerts are scheduled throughout the year.

Special events include a Spring Festival in April, a Civil War Encampment in June, a Torchlight Procession on the Fourth of July, and Salem Christmas in December. An Easter sunrise service has been held in God's Acre every year since 1772 and attracts thousands of visitors.

SIDE TRIPS

Historic **Bethabara** ("house of passage" in Hebrew) is the site of the first Moravian settlement in North Carolina. Archaeological research has uncovered the foundation walls and cellars of many of the original buildings. The 1756 **palisade**, a fort that gave refuge to outlying settlers in times of trouble, has been reconstructed. The 1788 **Gemein Haus** (Congregation House), a fine example of Moravian architecture, the 1782 **Potter's House,** and the 1803 **Brewer's House** have all been restored as exhibit buildings. The **Visitors' Center** contains exhibits on the early settlers, including many artifacts found on the site. Nature trails lead to the Moravian graveyard called **God's Acre.** Open Monday–Friday, 9:30 a.m.–4:30 p.m., and Saturday–Sunday, 1:30 p.m.–4:30 p.m., from Easter to Thanksgiving. For information, write to 2147 Bethabara Road, Winston-Salem, NC 27106; telephone (919) 924-8191. Admission is free.

Mother Ann Lee's Shakers or the United Society of Believers in Christ's Second Appearing

A studio portrait of three Shaker sisters: Emma Jane Neale (1847–1943), left; Sarah Neale (1849–1948), right; and Carrie Alice Wade (1872–1924), in back. Photograph courtesy of The Western Reserve Historical Society, Cleveland, Ohio.

BIOGRAPHICAL SKETCH OF MOTHER ANN LEE

Today, the best-known legacy of the Shakers is their highly prized, simple but elegant furniture rather than their religious beliefs. In the eighteenth and nineteenth centuries, the communal, celibate religious group was known for its exuberant worship services.

In America's communal and utopian experiments of the eighteenth, nineteenth, and early twentieth centuries, certain similarities emerge. Many of them rested on religious rather than secular principles. They were frequently a reaction against institutionalized Christian religion and a cry for a simpler, more primitive Christianity called Pietism. They frequently had mystical elements that included direct communication with the spirit world. They were typically founded in Europe and transplanted to America after repeated persecution, both legal and illegal. They were often Germanic. They were countercultural. They had charismatic leaders. And ALL of the leaders were male with the exception of the most successful communal experiment on American soil—the Shakers. Its leader was an English woman named Ann Lee.

Founder Ann Lee was an illiterate woman from Manchester, England. Biographically, documentation of her early life is sparse. Her baptism, marriage, and the death of a daughter are chronicled in church records. An extensive record of arrests and imprisonment also exists. Yes, Ann Lee was a convict who was arrested, convicted, and served time in prison both in England and America. Her crimes included profaning the Sabbath, disturbing the peace, and creating a public nuisance. It was not uncommon for charismatic religious leaders to have criminal records during the eighteenth and nineteenth centuries. With no separation of church and state in Europe, any transgression against the state church, including not attending Sunday services, was a crime.

Ann Lee (formerly Lees, the "s" was dropped in America) was born on February 29, 1736, to John Lees and his wife; she was the second of their eight children. Her mother has been described as religious. The family lived on Toad Lane in Manchester, England. Though hardworking John Lees was a blacksmith by day and a tailor by night, the family was poor. Manchester was a textile mill city, and laborers lived in unspeakably miserable conditions.

Ann's childhood was short. She was baptized in Christ Church, Manchester, on June 1, 1742, at age six. She never attended school, nor did she learn to read or write. At age eight, she began working twelve hours a day in the mills as a cutter of velvet. On Sundays, she helped clean the mill machinery. After her mother's death, Ann took on the added responsibility of caring for her younger siblings.

Ann was religious though she did not find much solace in the Church of England. After attending an outdoor revival held by George Whitefield in Manchester, she came away deeply impressed both by his message and his style.

Biographical Sketch of Mother Ann Lee

He spoke about the Holy Spirit's direct influence on a person's life. Whitefield was a zealous preacher who generated a great deal of emotional response in his audience.

By the time she was twenty-two, Ann had left the mills to work as a cook in the Manchester Infirmary, a mental hospital. Around that time, she began attending revival meetings led by Jane and James Wardley. The Wardleys were tailors from Bolton-on- the-Moors, not far from Manchester. Former Quakers, they headed a group called the Wardley Society. They were known for very emotional worship services that included open confession, impassioned preaching by Jane Wardley, and physical expressions by the congregation, including chanting, singing, shouting, shaking, and dancing. These physical movements garnered the group the derogatory name "Shaking Quakers." Jane Wardley experienced visions and other mystical manifestations about which she spoke to the congregation. The Wardleys believed that God was both male and female. Jesus Christ was a manifestation of the male aspect, but still to come was a Second Coming of Christ in female form.

Ann Lee married Abraham Standerin (the name was later changed to Stanley) on January 5, 1762, when she was twenty-six years old. Her husband, selected by her father, was also a blacksmith. They were married in the Anglican Church, signing the marriage registry with an X, as both were illiterate. The couple lived with Ann's father.

Ann gave birth to four children, three of whom died in infancy. A daughter, Elizabeth, died in early childhood. Her burial on October 7, 1766, was recorded in the cathedral registry. These tragedies caused Ann unremitting mental anguish. Consumed with grief and guilt, she spent sleepless nights calling out to God for help. She fasted until she was emaciated. She believed the death of her children was a punishment from God for her sins.

Ann eventually concluded that sexual behavior was a form of human depravity and that she and her husband should not have sexual relations. This led to many arguments between Ann and Abraham, who appealed to the local clergy. They sided with Abraham and told Ann that it was her Christian duty to submit to her husband. Ann remained adamant. Though unhappy with the arrangement, Abraham stayed with his wife and later joined the Shaking Quakers.

Ann's role in the Wardley group gradually increased until she was conducting meetings and preaching. Local authorities disapproved of the Shaker's noisy meetings. The warden raided a service held at the Lee house. Those who attended were arrested on a charge of profaning the Sabbath and confined in Manchester prison. The next morning, everyone was released except Ann Lee and her father who were imprisoned for several weeks.

In 1770, thirty-four-year-old Ann was arrested for disturbing the peace and sent to prison again. There she had a powerful vision. Consumed by religious ecstasy, she saw Adam and Eve in the Garden of Eden engaged in sexual intercourse. Found by God, the couple was expelled for their evil action. This confirmed her belief that sex was an enormous barrier between man and God, an insight that finally brought her the peace she had been searching for during the last decade. She felt reborn, free from sin at last, and anxious to share the newly discovered truth with others.

Released from prison, Ann embarked on a crusade to inform others of the evil of lust. Ann exhorted them to abandon the world of the flesh and enter the spirit world, where all sexual desire would disappear. Only celibate people could achieve true holiness.

Clearly transformed herself, Ann mesmerized her audiences with her intensity, strength, peace, and certitude. The Wardleys declared her the leader of their group, and she was addressed as Mother. Ann urged her followers to adopt celibacy and to confess their sins. Self-proclaimed sinners admitted their evil acts in lurid detail. Hostile crowds were drawn to these sensational meetings, where they mocked the penitents. On July 14, 1722, the local authorities charged Ann, her father, and two others with creating a public nuisance. At hearings held by Justice Peter Mainwaring in the Mule Inn, the Lees were sentenced to a month in prison.

The frenzied enthusiasm of Shaker worship combined with the outspoken opposition of the Shakers to the established Church of England created fear and outrage in many Manchester citizens. Rumors circulated about Shakers and witchcraft. More than once, Ann barely escaped harm when she was chased and threatened by angry mobs.

Undaunted by recurring imprisonment, on July 20, 1773, Ann, her sister, and two men disrupted a service at Christ Church in Manchester. This action resulted in a fine of twenty pounds. Unable to pay the fine, they were again imprisoned.

Because she appeared transformed after her earlier vision in prison, Ann Lee's followers declared that she exhibited godlike powers. Regarded as blasphemy by the Church of England and civil authorities, Ann was imprisoned. She was placed in solitary confinement without food or water for two weeks. In her weakened physical condition, it was equivalent to a death sentence.

Two weeks later, the prisoner miraculously walked out of her cell. However, a human being rather than the Divine had saved Ann. James Whittaker, a young, devoted follower, managed to slip into the prison each night with a pipe filled with milk and wine. He pushed the pipe stem through the keyhole of the prison cell, and Ann drank the liquid and survived.

Imprisoned yet again, Ann had another powerful spiritual experience. In this vision, she was filled with the spirit of Jesus Christ, who anointed her as his successor on earth. She became the incarnation of the Word of God, the Second Coming of Christ as a woman.[1]

When Ann revealed her experience to the other Believers, they proclaimed her the Word of God. Radiating holiness, Mother Ann affected her audiences deeply. She claimed it was not her voice but Christ's voice within her that spoke.

Ann did not claim she was God or divine. She and her followers did not believe that Jesus was divine, but that he was the male incarnation of the spirit

Biographical Sketch of Mother Ann Lee

of God. She was the female incarnation of the spirit of God. Eventually, Shaker doctrine declared that Mother Ann, who was the Second Coming of Christ in its female aspect, had fulfilled the millennium. This belief developed more strongly after her death than during her lifetime.

The picture that emerges of Mother Ann Lee is one of an inspired and saintly woman. Known for her preaching ability, she could make a congregation weep or shout with joy. She convinced many followers that she had been given the truth. She was known to be loving, strong, energetic, kind, gentle, modest, and hardworking, with an uncanny ability to look into people's hearts. She was deeply loved by other Shakers.

No photograph or drawing exists of Mother Ann Lee. She has been depicted as a short, robust woman with penetrating blue eyes. The words beautiful, radiant, and glowing were frequently used to describe Ann, and whether physical beauty or spiritual qualities are being described is difficult to discern.

Seeking freedom from unremitting persecution for her religious beliefs and practices, Mother Ann contemplated immigrating to the American colonies. She received a sign that God wanted her to take her church to where many waited to join. Confirming the decision, James Whittaker had a vision in which he saw a large tree whose leaves shone like a burning torch. Whittaker interpreted that sign to mean that he was to help plant the tree of faith in the New World.[2]

A small party of nine Shakers: Ann, her husband, her brother William, her niece Nancy Lee, John and Richard Hocknell, James Whittaker, Mary Partington, and James Shepherd, left Liverpool aboard the *Mariah* on May 19, 1774, and docked at New York City on August 6, 1774. The small band of Believers found lodging and jobs. Though Ann was a washerwoman and Abraham was a blacksmith, their meager wages still left them impoverished, as were the other Shakers. Abraham, who never reconciled himself to a sexless marriage, left Ann for another woman within a year of reaching New York.

The Believers had arrived in New York at a tumultuous political moment in American history. Colonial resentment of English rule had resulted in anti-British actions. The colonies were ready to revolt. The small band of British pacifists resolved to leave New York City, and in the summer of 1775, John Hocknell sailed up the Hudson River to Albany looking for land to purchase. He found a tract of woods eight miles northwest of Albany owned by Stephen Van Rensselaer, a Dutch patroon. Instead of selling the land, Van Rensselaer agreed to lease it to the Shakers in perpetuity. The land was called Niskeyuna, an Indian term meaning "Where the Water Flows," because of its winding river. The Dutch name for the property was Watervliet. Mother Ann was elated that they had finally found a home in which to practice their religion remote from the eyes of the world.

Before they could move to Watervliet, Hocknell returned to England to liquidate his property and to get his family. He and his relatives, along with the John Partington family, landed in Philadelphia Christmas Day, 1775. The religious group was forced to wait until the ice melted on the river before they could travel to their new home. However, William Lee and James Whittaker had spent the previous autumn clearing the land, and Mother Ann had visited Watervliet several times already. Arriving in the spring of 1776, the Believers narrowly escaped the capture of New York City by General Howe, the British commander who had forced out George Washington and his colonial troops.

Much hard work faced the pioneers at Niskeyuna. They cleared and drained the land, built cabins, and planted crops. They were plagued with meager food supplies, snakes and insects, wild animals, sickness, fever, and harsh winters. Their neighbors were Mahican Indians who, displaced by whites, had relocated in the area. Mother Ann visited them and smoked a peace pipe with them. As so many others, the Mahicans recognized the goodness of Mother Ann and dubbed her "Good Woman." The Native Americans generously taught the Shakers to grow corn, dry seeds, weave baskets, make herbal medicines and dyes, ice fish, and track wild animals. The help of these Native Americans was invaluable to the small band's survival in the harsh environment.

The Believers had come to the New World to spread their religion to others, and when, after several years, no converts had been made, they were very disappointed. It was at this time that Joseph Meacham Jr. was attracted to the group. Meacham, a Separate Baptist lay minister in New Lebanon, was active in the New Light stir, a series of revivals in 1779 in New York and Massachusetts. Revivalists predicted that Christ's Second Coming was imminent. At frenzied religious events, participants went into trances, spoke in tongues, and prophesied. When Christ did not appear, ecstasy gave way to despair.

When word about a small band of religious folk who claimed that Christ's Second Coming had already occurred in the form of a female spread to the disappointed revivalists, some decided to investigate. Calvin Harlow, an associate of Meacham, traveled to Niskeyuna and questioned Ann Lee. Based on Paul's admonition against female leaders in the Church, Harlow demanded an explanation for a female claiming to be Christ's Second Coming. Ann's answer was a parable about a family in which children were subject to both parents, and the wife was subject to the husband. If he was absent, then the woman was the head of the family. In the absence of Christ, Mother Ann was the head of Christ's family.

When Meacham learned of Ann's answer, he was impressed. After he visited Niskeyuna in May 1780, spoke with Mother Ann, and observed the worship services, Meacham became the first convert to Shakerism in the New World. His wife, children, father, and others from the New Light movement joined him. Word of Meacham's conversion attracted more visitors to Niskeyuna, many of whom joined the community.

Coming to America did not end the Shaker's legal problems, which now became political rather than religious. During the American Revolution, rebellious colonials considered British Loyalists in the colonies traitors. New York established a body of "Commissioners for detecting and defeating Conspiracies," and by mid-1780, the Albany commissioners suspected that some Shakers were British sympathizers. Brother David Darrow, apprehended while driving a flock of sheep to Niskeyuna, was accused of bringing the sheep to the enemy. When, at his hearing, Darrow as well as John Hocknell and Joseph Meacham said that they would never bear arms and would try to persuade others not to also, they were imprisoned.

On July 26, 1780, John Partington, William Lee, Ann Lee, James Whittaker, Calvin Harlow, and Mary Partington were arrested for "dissuading the friends to the American cause from taking up Arms in defence of their Liberties." Admitting to these actions, the Shakers were jailed. The men were released in mid-November, and Ann was released in early December after William Lee pleaded with Governor George Clinton.[3]

Mother Ann, accompanied by her brother William and James Whittaker, went on a journey throughout Massachusetts and Connecticut, from May 1781 to September 1783, to visit the converts who had visited Niskeyuna. They stayed at their homes and held public meetings that attracted both new converts and enemies. At times, they were physically attacked by mobs, dragged from their beds, whipped, beaten, and driven out of town. These attacks probably were a contributing factor to William and Ann Lee's early deaths.

William Lee died at Niskeyuna on July 21, 1784. Only two months later, on September 8, Ann Lee died at age forty-eight, possibly the victim of mob violence.[4]

Although many groups formed around a charismatic person dissolve after the leader's death, the Shakers survived and in fact thrived for more than a century after Mother Ann's death. In America, Ann Lee headed her small but growing number of followers for only ten years, yet a series of competent leaders directed thousands of Shakers in nineteen communities for more than a hundred years.

The gravestone of the English founder of the Shakers, Mother Ann Lee, in the Shaker Cemetery at Watervliet, New York, the first Shaker community. Photograph by Patricia A. Gutek.

Mother Ann Lee's Shakers

Even though Ann Lee was without doubt the spiritual leader of the Shakers, she shared administrative responsibilities with her brother William and James Whittaker. After William and Ann's deaths, Whittaker assumed the leadership of the society. Not everyone accepted him as head, including two of the founding Shakers, James Shepherd and Richard Hocknell. They and John Partington left the society.

James Whittaker, who is said to have been raised by Mother Ann, died three years after her at age thirty-seven. Mother Ann had led the Shakers during their fluid and revivalistic founding years. Father James's abbreviated tenure was characterized by organizational efforts to gather scattered converts in New England into family units. Whittaker also supervised the erection of the first Shaker meetinghouse at New Lebanon, New York, in 1785.

Whittaker was succeeded as lead elder by Joseph Meacham Jr., who Ann Lee repeatedly predicted would gather the church into gospel order. He appointed Lucy Wright as lead eldress to equally share authority, thus formalizing the male-female duality of Shaker leadership. From that time on, where there was an elder, there was an eldress, and where there was a deacon, there was a deaconess.

The selection of Meacham and Wright, who were both American converts, signaled the end of the founding English Shakers' leadership. Lucy Wright, born in Pittsfield in 1760, was married to Elizur Goodrich, a Richmond, Massachusetts, merchant. The young couple converted after visiting Mother Ann at Niskeyuna. In 1781, Ann Lee appointed Lucy as head of sisters' affairs at Niskeyuna. Her remarkable organizational skills led Joseph Meacham to select her as eldress at New Lebanon.

Structure and organization would be the priorities of the leaders during the next several decades. Mother Ann had provided the spiritual impetus, while her successors were concerned with unifying Believers by formulating doctrines, laws, covenants, rituals, and establishing governing structures. Obedience to those in authority was emphasized.

Up to this time, Shakers had followed conventional individualistic residential patterns. Members, who had lived on their own farms, shared beliefs and met for religious meetings. Meacham and Wright decided that scattered Believers should live together communally in extended family units far away from non-Believers, who were collectively termed "the world" or "world's people." This process was called "gathering."

Father Joseph, who drew up a covenant for new members to sign, formalized communalism in 1795. In it, converts irrevocably consecrated their property to the Shakers. Property included land, animals, household goods, tools, and cash. Many contributions were very small, though others were substantial. New communities often began on land donated by a convert. When entire families joined, children of course brought no possessions of value. Deacons and Deaconesses in each family then administered economic affairs. They not only oversaw finances but also provided food, clothing, and housing equally to all family members. Wages were not paid.

Biographical Sketch of Mother Ann Lee

The first gathering occurred at New Lebanon, which also became the headquarters of the lead ministry. A meetinghouse was built at New Lebanon, and the first meeting was held on January 29, 1786. In 1790, communities were organized at Hancock, Massachusetts, and Enfield, Connecticut; in 1792, at Canterbury, New Hampshire, and Tyringham, Massachusetts; in 1793, at Enfield, New Hampshire, Shirley, Massachusetts, Harvard, Massachusetts, and Alfred, Maine; and in 1794, at New Gloucester, Maine.

Shakers formed nineteen communities in eight states. Typically, within each community were several families who were ranked spiritually. The Church or Founding Family was the highest or most spiritually advanced. Each family had between 30 and 100 people and was governed by two elders and two eldresses.

Families lived together in one or more dwelling houses with shared sleeping rooms, large dining rooms, kitchens, and meeting rooms. Although men and women resided in the same building, dwelling houses were designed to minimize contact between the sexes. They had double doors, one for the men and one for the women, wide hallways, and parallel staircases for each gender. Retiring rooms or bedrooms for men and women were either on different floors or separate sides of the building. The dining room was also segregated, with men and women eating at separate tables on different sides of the room.

Near the dwelling house were the family's shops, mills, barns, sheds, pens, stables, gardens, and fields. Each family was an economic unit and tried to provide for most of their own needs in terms of food, shelter, and clothing. Though Shaker women had leadership roles, work assignments followed traditional gender lines, with women cooking, cleaning, weaving, sewing, knitting, doing laundry, and caring for children while men farmed and plied trades like blacksmithing and carpentry in the workshops.

Two or three communities constituted a bishopric. In the First Bishopric were Watervliet and New Lebanon, New York. In the Second Bishopric were Hancock, Tyringham, and Enfield, Connecticut. In the third Bishopric were the communities at Alfred, Gorham, and New Gloucester, Maine.

Since people were not born into the celibate Shaker religion, missionary activities were necessary to attract converts. Because Mother Ann and her associates' trip through New England had resulted in physical attacks, Father James Whittaker suspended missionary journeys. He felt converts could be attracted through publications about the Shakers. Later, using a clever marketing technique, missionaries targeted locations where religious revivals were taking place to preach. Those drawn to the revivals were frequently still searching for their religious identity and were receptive to the Shaker message.

Father Joseph Meacham resigned as lead Elder in 1796, several months before his death in August. Mother Lucy Wright remained the leader. *Millennial Laws* was the formalization of Shaker laws and worship. Prior to 1821, rules were communicated verbally and varied somewhat from village to village. Assembled by Brother Freegift Wells of Watervliet, the *Laws* were a written record of regulations and admonitions, many of which had been observed for decades. Topics included confession of sin, Sabbath practices, separation of the sexes, financial policies for the deacons, rules for dealing with the world, fire safety, neatness, table manners, and care of animals.

Mother Lucy expressed reservations about the publication of the *Millennial Laws* and refused to have it distributed. She felt that a written record would inhibit flexibility in future leaders, and she feared that it would result in criticism of the Shakers if it got into the hands of the world. After her death in February 1821, copies of the laws were given to all Shaker families.[5]

Mother Lucy regularized Shaker dress between 1805 and 1815 and stressed modesty not fashion. Brethren wore long, baggy trousers, and sisters wore long gowns, high collars, and neck handkerchiefs.

Spiritualism, communication from the spirit world through people called mediums, played a role in Shakerism from the beginning. Mother Ann Lee had visions that were foundational to Shakerism, including learning that Adam and Eve's carnal sin was the cause of their removal from the Garden of Eden, and the need to relocate in America, where Shakerism would thrive and grow, which it did. Founding father James Whittaker also had visions. Visions, dreams, voices, prophecies, and healings occurred at Shaker villages prior to the late 1830s, when a period of intense spiritualism began.

Mother Ann's Work, or the Era of Manifestations, refers to a period of spiritualistic activity that extended from the late 1830s to the early 1850s. Verbal and written messages, songs, dances, and artistic expressions were received from spirit world inhabitants, including Mother Ann, historical figures, family members, and angels, by human Shakers, called mediums or visionaries, who often exhibited bodily movements, including trances, shaking, and twirling. This period of Shaker history has been interpreted as highly religious, confirming the exuberant joy and enthusiasm of Shakerism, or as evidence of weird, strange people delusional enough to believe they could communicate with the dead. However it is viewed, the supernatural phenomenon was contagious and eventually spread to every Shaker community, where large numbers of Believers directly participated in it.

The earliest manifestations occurred at Watervliet, New York, in the Girls' Order during the winter of 1837–38. Young women ages ten to fourteen had visions and received messages, termed "gifts," from spirits. Learning of the visions, Believers in Shaker communities in the East, followed by those in the West, began having supernatural experiences.

The messages confirmed beliefs, gave comfort or admonitions, counseled or encouraged. In addition to written and verbal messages, some recipients received spiritual gifts of invisible objects, including "colorful balls and other playthings, golden chains and jeweled necklaces, fine clothing, treasure boxes, fruit baskets, musical instruments, lovely handkerchiefs, birds, flowers." The spirit manifestations often involved mime in which the mediums engaged in rituals that mimicked "eating, drinking, washing, planting," and other activities.[6]

Biographical Sketch of Mother Ann Lee

Curious non-Believers who heard about the visitations from the spiritual world flocked to Shaker meetings, which were open to the public. After American Indian spirits communicated with mediums who then behaved wildly, the ministry decided in 1842 to close Shaker worship services to outsiders to avoid ridicule and criticism. Also, visits by Holy Mother Wisdom, the female aspect of the Deity, had been received, and these profoundly holy and sacred occurrences needed to be treated with great solemnity. During this spiritualistic period, the Shakers began holding outdoor "Passover" feasts on carefully prepared sites in each village twice a year, in spring and fall.

Authority became a problem during the period of Mother's Work. The youngest and newest members rather than the leaders received many spiritual gifts. Shaker authority flowed downward from the lead ministry, through the elders and deacons of each family to the rank and file membership. Because the young mediums received messages directly from Mother Ann Lee, other founding Shakers, and Holy Mother Wisdom whose holiness superseded any living Shaker, traditional authority was challenged.

Most gifts were considered authentic and were regarded as tremendous blessings, although occasionally the leadership found it necessary to distinguish between true and false revelations. Inexperienced Believers might not be able to recognize that false revelations would come from an evil spirit.

In the fall of 1841, a message was received that prohibited the consumption of pork, tea, and coffee. This sparked a storm of controversy. A prior unresolved conflict in the society had concerned vegetarianism, with the young in favor of it and the older members opposed to it. Although some doubted the message's authenticity, a ruling from the lead ministry supported it. In 1855, the ban against tea and coffee was lifted. Members had already resumed eating pork. By the mid-1840s, spiritual manifestations had begun decreasing, and by the 1850s had faded completely.

Apostasy was an ongoing problem in Shakerism as in other communal religious groups. Adults who joined and initially believed became disenchanted. Children raised in the communities decided to leave when they reached adulthood. Prohibitions against sex and marriage were particularly difficult for young adults, some of whom left for that reason. There were power struggles in which the person who lost would leave. Sometimes sisters or brethren who were considered sinful and unrepentant were excommunicated. Even visionaries left after the spiritualist movement waned. The apostasy rate was highest among those between the ages of sixteen and twenty-nine. On their departure from the Shakers, apostates generally received clothing, cash, and tools if they had a trade.

Some who left Shakerism simply blended into the world, and others embarked on lifelong crusades of revenge and hatred, severely attacking the Shakers' reputation in publications. An early and prolific apostate was Valentine Rathbun, a Separate Baptist minister from Pittsfield, Massachusetts. Rathbun, many from his congregation, and several family members converted in 1780 after a visit to the twelve Shakers at Niskeyuna. A few months later, possibly in reaction to not being appointed an elder as he believed he had been promised, Rathbun left.

In an effort to expose and destroy the Shakers, Rathbun wrote in 1781 *An Account of the Matter, Form, and Manner of a New and Strange Religion, Taught and Propagated by a Number of Europeans, Living in a Place called Nisqueunia, in the State of New-York*. One of the earliest published accounts of Shaker life, it is completely negative. Rathbun accused the Shakers of witchcraft, of being British collaborators during the Revolution, and of deceitfulness toward potential converts. Describing Shaker meetings as noisy sessions of commotion and bedlam, he claimed some participants hooted like owls, crowed like roosters, hissed like ganders, and ran naked through the woods.[7]

In the 1870s, long after the period of manifestations ended, many Believers became concerned about a lack of religious vitality, as evidenced by membership decline. According to the 1870 census, there were 1,444 Shakers in the eastern communities, down 40 percent from a high of 2,427 in 1840. In an effort to revitalize and add new blood, a missionary program was undertaken. Selected members lectured at public meetings, accompanied by singers from Canterbury as well as dancers. The missionaries generated large crowds, as there was an extraordinary interest in Shakerism. Another missionary tool was a publication begun in 1871 called *The Shaker*, which explained their tenets and beliefs. Frederick Evans, one of the most prominent missionaries, also preached in England. His "Autobiography of a Shaker" was published in the *Atlantic Monthly* in 1869 and later as a book.

Still, the numbers continued to decline. After 1875, Shaker villages began to close; the first was Tyringham, Massachusetts, in 1875, followed by the Ohio communities of North Union in 1889, Groveland in 1892, and Watervliet in 1900. The year 1907 witnessed the end of Ohio's Whitewater village, succeeded by Shirley, Massachusetts, in 1908, Pleasant Hill, Kentucky, and Union Village, Ohio, in 1910, Enfield, Connecticut, in 1917, and Enfield, New Hampshire in 1918. That same year saw the termination of the Harvard, Massachusetts, community, then South Union, Kentucky, in 1922. The Alfred, Maine, community disbanded in 1931, Watervliet, New York, in 1938, and New Lebanon, New York, in 1947. The Hancock, Massachusetts, village closed in 1960.

The year 1974 marked the 200th anniversary of the arrival in America of Ann Lee and her fellow Shakers. At that time, two Shaker villages remained: Canterbury, New Hampshire, and Sabbathday Lake, Maine. However, in 1972, the few Shakers still residing at Canterbury, New Hampshire, had turned their property over to a preservation group to establish an outdoor museum. All the Canterbury Shakers have since died. Sabbathday Lake Village is the only active Shaker community that exists today.

Museum villages have been established at Pleasant Hill and South Union, Kentucky; Sabbathday Lake, Maine; Hancock, Massachusetts; Canterbury, New Hampshire; and Mount Lebanon, New York. There is also a fine collection of Shaker furniture and artifacts at the Shaker Museum in Chatham, New York.

MOUNT LEBANON
SHAKER VILLAGE
1787–1947, New Lebanon, New York
NR, NHL, HABS

ADDRESS: P.O. Box 628, New Lebanon, NY 12125
TELEPHONE: (518) 794-9500
LOCATION: In eastern New York, southeast of Albany, on Route 20, near the Massa-
chusetts border, 11 miles west of Pittsfield, Massachusetts.
OPEN: Daily, 9:30 a.m.–5:00 p.m., Memorial Day weekend–Labor Day weekend; Fri-
day–Sunday, 9:30 a.m.–5:00 p.m., Labor Day–October 31.
ADMISSION: Adults, $5; seniors, $4; children 6–17, $3; family rate, $13.
RESTAURANTS: No.
SHOPS: Gift shop.
FACILITIES: Self-guided tour; guided tours on weekends.

OVERVIEW

Executive headquarters of the United Society of Believers in Christ's Second Appearing from 1787 to 1947, Mount Lebanon was the second community founded by the Shakers. Elders from the other eighteen Shaker villages
reported to and took direction from the lead ministry at Mount Lebanon. The
central ministry's administrative duties included appointing elders at other communities, removing ineffective leaders, dealing with apostates, defining economic policies, developing and enforcing moral and religious rules, opening
and closing villages, and dealing with civil authorities regarding military service, pacifism, taxes, and litigation.

Today, Mount Lebanon is the least restored of the Shaker museum villages. Although a large number of original buildings remain at the site, most of
them are occupied by the Darrow School and are not open to the public. Tourists usually visit two or three buildings. If a guide is available, several additional
buildings can be visited. There are plans for further restoration, but progress
has been slow.

Yet, it is at Mount Lebanon that visitors can truly experience a sense of a
Shaker village. In a pastoral setting, strung along a winding road are clusters of
buildings from the Church, North, and Center families. Walking up the old
Albany- Boston Post Road, with a little imagination visitors may feel that they
are indeed in a place separated from the world. As Charles Nordhoff wrote in
1875: "Mount Lebanon lies beautifully among the hills of Berkshire . . . admira-
bly placed on the hillside to which it clings, securing it good drainage, abundant water, sunshine, and the easy command of water-power. Whoever selected
the spot had an excellent eye for beauty and utility in a country site. The views
are lovely, broad and varied; the air is pure and bracing; and, in short, a com-

pany of people desiring to seclude themselves from the world could hardly have chosen a more delightful spot."[1]

HISTORY

Mount Lebanon was an active Shaker village from 1787 to 1947 and home to the central ministry of the Believers. Shaker leadership as conceived by Joseph Meacham, the first American elder to succeed the English founders, was a hierarchy in which authority flowed in a top-down direction from the central ministry, which usually consisted of two elders and two eldresses. Immediately beneath them were the bishopric ministries, consisting of two elders and two eldresses appointed by the central ministry. Each bishopric was comprised of several villages. Village ministries constituted the next level of authority, followed by the elders of each family in the village. Religious and economic responsibilities were administered separately, with religious authority vested in elders and economic responsibilities in deacons.

Members of the central ministry who presided over a network of eighteen large villages from Maine to Kentucky held extremely powerful positions religiously, socially, and economically. Obedience to authority figures was based on the premise that leaders were divinely inspired. As Hervey Elkins said in his "Fifteen Years in the Senior Order of the Shakers," published in 1853, "All are to regard their spiritual leaders as mediators between God and their own souls; and these links of divine communication, successively descending from Power and Wisdom, who constitute the dual God, to their Son and Daughter, Jesus and Ann, and from them to Ann's successors . . . this concatenated system of spiritual delegation is the river of life, whose salutary waters flow through the celestial sphere for the cleansing and redemption of souls."[2]

The first community established by Mother Ann Lee and the founding Shakers was at Niskeyuna, also known as Watervliet, New York, in 1776. A lengthy missionary trip through New England by Mother Ann and several followers made many converts, some of whom resided in the New Lebanon area. The first gathering occurred at New Lebanon on property donated by converts.

James Whittaker supervised the erection of the first Shaker meetinghouse there in 1785, and the first meeting was held on January 29, 1786. Construction of communal buildings included the Great House built in 1788, the Brick House in 1789, and the Bake House in 1790. In 1791, construction was started on buildings for the Second Family.

When Joseph Meacham succeeded James Whittaker as lead elder in late 1787, the headquarters of the lead ministry was moved from Watervliet to New Lebanon. Meacham selected Lucy Wright, who had served as Ann Lee's head of sisters' affairs at Niskeyuna because of her remarkable organizational skills, as lead eldress at New Lebanon.

While Mother Ann had been the inspiration for the Believers, Meacham was the organizer of the sect. At New Lebanon, Meacham developed the prototype for other Shaker villages. He formulated the concept of relatively self-sufficient economic family units of 100 people or less who lived communally, living, eating, and working together. Several families, each with its own living facilities, constituted a village. Families were ranked as to their degree of holiness, with the Church or founding family the highest rank and the family containing new members the lowest rank. Other families were commonly named Second, West, South, North, and East.

Although Shaker meetings were initially characterized by charismatic expressions of worship with unchoreographed dancing, speaking in tongues, ecstatic songs without identifiable words, and visions from the spirit world, Meacham introduced pattern, structure, and communalism to the Shakers, and his work was continued by his successors. The once verbal covenant of membership was written in 1795. Songbooks were printed. Dances were choreographed. Rules and regulations pertaining to just about every aspect of Shaker life were written and distributed to members.

As lead ministers, Joseph Meacham and Lucy Wright oversaw the initial gathering of converts into communities at other locations. The elders appointed for each community were drawn from the membership at New Lebanon. When Meacham died in August 1796, Lucy Wright served as leader of the sect for the next twenty-five years. She organized a Gathering Order of missionaries who sought converts throughout New England. New Believers joined New Lebanon's North family, which was considered a novitiate family, confessed their sins, became probationary members, and worked without compensation. When judged ready by the elders, a new Believer was moved to one of the other families.

In 1805, Mother Lucy authorized a western missionary expedition by John Meacham, Issachar Bates, and Benjamin Seth Youngs through the Ohio Valley into southern Ohio and Kentucky. This expedition resulted in the establishment of Shaker communities in the West.

New Lebanon was a prosperous community with 6,000 acres and 125 buildings. Primarily engaged in agriculture, the community also produced and sold garden seeds, herbs, chairs, flat brooms, leather goods, and baskets.

Believers lived in eight families: the Church, Center, North, South, East, and Second families at New Lebanon, and the Upper and Lower Canaan families in adjacent Canaan. During New Lebanon's 160-year history, its population varied considerably, starting with 221 in 1790, growing to more than 300 between 1800 and 1820, and reaching more than 400 between 1830 and 1850. Resident membership peaked at 550 in 1860 before declining to more than 300 in the 1870s and 1880s and to 124 by 1900.[3] When the community closed in 1947, only two sisters remained.

In the 1830s and 40s, the occurrences of spiritual gifts, that is, communication with the spirit world in the form of visions, dreams, voices, and prophecies transmitted through human mediums, accelerated throughout the Shaker world. The central ministry affirmed their authenticity but admonished that "the gifts" from God "be used to support union and order within the society."[4]

Mother Ann Lee's Shakers

The intense spiritualism of this period was in the Shakers' charismatic tradition. The bizarre behavior of the human mediums or instruments attracted many spectators to the meetings, which were subsequently closed to outsiders by order of the central ministry in 1842.

The first outdoor Passover feast was held on a site called the Mount of Olives on East Mountain at New Lebanon, now renamed "Holy Mount." Members of other communities attending this ritual were then directed to hold similar ceremonies.

Visionaries continued to receive new rules and regulations, leading the central ministry to revise the *Millennial Laws* in 1845. In 1846, eight young members of the Church family at New Lebanon, two of whom were instruments, apostatized, which greatly disturbed many Shakers and weakened their faith in the spiritual gifts.

The name of the New Lebanon community was changed to Mount Lebanon in 1861 when a post office was established. During the period of Mother's Work, it was renamed "Holy Mount."

The Civil War caused problems for the Shakers, who were pacifists. Their official position, outlined by the central ministry, was that "Believers, who are obeyers, cannot, under any circumstances engage in military servitude of any name or nature."[5] Frederick W. Evans, an elder of the North family, negotiated resistor status for young Shaker brethren in a meeting he and Benjamin Gates had with Abraham Lincoln in Washington in 1862. The brethren developed a fondness for Lincoln, sent him a chair, which he thanked them for, and, just weeks before the president was assassinated, invited him to take a much-needed rest at Mount Lebanon.

Elder Frederick Evans (1892) surrounded by members of the Mount Lebanon North family, which he served as an elder for fifty-seven years. Photograph courtesy of the Shaker Museum and Library, Old Chatham, New York.

Mount Lebanon Shaker Village

Charles Nordhoff, who visited Mount Lebanon in 1874, said, "I have found all or nearly all the Shaker people—polite, patient, noiseless in their motions except during their 'meetings' or worship, when they are sometimes quite noisy; scrupulously neat, and much given to attend to their own business. The Sabbath quiet and stillness which prevailed I attributed to the fact that there had been a death in the family, and the funeral was to be held that morning; but I discovered afterward that an eternal Sabbath stillness reigns in a Shaker family—there being no noise or confusion, or hum of busy industry at any time, although they are a most industrious people."[6]

Fire set by an arsonist destroyed eight uninsured Church family buildings with an estimated value of $100,000 on February 6, 1875. Later that same month, the herb house and its valuable contents burned at an estimated loss of $50,000.

Declines in membership and financial hardship hit all the Shaker villages hard. In 1930, the Church family property at Mount Lebanon, consisting of forty buildings and 300 acres, was sold for $75,000 to the Lebanon School, later renamed the Darrow School. Mount Lebanon closed October 15, 1947, and its two remaining members moved to Hancock. Most of the North family property was initially sold to a religious society, but in the late 1960s, the Darrow School acquired it. In the late 1970s and early 1980s, the school acquired more of the North family land and the remains of the Stone Barn, which had burned in 1972.

In 1991, Mount Lebanon Shaker Village, a nonprofit corporation formed to maintain, preserve, and restore the buildings, purchased the twenty-five extant buildings of the Church, Center, and North families from Darrow School. While the process of preservation is ongoing, the majority of the buildings have been leased back to the school.

TOUR

Mount Lebanon Shaker Village, a nonprofit corporation, owns twenty-five buildings from the North, Church, and Center families. Those leased to the Darrow School may be viewed from the outside.

Tickets for the self-guided tour are sold in the 1838 **Granary**. This North family two- story, wood frame building was used to store seeds and grain. It now houses the **gift shop,** which stocks a variety of books related to Shakerism as well as craft items.

The 1854 **Washhouse** was converted from a woodshed to a laundry facility in the 1860s. The large three-story frame building contained water-powered laundry equipment in the basement, with ironing and drying equipment on the first floor. The unfurnished building retains its built-in drying racks and has a classroom, as the washhouse was also used as a school. Agricultural equipment is also displayed.

The 1829 **Brethren's Workshop**, a five-story brick building, now houses the Mount Lebanon Shaker Village office.

The 1860 **Plant Nursery** is a small wooden structure that served as a garden seed house.

Although it burned in September 1972, the walls of the North family's **Stone Barn** remain, indicating how large and impressive the 1859 structure was. The 196-by-50-foot barn was designed by George Wickersham and built by a Lenox, Massachusetts, company at a cost of $20,000. Five stories high, cattle stalls were on the first floor, and hay and other crops were stored on the second and third floors.

The **Darrow School** occupies the 1835 **Second Dwelling House**, the 1840 **Farm Deacon's Shop**, the 1838 **Tannery**, the 1875 **Ministry House**, the 1875 **Dwelling House**, the **Dairy**, an eighteenth-century structure that predates the Shakers occupation, the 1826 **Brethren's Workshop, Cherry Lane Cottage,** the **Sheep Barn**, the 1864 **Valentine Cottage**, the **Medicine Shop, Ann Lee Cottage**, the 1839 **Shaker Schoolhouse**, the 1857 **Shaker Infirmary**, the 1827 **Trustees' Office and Store**, and the 1852 **Sisters Shop and Store**.

HANCOCK SHAKER VILLAGE
1790–1959, Pittsfield, Massachusetts
NR, NHL

ADDRESS: P.O. Box 898, Pittsfield, MA 01202
TELEPHONE: (413) 443-0188
LOCATION: In the Berkshire Hills of western Massachusetts, 5 miles west of Pittsfield, at the junction of Routes 20 and 41.
OPEN: Daily, 9:30 a.m.–5:00 p.m., May 1–October 31; 10:00 a.m.–3:00 p.m., April and November; tours by appointment only, December–March.
ADMISSION: Adults, $10; children 6–17, $5; families, $25.
RESTAURANTS: Village Café; Saturday evening candlelight dinner in Believers' Dining Room, from mid-July through mid- October.
SHOPS: Village Shop with reproduction Shaker furniture and furniture kits, crafts, books, and herb products.
FACILITIES: 1,200 acres; craft demonstrations; historic farm and gardens; orientation films; children's summertime discovery room; special events; craft workshops; twice-yearly tours for sight- and hearing-impaired persons.

OVERVIEW

Hancock Shaker Village is the site of a Shaker community founded over 200 years ago—one of nineteen American communities founded by the communal religious group. About 300 Believers lived, worked and worshipped at Hancock during its 170 years of existence from 1790 to 1960. Twenty original Shaker buildings have been restored at this museum village situated on 1,200 acres in western Massachusetts' picturesque Berkshire Hills. Hancock has an impressive collection of original Shaker furniture, tools and equipment, household objects, textiles, and spirit drawings displayed in room settings or in gallery exhibits. Because the Shakers at Hancock were engaged primarily in agriculture, farming activities and gardens are also a significant aspect of this outdoor museum of Shaker life and crafts.

HISTORY

On her missionary tour of New England, Mother Ann arrived in Hancock, Massachusetts, in August 1783. She stayed at the home of Daniel Goodrich and held meetings there, which were sometimes disrupted by mobs of opponents. Valentine Rathbun, an early Shaker convert who had renounced his membership in bitterness, urged the hostile crowd on.

Mother Ann and her associates retreated to nearby Richmond, where they were arrested on charges of blasphemy and disorderly conduct. The Richmond Board of Justices fined them twenty dollars and ordered them to leave the state. Ignoring that order, the Shakers went to the Hancock home of Nathan and Hannah Goodrich and resumed preaching to large crowds. Rathbun, again, led a mob that disrupted the meetings and threatened to harm their leaders.

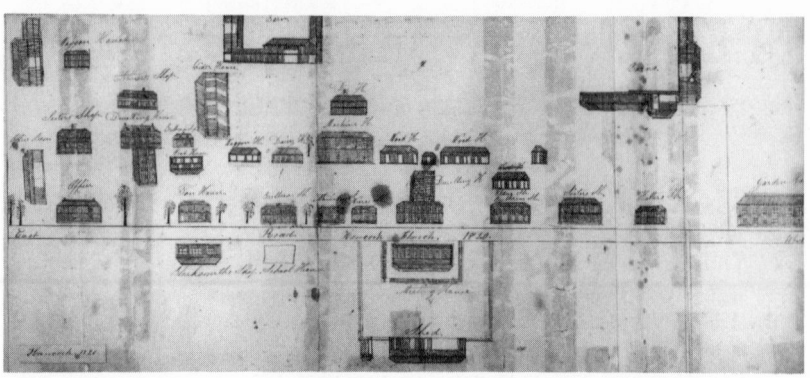

Pen-and-ink sketch (1820) of the Shaker village at Hancock, Massachusetts.
Photograph courtesy of the Shaker Museum and Library, Old Chatham, New York.

Ann and William Lee assured the unruly crowd that they would leave the
following day, which they did. They returned to Niskeyuna, New York, in the
fall.[1]

The Hancock Believers laid the foundation for a meetinghouse, where
they could worship, on August 30, 1786. Framed by Moses Johnson, it was 44-
by-32 feet with a large meeting room on the first floor and rooms for the ministry upstairs. In 1790, Elder Joseph Meacham dispatched Elder Henry Clough
and two other brethren to Hancock to bring the Believers there into gospel
order, that is, to establish a community. Hancock's first communal meal was
held on Christmas in 1790, and the formal gathering of the Hancock Church
family, presided over by Father Joseph Meacham, occurred on January 14, 1791.
Nathaniel Deming and Cassandana Goodrich constituted the first ministry at
Hancock.

The Goodrich, Talcott, and Deming families deeded over farms in the
Hancock area to the Shakers. The Church family was located on Daniel and
Anna Goodrich's farm. The Second family, also established in January 1791,
was located on the John Deming farm in West Pittsfield. The West family
originated on the Talcott farm in 1792, and the East family settled on the
Bryington farm in West Pittsfield in October 1793.

Reuben Rathbun was the first elder of the Church family and Eunice
Deming was the first eldress. Reuben was the son of Valentine Rathbun, the
embittered former Shaker who published anti-Shaker diatribes. At Hancock,
Reuben grew increasingly dissatisfied. He criticized the appointment of Deming
and Goodrich as ministry elders and expressed doubt that the Second Coming
of Christ had occurred. He said that being a Believer did not end sexual desires
as promised, that many Shakers did not lead exemplary lives, that the children
were not being educated in humanitarian principles, and that those who left
the church were unfairly treated.

Reuben was replaced as Church family elder during early summer 1799. He and Sister Elizabeth Deming left the community on July 24, 1799, and subsequently married and had a son. In 1800, Reuben published an exposé of the Shakers in which he alleged that Mother Ann was frequently drunk and violent.[2]

Like the other Shakers, the Hancock Believers were communal. In 1791, they verbally agreed to consecrate their property and service. In 1796, they drew up their first written covenant, pledging their possessions and their devotion to the service of God and the gospel forever. They also promised never to bring claims for property or services against the society or its members.

The early decades of the nineteenth century brought an increase to the ranks and prosperity of the Hancock Shakers. By 1803, there were 142 people in five families. The population had grown to 317 by 1820 and to 338 by 1830.

Agriculture was the major pursuit at Hancock, with 2,000 acres under cultivation. A machine shop was built in 1790 with an overshot wheel powered by a waterpower system, which also provided water to the barns, stables, washing rooms, and saw mill. By 1795, a dairy was in operation.

In 1820, the Church family had thirty-four buildings, including a meetinghouse, two dwelling houses, an office, a schoolhouse, a machine shop, nurse's shop, dye shop, tan shop, blacksmith shop, hatter's shop, a cider house, and four barns, as well as brethrens', sisters', and elders' shops.

In the Brethren's Shop, built in the late 1790s, tradesmen made barrels, tin objects, brooms, oval and round boxes, clocks, harnesses, shoes, chairs, and other furniture. Items produced and sold by Hancock villagers included garden seeds, medicinal herbs, flat brooms, wagons, plows, leather, hats, cars, measures, wire sieves, flax combs, woodenware, tubs, pails, cheese hoops, churns, and table swifts. The sisters produced and sold palm-leaf bonnets, cloaks, baskets, and knitted goods.

In 1826, the Church family built a unique round stone barn for their expanding dairy business. The round structure was ninety feet in diameter with limestone and granite walls one yard thick. It accommodated fifty-two cows, which fed from a central haymow. A ground floor ramp led to a circular track so that hay wagons could unload their hay and proceed back down. In the center of the mow was a ventilating shaft through which the steam from the hay could escape. In December 1864, the barn caught on fire but was rebuilt with some modifications.

A Hancock resident's day involved hard work, plentiful meals, and worship. Believers ate breakfast at 6:30 a.m., dinner at noon, and supper at 6:00 p.m.; all meals were eaten in silence. Four evenings a week, families gathered in the meeting rooms of their dwellings to dance and pray. Union meetings were held on the other evenings. At these meetings, designed by Joseph Meacham, pairs of sisters and brothers sat on chairs facing each other and conversed on specified topics, read aloud, or sang. The purpose of union meetings was to have supervised interaction between the sexes in the celibate society.

Mother Ann Lee's Shakers

During the Shakers' period of spiritual renewal in the early 1840s, Hancock Village was renamed the City of Peace, and a wooded mountain near the settlement, which they named Mount Sinai, was chosen for the community's feast grounds. A third of an acre was cleared and leveled. Twice a year, in spring and fall, the membership engaged in elaborate spiritual exercises at Mount Sinai. The ministry provided vividly colorful spiritual garments to wear. They believed angels accompanied them on their morning climb up the mountain, where the assembly sang and danced. They spiritually scrubbed each other, brethren to brethren and sister to sister. Mediums received spiritual gifts of silver and gold, which were presented to the members. After a ten-year period, the Mount Sinai rituals were discontinued.

During this period, there were frequent communications with the spirit world. Individual Shakers, the instruments or mediums, received spiritual manifestations from the spirit world, including visions, dreams, prophecies, songs, dances, and drawings. Messages arrived from Mother Ann Lee, Holy Mother Wisdom, angels, American Indians, and deceased Shaker elders and famous leaders.

Hannah Cohoon and Polly Collins received inspired artwork, called spirit drawings. Hannah and her two children joined the community when she was thirty-five. Four of Hannah's paintings remain and are probably the most well-known Shaker art. Two show the Shaker Tree of Life as described in a vision by Father James Whittaker, a third depicts mulberry trees, and the fourth is a basket of apples. Each is accompanied by a written explanation of its religious significance. Polly Collins, who joined at age twelve, produced at least fifteen watercolor paintings between 1841 and 1859.

After the period of spiritualism ended, the drawings were placed in drawers and forgotten. In the 1920s, Sister Alice Smith showed a spirit drawing to Edward Deming Andrews, a scholar on the Shakers and a collector who lived near Hancock. He was most impressed. Shaker drawings are a valuable addition to American folk art, and this extensive collection is one of the outstanding features of the Hancock restoration.

In August 1851, authors Nathaniel Hawthorne and Herman Melville visited Hancock Village. Hawthorne published his negative reactions to the Shakers in *American Notebooks*. After visiting a dwelling house, he wrote that "everything [was] so neat that it was a pain and constraint to look at it." Hawthorne claimed that two people slept in narrow beds, and there were no bathing facilities. He said that "all their miserable presence of cleanliness and neatness is the thinnest superficiality; and that the Shakers are and must need be a filthy set." Apparently not finding anything to praise in the Shaker lifestyle, he concluded "the sooner the sect is extinct the better."[3]

Pacifism was a principle that repeatedly caused problems for the Shakers. During the Revolutionary War, they were accused of being pro-British traitors when they preached about the evil of bearing arms. In 1823, twenty-three New Lebanon brethren moved to Hancock because they were eligible for conscription in New York but not in Massachusetts, where conscientious objectors were excused from military service. A year later, twenty-seven more brethren arrived.

During the Civil War, brethren were summoned to appear at their local draft boards. Elder Frederick Evans and Benjamin Gates carried a proposal to President Abraham Lincoln that he ultimately accepted. They suggested that the $600,000 in back wages the government owed the brethren who had served in the military prior to joining the Shakers, and which the ministry refused to let them collect, be allowed to cancel out the muster fines of $28,000 owed by the Shakers.[4]

The Civil War took its toll on Hancock's seed industry as all of its southern markets dried up. Another factor in the seed market decline was the transcontinental railroad, which opened national markets to large seed farms in the Midwest. Their once thriving medicinal herb business waned because of competition by pharmaceutical companies in the 1860s and 70s. The tannery closed in the 1860s, when the Tillotson Tanning Mill in nearby Pittsfield expanded.

From a peak population of 338 people organized into six families in the 1830s, membership dropped to under 200 by 1853. The South family closed in 1849. By 1900, three of the six families had closed. Although the community would continue for another century, its numbers gradually declined until only three sisters remained in 1959, the year that the central ministry at Canterbury, New Hampshire, closed Hancock.

Membership dropped for a variety of reasons. Old age and illness took a toll. Fourteen members died in a typhus epidemic in 1813. People lost faith in Shaker doctrines. Children raised by the Shakers chose not to join when they reached adulthood. This was a great loss because the economy and leadership of each family depended very heavily on young adults. Families composed primarily of children and the aged could not provide the manual labor and skill at trades necessary to maintain themselves financially. Shakers fell in love with each other. Sometimes when the community woke up in the morning, they were unpleasantly surprised to find a couple of people missing. Barnabas Sprague, second elder at the Hancock East family, and Selia Demsy left in April 1854 and were married.[5]

In the late 1860s, Hancock Shakers still were primarily farmers, having nearly a thousand acres planted with hay, Indian corn, oats, barley, rye, and potatoes. As farming became more mechanized, the Shakers acquired agricultural machinery when it became available. Even though farming was less labor intensive, workers were hired as the number of able-bodied brethren declined dramatically. In 1870, fifty men and seventy-five women lived at Hancock; in 1880, there were twenty-seven men and fifty-four women, and by 1900, there were only two men, ages fifty-three and sixty-five, and forty-one women, including ten over sixty and sixteen under age sixteen.

By 1900, only the Church, Second and East families remained in Hancock village. Fifteen hired men were living there, which resulted in romantic liaisons with some sisters. In 1900, Sister Edith Hall married Comfort Sykes, and in 1905, Eldress Emma J. Thayer married Paul J. Audette. Both men were outside workers.[6] In 1911, the East family was sold and the sisters moved to the Second family. Next, the Second family closed, leaving only the Church family. To reduce taxes, many buildings were dismantled during the 1930s and 1940s. The round stone barn was abandoned in 1932 because of a state regulation against cows being kept on wooden floors. The meetinghouse was taken down in 1938.

In the 1930s or 40s, Hancock's schoolhouse, built between 1820 and 1830, was sold and moved. The Hancock Shaker school, which was established in 1792, made a separate school district in 1800, and a public school in 1817, had operated in a variety of buildings. A school continued to operate in the brick dwelling until 1942.

In 1947, the remaining six members of the Mount Lebanon village joined the Hancock community. When the central ministry closed the community in 1960, 550 acres of woodland were transferred to the state of Massachusetts to become part of the Pittsfield State Forest in exchange for maintenance of the cemetery. Eldress Fannie Estabrook and Sisters Adeline Patterson and Mary Dahn were the only residents left at Hancock.

In October 1960, after 170 years as a Shaker village, 974 acres and twenty-one buildings were sold for $125,000 to Shaker Community, Inc., a group of local citizens who wanted to develop the site for an outdoor museum interpreting the Shaker way of life. Restoration of the buildings started soon after.

TOUR

At Hancock Shaker Village, twenty of the approximately sixty buildings that belonged to the Church family have been restored.

The **Visitors' Center**, where tickets are sold and tour information is available, is housed in a modern wooden building. Visitors are advised to allow at least two hours for touring the village; we spent an enjoyable five and one-half hours, including a lunch break. The **lunchroom** is located in the center, which also houses the **Village Shop**, where books, Shaker crafts, some needlework kits, herbs, and furniture are sold.

The six-story **Brick Dwelling**, built in 1830, was home for the 100 members of the Church family, who slept, cooked, ate, and worshiped here. On the lowest floor, you'll find the kitchen, a very large room with a brick oven capable of baking fifty loaves of bread at a time. The kitchen had running water and wood-fired appliances for boiling, steaming, deep frying, and grilling; these are still used today by interpreters to prepare food from Shaker recipes.

The Brick Dwelling housed both men and women, who used separate entrances and staircases. At meals, men sat on the east side of the dining room and women on the west at long tables. The small dining room was for elders and eldresses, who always ate apart from the others.

Today, visitors can enjoy Saturday evening candlelight dinners in summer and fall, which are served in the **Believers' Dining Room** of the Brick Dwelling.

Some of the retiring rooms on the upper floors in the dwelling house are furnished to portray rooms in other buildings that have since been demolished. Consequently, there is a deacon's office, a deaconess's sewing room, an infirmary (which contains cradles for sick adults), and a pharmacy. All the furniture in the Hancock restoration is Shaker, and much of it was made in Hancock.

One of the highlights of Hancock Shaker Village is the imposing **Round Stone Barn**. The three-story dairy barn, built in 1826, was twice destroyed by fire and faithfully reconstructed, the last time in 1968. Inside, the scope of the barn is majestic. The soaring ceiling, with its cupola, and the huge open space give it the feeling of a cathedral, not a barn. However, the Shakers built it this way for functional reasons; one man could easily feed fifty-two head of cattle working the circular area. The hay was stored in a central area. All three levels are ramped, which enabled wagons pulled by teams of horses to reach the highest level for unloading hay. Still considered an architectural treasure, the round barn alone justifies a visit to Hancock.

The **Meetinghouse**, designed and built by Moses Johnson in 1793, was originally located in Shirley, Massachusetts, but was moved to Hancock in 1962. It replaced the original Hancock meetinghouse, also built by Johnson, which had been dismantled by the Shakers in 1938 because it had fallen into disuse. Like Johnson's other meetinghouses, it is a two-story, white frame building with a gambrel roof and two front entrances, one for men and one for women. Its built-in benches, where visitors sat while observing the Shakers at worship, are original. Docents discuss Shaker religious practices and music in the meetinghouse.

The **Ministry Shop**, constructed around 1874, was where the two elders and two eldresses, who constituted the ministry, carried out their administrative duties. Like the other members of the community, the ministry was required to do manual labor, so the building had both administration offices and craft workshops.

Many Shaker crafts are demonstrated at Hancock. Visitors can watch the making of oval boxes, brooms, and chairs at the 1795 **Brethren's Workshop** and weaving and spinning in the 1795 **Sisters' Dairy and Weave Shop**. There is a blacksmith's shop and a cabinetmaker in the 1835 **Tan House**, which also has equipment for making apple cider. A printing office is in the **Hired Men's Shop and Print Shop**.

The 1790 **Machine Shop and Laundry** is the oldest building at Hancock. It contains early water-powered machinery and institution-size facilities for washing. Its ironing room has a conical stove that warmed twenty-five irons at a time. There is an herb and seed exhibit upstairs.

The **Schoolhouse** is a reconstruction on the original foundation. The original schoolhouse was moved to nearby Route 41.

The **Trustees' Office and Store** was the site of the offices of the trustees, who were charged with regulating trade and administering the lands, monies, and property of the family, as well as with conducting business with all visitors to Hancock. The office, built in 1830, was remodeled in 1895, and the austere Shaker building was converted into a High-Victorian structure with a tower, bay windows, bracketed porches, awnings, and machine-turned woodwork, reflecting the changing tastes of the Shakers.

The brick 1878 **Poultry House** now houses a research library on its second floor, and the first floor is used for changing exhibits and an orientation program.

Increasing emphasis has been placed on recreating agrarian activities at Hancock during recent years. Hancock was a self- sustaining agricultural village. Farming and raising livestock, rather than furniture making or crafts, were the major activities. An herb garden, an heirloom vegetable garden, and historic breeds of livestock represent Hancock's agricultural heritage. The **vegetable garden** is planted with many documented Shaker seed varieties. Gardeners use cultivation techniques from the mid-1800s. There are 120 varieties of herbs, both culinary and medicinal, in the **herb garden**. The Shakers were well known for their high-quality seeds and herbs, and both industries flourished at Hancock. **Museum animals** include a flock of Merino sheep, striped Dominique and white Wyandotte chickens, work horses, Brown Swiss oxen, and short horn cows. Garden tours and farm animal talks are given daily.

During July and August, the **Village's Discovery Room** has hands-on activities that introduce visitors of all ages to nineteenth-century life. Visitors may try spinning, weaving on a loom, writing with a quill pen on a slate, or weaving a basket. Shaker-style clothing can be tried on, and there are toys and games for youngsters.

Annual special events include Shearing Days with sheep shearing and other spring farm activities at the end of May; an Americana Artisans' Crafts Show in mid-July; an Antiques Show the last weekend in August; Autumn Weekend the first weekend in October; Christmas Festival the first weekend in December; Winter Week in February; craft workshops for adults and children several times a year; tours for sight- or hearing-impaired visitors twice a year; and candlelight Shaker dinners on Saturday nights from mid-July through mid-October.

CANTERBURY SHAKER VILLAGE
1792–1992, Canterbury, New Hampshire
NR, NHL

ADDRESS: 288 Shaker Road, Canterbury, NH 03224
TELEPHONE: (603) 783-9511
LOCATION: In south central New Hampshire, 15 miles north of Concord; follow
signs from I-93 Exit 18.
OPEN: Monday–Saturday, 10:00 a.m.–5:00 p.m., and Sunday, noon–5:00 p.m., May–
October; Friday–Saturday, 10:00 a.m.–5:00 p.m., and Sunday, noon–5:00 p.m.,
April, November, and December.
ADMISSION: Adults, $7.50; children 6–16, $3.75; family (2 adults and children under
16), $20.00. Candlelight Dinner and Tour: $32.00 per person. Special Events:
adults, $6.00; children 6–16, $3.00.
RESTAURANTS: Creamery Restaurant open daily for lunch, Sunday for brunch, and
Friday and Saturday evenings for candlelight dinners; Summer Kitchen.
SHOPS: Carriage House Gift Shop.
FACILITIES: Special events; picnic area; workshops on Shaker crafts; guided tours;
nature trails; weekend candlelight dinners.

OVERVIEW

A village of twenty-four original Shaker buildings on a hillside surrounded
by woods and fields remains as a symbol of peace and tranquility in rural New
Hampshire. All Shaker villages are unique, wonderful places to visit, but Canterbury is special because it was, until very recently, one of only two Shaker
communities that existed to the present day.

During the early 1970s, the remaining handful of sisters turned their property over to a nonprofit organization for a museum in which they would share
control. Thus, preservation efforts began before the Shakers actually ended
their tenure at Canterbury, and the sisters were active participants in the historic interpretation of the site. During the next two decades, Shaker sisters
who had been members of the community since childhood routinely welcomed
fortunate museum visitors.

For 200 years, until 1992 when the last sister died, Canterbury Shaker
Village was an active Shaker community. Now, it is a fine museum village where
restored original buildings are on their original site. Guided tours of selected
buildings are given, and restoration is ongoing. In 1993, Canterbury Shaker
Village was designated a National Historic Landmark.

HISTORY

Canterbury Village, chartered in 1792, was the seventh Shaker community founded in America and an active Shaker community for 200 years. Approximately 2,500 people lived in the village, some for a short time, others for
most of their lives. In 1965, Canterbury closed the covenant and accepted no

new members. When Sister Ethel Hudson died in 1992 at age ninety-six, the Canterbury community of Shakers ended.

The Canterbury community began with meetings held at Benjamin Whitcher's home in the 1780s. Eventually, he donated his 100-acre farm as the communal site for the Church family. The Shaker architect Moses Johnson built Canterbury's meetinghouse in 1792. The central ministry of Joseph Meacham and Lucy Wright appointed Job Bishop and Hannah Goodrich as Canterbury's male and female elders.

By 1850, the village had 100 buildings on 4,000 acres with 300 residents who were divided into four families: Church, Second, West, and North. Because Canterbury did not have a convenient water source to power its nine mills used in the manufacture of wood products, they constructed a system of millponds and ditches using reservoirs, dams, sluices, and spillways to bring water a distance of two miles.

Although agriculture was the primary economic pursuit, there was a substantial industrial complex at Canterbury, including a printshop that served the entire Shaker movement. An 1875 visitor, Charles Nordhoff, wrote: "Agriculture they believe to be the true base of community life, and if their land were fertile they would be glad to leave off manufacturing entirely. But on such land as they have they can not make a living."[1] According to Nordhoff's account:

> This society is prosperous. It owns three thousand acres of rather poor farming land, some of which is in wood and timber. It has also a farm in Western New York, where it maintains eight hundred sheep. Its industries are varied: they make large washing-machines and mangles for hotels and public institutions, weave woolen cloths and flannels, make sarsaparilla sirup, checkerberry oil, and knit woolen socks. They also make brooms, and sell hay; have a sawmill; make much of what they use; and they keep excellent stock, having one enormous and admirably arranged barn. The sisters also make fancy articles, for which they have a good market from the summer visitors to the mountains, with whom the Canterbury Shakers are justly favorites.
>
> Their buildings are very complete and in excellent order. They have a steam laundry, with mangle, and an admirably arranged ironing-room; a fine and thoroughly fitted schoolhouse, with a melodeon, and a special music-room; an infirmary for the feeble and sick, in which there is a fearful quantity of drugs; and they take twelve or fifteen newspapers, and have a library of four hundred volumes, including history, voyages, travels, scientific works, and stories for children, but no novels.[2]

One of Canterbury's most successful products was the Dorothy cloak, designed by Eldress Dorothy Durgin and worn by Frances Cleveland, President Grover Cleveland's wife, at the 1893 inaugural ball. The cape became the rage among Victorian women.

Family cloak-sewing room (c. 1903). The Shaker cloak was so popular that Mrs. Grover Cleveland wore one to her husband's inauguration. Photograph courtesy of the Shaker Museum and Library, Old Chatham, New York.

Nordhoff's description highlights several changes that occurred over time in the village and restrictions that were dropped. He mentions a melodeon, although musical instruments had originally been banned. In addition, an orchestra was formed at Canterbury toward the end of the nineteenth century, and a quartet, "Qui Viva Quartette," consisting of Jenny Fish, Josephine Wilson, Cora Helena Sarle, and Jessie Evans under the direction of Dorothy Durgin, gave concerts for other Shakers and the world's people. Another former prohibition had been against reading newspapers and books other than the Bible and a few religious volumes. In 1953, the sisters were given a television set by a friend.

Like all Shaker communities, Canterbury began a steady decline about the time of the Civil War. In 1972, the three remaining Shakers turned over their twenty-four buildings and 694 acres to Shaker Village, Inc., a nonprofit organization. There are no Shakers left at Canterbury, as Bertha Lindsay, its last eldress, died in October 1990 at age ninety-three, and Ethel Hudson, its last sister, died in 1992 at age ninety-six.

TOUR

Canterbury is situated on a hilltop surrounded by 694 acres of pastoral land. Its twenty-four buildings, many of which are New England-style white frame structures, form a serene cluster. These remaining buildings originally belonged to the Church family. Knowledgeable guides take visitors through the buildings on guided tours.

Mother Ann Lee's Shakers

The **Moses Johnson Meetinghouse**, the village's first building, was completed on September 22, 1792. Like many other Johnson meetinghouses, it is a Federal-style, white frame meetinghouse with a gambrel roof. Initially, all interior woodwork was painted a dark blue, as prescribed by the *Millennial Laws*, and the woodwork in the upstairs rooms still retains its 200-year-old paint. Woodwork in the meeting room was repainted light blue in 1878. The building houses exhibits of Shaker-made furniture, baskets, medicines, and stoves.

The **Ministry's Shop** was built in 1848. Traditionally, the elders and eldresses lived on the upper floors of the meetinghouse; but as time passed, they occupied a separate building, in which they worked, slept, and carried out their administrative duties. Today, the building's sleeping rooms, workrooms, and offices are furnished with Shaker furniture, much of it made at Canterbury. Elder Henry Blinn, who was a beekeeper, dentist, and carpenter, made the bookcase desk displayed in his office.

The **Sisters' Shop**, a white frame, two-story building, dates from 1817. Shakers made their own clothing, and much of the sewing was handled in this shop. Many sisters were involved in cutting and sewing the extremely popular broadcloth Dorothy cloaks. The room in which the cloaks were made features built-in cupboards and a tailoring bench, a combination tailor's table and chest of drawers designed especially for this work.

Doing laundry was another task assigned to the sisters. In the 1795 **Laundry** at Canterbury, clothes, cleaned in a mechanical washing machine, a Shaker invention, were brought upstairs in a laundry elevator and hung on wooden racks. A steam- operated boiler was used for heating the building and drying the clothes. The laundry has its original soapstone sinks, washing machines, mangle, extractor, laundry elevator, and steam drying cabinet. The building also contains the original steam-powered woodworking shop.

School was first taught at Canterbury in 1801 by Hannah Bronsen; she used a room in the **Blacksmith's Shop**. A one-room **Schoolhouse** was built in 1823. The traditional Shaker curriculum was expanded to include agriculture, history, geography, botany, physiology, music, drawing, and elocution.

In 1863, the schoolhouse became a two-story building. Because it was too far from the Church family, it was moved, and a new first floor was added under the original building. It was considered easier to add four walls than to replace the roof. Therefore, the second floor of the schoolhouse is forty years older than the first. Moving or adding to buildings was a common practice among the Shakers, along with recycling buildings for other uses. Structures no longer being used were usually torn down.

The restored 1806 **Carpenter Shop** houses woodcrafts such as dovetailing demonstrations, oval box making, and ash basketry. Shaker-inspired furniture and accessories displayed in the **Carpenter Shop Gallery** are for sale.

The 1819 **Horse Barn**, which has been restored to the 1910 period, is used to exhibit horse-drawn equipment, including Shaker sleighs and carriages and a Concord Coach.

Canterbury Shaker Village

Schoolroom at Canterbury, New Hampshire. Photographed by W. G. C. Kimball (1875). Photograph courtesy of the Shaker Museum and Library, Old Chatham, New York.

Canterbury's **Infirmary** was built in 1811 and remodeled in 1849 and 1892. It is said to be the oldest extant community healthcare facility in New Hampshire. Patient rooms reflect 1848 and 1892 periods. There is a pharmacy with shelves lined with bottles containing extracts, oils, and powders. In the dental care area are a dental chair, dental tools, and a foot-pedaled drill. There is an original kitchen and nurses' quarters. The Canterbury Shakers were known for their patent medicines, particularly Brother Thomas Corbett's Syrup of Sarsaparilla, which was prepared from roots, herbs, and berries grown, selected, and discovered by the Shakers. Advertised as a great purifier of the blood and other fluids of the body, it was said to have beneficial effects on cases of dyspepsia, indigestion, thin watery blood, malaria and liver complaint, weak nerves, lungs, kidneys and urinary organs, consumption, emaciation, exhaustion of delicate females, nursing mothers, sickly children and the aged. Sounds like it could do anything but set broken bones.

The **production garden** and **Physician's Botanical Garden** have been moved to their original terraced setting, and all the plants are identified. There is a self-guided nature trail around **Turning Mill Pond**. A self-guiding pamphlet describes the archeological mill ruins, a series of dams and sluiceways, and the flora and fauna. Another nature trail to **Carding Mill Pond** passes additional mill ruins.

Canterbury has also been particularly known for Shaker crafts. Workshops given by fine craftspeople are offered in broom making, herbal arts, basketry, woodworking, and weaving.

In the restored **Carriage House**, craftspeople demonstrate basketry, tinsmithing, woodworking, and sewing. These products are among the items sold in the **gift shop**, which is located in the carriage house. A herbalist has cultivated sixty-two varieties of medicinal and culinary herbs, and some of these are sold in the shop.

Annual special events at Canterbury include Wood Day and Herb Day in May, Mother Ann Day and the Antique Show and Sale in August, Wool Day in September, and Harvest Day in October.

THE SHAKER MUSEUM
1794–Present, Poland Spring, Maine
NR, NHL, HABS

ADDRESS: R.R. #1, Box 640, Poland Spring, ME 04274
TELEPHONE: (207) 926-4597
LOCATION: In south central Maine, between Portland and Lewiston, on Route 26; 8 miles north of Gray, ME Turnpike Exit 11; 8 miles south of Auburn, ME Turnpike Exit 12.
OPEN: Monday–Saturday, 10:00 a.m.–4:30 p.m., Memorial Day–Columbus Day.
ADMISSION: Guided Introductory Tour: adults, $4.00; children 6–12, $2.00. Guided Extended Tour: adults, $5.50; children 6–12, $2.50.
RESTAURANTS: No.
SHOPS: Museum Shop; Shaker Store.
FACILITIES: Active Shaker community; seventeen original buildings; craft demonstrations; workshops; special events; library and archives.

OVERVIEW

The year 1994 marked the bicentennial of the founding of the Sabbathday Lake Shaker Village, still an active, though quite small, Shaker community today. The Shaker Museum, founded in 1931, and the over 200-year-old living Shaker religious community share a picturesque site in rural Maine. "Chosen Land" is the return address on a letter we received from a Sabbathday Lake brother. The phrase seems apt when you come upon a cluster of white frame buildings, pinewoods, the shining lake from which the village takes its name, sheep grazing in the pasture, apple orchards on the hill, and carefully tended herb gardens.

More than a dozen original Shaker structures, some of which are museum buildings and others that are occupied by a handful of sisters and brothers, remain at Sabbathday Lake. As with all the Shaker villages we have seen, the impressive architecture, pastoral setting, well-done preservation and restoration, and exquisite furniture are worth any detour necessary to make the visit. The fact that it is a living community adds a special dimension to this historic site. When you meet a Shaker sister or brother who patiently answers your questions, it is a totally different experience from dealing with a museum guide whose job requires dressing in a Shaker costume.

In addition to the historic buildings, the museum has fine collections of Shaker furniture, folk and decorative arts, tin and woodenware, textiles, early American tools, and farm implements.

HISTORY

In November 1782, Elisha Pote, Nathan Freeman, and Joseph Stone, Shaker missionaries from Gorham, Maine, traveled to the New Gloucester area.

The Shaker Museum

Revival meetings among the Freewill Baptists being held there had drawn large crowds. The Shakers were successful in converting several members of that congregation.

On April 19, 1794, the New Gloucester United Society of Believers in Christ's Second Coming, later known as Sabbathday Lake, was founded. The lake derived its name from a tradition that in the 1700s backwoodsmen often gathered at the lake to visit on Sundays. Initially, New Gloucester converts met at Gohan Wilson's farmhouse. In 1793, Lucy Wright and Joseph Meacham appointed John Barnes and Sarah Kendal as leaders at Alfred and Sabbathday Lake, Maine.

Before long, the work of building a community began. The first order of business was erecting a meetinghouse, their place of worship. Moses Johnson, a Shaker brother and architect, designed, framed, and built the meetinghouse in June 1794. In 1795, a three-and-a-half-story central dwelling house was erected across from the meetinghouse.

The two Maine communities, Alfred and New Gloucester, were remote, over 200 miles from the lead ministry at New Lebanon, New York. This led to a degree of independence not shared by other eastern Shaker communities. Elders were elected at New Gloucester and then confirmed, rather than appointed by, the central ministry.

The 1794 Meetinghouse, built by master builder Moses Johnson. An ell was added to the north side in 1839. Photograph by Patricia A. Gutek.

Mother Ann Lee's Shakers

The village of Sabbathday Lake grew as new members joined. A number of large families joined together including twenty- four members of the Briggs family, twenty-nine members of the Holmes family, and thirty-two members of the Merrill family. As the population increased, other buildings were added, forming three parallel rows on both sides of what is now Route 26. When the family outgrew it, the central dwelling house was moved sixty-five feet north-east and replaced with a five-story brick dwelling house, completed in 1884. The 1795 house was then torn down.

The New Gloucester community became involved in many businesses, including tannery and cooper shops; herb and garden seeds; lumber; and flour, carding, and spinning mills. They also practiced crafts, including furniture making and basketry. Another successful enterprise was the production of Tamar Laxative.

Peak population at New Gloucester was 139 members in 1820. Between 1820 and 1860, the community had more than 100 members, but after that the numbers declined. The community in Gorham, Maine, ended in 1819. In 1830, the central ministry directed the ministry at Canterbury to supervise the Alfred and New Gloucester communities because they were experiencing some internal discord.

During the period of spirituality called the Era of Mother's Work—the late 1830s to the late 1850s—Sabbathday Lake adopted the name "Chosen Land."

A new mill built in the mid-1850s was initially successful, but by 1859, the village was in debt because of unwise speculation by trustee Ransom Gilman. He had borrowed money to buy wheat in Chicago and then had it shipped to the village, where it was ground into flour with the expectation that it would be sold at a profit. The scheme failed, primarily due to an economic recession in 1857, leaving the community with a $14,000 debt, which they were unable to pay. The central ministry at New Lebanon took control of their financial affairs and assessed the other villages a tax to offset the debt. Charles Vining, Gilman's successor, embezzled $5,000 and incurred additional debt before leaving the society. Engaging in further mischief, Isaiah Wentworth, the trustee of the Poland Hill family, incurred debts and mortgaged property. Elder Otis Sawyer finally removed Wentworth from his position in 1867.[1] Consequently, the Sabbathday Lake community struggled financially for years.

By 1882, the Poland Hill family had only nineteen members. Its property, 500 acres and eighteen major buildings, was sold for $7,500 in 1899. In 1931, the Alfred, Maine, community merged with Sabbathday Lake.

Services had not been held in the meetinghouse from 1888 until 1963, when a resurgence of religious activity attracted new converts. Among these new converts to Shakerism was Theodore Johnson, who organized weekly Bible classes and delivered sermons during meetings. Johnson became director of the village museum and library. He served as editor of the *Shaker Quarterly*, which began publication in 1961. He also edited the *Millennial Laws* of 1821 and Calvin Green's biography of Joseph Meacham. Johnson died in 1986.

A spirit drawing from Mother Ann to Amy Reed dated January 7, 1848. The instrument, or medium who received the drawing, was Sarah Bates. Photograph courtesy of the Shaker Museum and Library, Old Chatham, New York.

By the 1960s, only two active Shaker communities remained—Canterbury and Sabbathday Lake. In a now historical dispute, these two groups differed on the appropriate future of Shakerism. While serious converts were welcomed at Sabbathday Lake, Canterbury sisters took the position that no Shakers could be admitted to the society because the covenant was closed. All of the Canterbury sisters have died, which leaves the last Shaker community at Sabbathday Lake. Its members raise sheep for wool, harvest herbs for culinary use, and are active in community service.

The Shaker Museum, founded by Sister Ethel Peacock in 1931, exhibits artifacts made and used at the community the past three centuries.

TOUR

Seventeen original buildings remain on the site. All the buildings are eighteenth- and nineteenth- century frame except the **Dwelling House**, which is brick. Originally, the Shakers owned 2,700 acres; now, they have 1,900.

The Introductory Tour is a guided tour of the 1794 **Meetinghouse** and the 1839 **Ministry's Shop**; the Extended Tour includes those two buildings and the 1821 **Sisters' Shop** and the 1816 **Spin House**.

The **Boy's Shop** now serves as the **Reception Center**. It is a white, two-story building built in 1850; and although it was partially destroyed by fire in 1965, the facade is original. The building was used to house young Shaker boys until they reached their midteens, along with the brothers who took care of them.

The first floor houses a **bookstore** with a good collection of Shaker books and some reproduction Shaker items. The four rooms on the second floor are furnished with original Shaker furniture, most of it from Sabbathday Lake.

Mother Ann Lee's Shakers

The 1794 **Meetinghouse**, which now serves as the Shaker Museum, was the first building on this site. It was one of ten Shaker meetinghouses built by Moses Johnson, all with gambrel roofs. Chimney bricks were made by brethren near the Sabbathday Lake, and the nails were handmade by Joseph Briggs. In 1839, an ell was added to the north side.

Religious services are still held in the first-floor meeting room; on Sundays, they are open to the public. A divided stairway leads to the second floor, where Shaker costumes are displayed. The four rooms on the second floor originally housed the two elders and two eldresses who headed the community. Among the notable items contained in the rooms are a weasel, the Shaker invention used to measure a skein of yarn; chair tilters (one of the few Shaker inventions ever patented); and a sewing desk made by Joshua Bussell. One of the rooms displays a rare Shaker quilt, which is quilted but not pieced. The three rooms on the third floor were used as guest rooms for visiting ministers. All the rooms have built-in cupboards.

Because the lack of insulation made the meetinghouse extremely cold to live in, the elders moved into the **Ministry's Shop**, which was built in 1839 with insulated walls. The two elders and two eldresses used this building as both home and workplace. As the spiritual leaders, they governed the community. In addition to their administrative duties, they were required to do physical labor or craft work, so the building contains a sewing room and a tailor's room, as well as offices.

The three back rooms of the Ministry's Shop are used for temporary exhibits that have included displays about Shaker food, important leaders, and Victorian Shaker craftsmanship.

The **Sisters' Shop**, originally used as a laundry, houses a mail-order herb business on its second floor. From barrels of herbs, sisters fill small metal cans. Herb can labels are printed in the community **printshop**. This is only one of the businesses operating here; being self- supporting is a Shaker principle.

In your tour of the Sisters' Shop, you will see the original washing machine, invented by the Shakers, and a large press that chemically treated material. Permanent-press material was also a Shaker invention.

In the 1816 **Spin House** is an exhibit on the village's sawmill, called the **Great Mill**. The Sabbathday Lake Shakers began their lumbering business as early as 1796. The Great Mill, built in 1853 and operated until 1941, was sixty feet long, twenty-one feet wide, and three stories high. On exhibit are over a hundred mill production items and artifacts.

The 1880 New Gloucester Shaker **Schoolhouse** has been restored and houses the Shaker **Library** and **Archives**. Designed by Brother Hewitt Chandler and staffed by Shakers, the school served both Shaker and New Gloucester children until 1950. Sold by the town and moved by the purchaser, the school was acquired by the United Society of Shakers at Sabbathday Lake in 1986 and returned to its original site. Library collections focus on the Shakers, especially those in Maine, and include material on other American religious sects and communal groups. The Library, established in 1882 by Elder Otis Sawyer, has an outstanding collection of Shaker materials. It is open year round. Appointments are preferred.

There are **orchards** and **herb gardens** at the village as well as a **cemetery**. There are no individual markers, just the inscription "Shakers."

Workshops are offered each summer on topics such as planting herb gardens, rug braiding, patchwork, loom weaving, basketry, oval box making, and architectural photography.

SHAKER VILLAGE
OF PLEASANT HILL
1807–1910, Harrodsburg, Kentucky
NR, NHL

ADDRESS: 3500 Lexington Road, Harrodsburg, KY 40330

TELEPHONE: (606) 734-5411

LOCATION: In central Kentucky, 25 miles southwest of Lexington and 7 miles northeast of Harrodsburg; on US 68.

OPEN: Daily, 9:30 a.m.–5:00 p.m., mid-March–November; some exhibition buildings closed December–mid-March.

ADMISSION: Village: adults, $8.50; students 12–17, $4.00; children 6–11, $2.00; family (2 adults and unlimited children), $20.00. Riverboat: adults, $5.50; students 12–17, $3.50; children 6–11, $2.00. Combination Village/Boat: adults, $11.50; students 12–17, $6.00; children 6–11, $3.00; family, $27.50.

RESTAURANTS: Trustees' Office Restaurant (reservations essential); Summer Kitchen in West Family Dwelling.

SHOPS: Post Office craft shop; Carpenters' Shop craft shop.

FACILITIES: Paddlewheel riverboat rides; craft demonstrations; conference facilities; music and dance programs; winter weekends; special events; overnight accommodations in historic buildings.

OVERVIEW

One of two Shaker communities in Kentucky, Shaker Village of Pleasant Hill recreates aspects of the lifestyle of the American communal religious group who lived there for more than a century. Though there are no longer Shaker brothers and sisters at Pleasant Hill, the Shaker spirit permeates the site today. Picturesquely situated in Kentucky bluegrass country, the museum village is surrounded by 2,700 acres of rolling fields edged in stacked flagstone fences. An evening mist often envelops the site, contributing to its aura of separation from the modern world. First-time visitors to Pleasant Hill are struck by a sense of harmony in everything they see, from the orderliness of the setting to the pleasing proportions of buildings, to the elegant simplicity of the furniture, to the plain utilitarianism of the tools. White picket fences, stone walkways, lanterns hung on posts, and guides in Shaker costumes add to the sense of rural serenity.

Lodging and dining rooms retain a historically authentic atmosphere. There are eighty guest rooms in fifteen original Shaker buildings. Even though these buildings are restored to nineteenth-century standards, the guest rooms are heated, air- conditioned, electrified, and have their own bathrooms. They are furnished with reproduction Shaker rockers, beds, desks, and handwoven rugs. The dining rooms are in the Trustees' House. Meals are moderately priced, and

Edward R. Hamilton *Bookseller Company*

PO Box 15, Falls Village, CT 06031-0015

6

16970314
Ralph S Wilcox
320 N Summit St
Little Rock, AR 72205-4454

146316045   BATCH   20144245

SHIP TO:
Ralph S Wilcox
1500 Tower Bldg
323 Center St
Little Rock, AR 72201

ORDER RECEIVED: 11/4/2010
AMOUNT PREPAID: $29.35
ITEMS ORDERED: 3
ITEMS SHIPPED: 3

THE FOLLOWING ITEMS HAVE BEEN SHIPPED:

0-52	1	61Q3-P	Haiti: The Tumultuous History--From Pear	9.95	2455153
0-88	1	33T0-P	Visiting Utopian Communities: A Guide to	3.95	2454866
1-36	1	41P5-P	Two Wheels Through Terror: Diary of a So	11.95	2474999

Postage and Handling $3.50

If ITEMS ORDERED and ITEMS SHIPPED shown above agree, your order is complete. If any items were not shipped, a second shipment and/or a refund by bank check will be made as soon as possible, but in no case later than 60 days.

If all items were shipped but a credit was due you, a refund check has been mailed to you separately.

If you receive a damaged, defective, or incorrect item please do NOT return it. Just let us know what is wrong and we will correct it.

You may return any item for a refund of its purchase price. You pay only the postage.

the Shaker and Kentucky recipes showcase American cuisine at its finest: fresh foods properly prepared and beautifully served. No alcohol is sold.

HISTORY

On January 1, 1805, three Shaker missionaries from New Lebanon, New York, traveled 1,200 miles to Kentucky. They had heard about the Great Kentucky Revival, in which a wave of camp meetings had reawakened religious sentiments among thousands of people. After making some converts, the Shaker group gathered on Shawnee Run, a few miles from Harrodsburg.

Two years later, in 1807, a permanent settlement was established on the elevation that came to be called Pleasant Hill. In January 1809, two elders and two eldresses were sent from Union Village in Ohio to form the first ministry. In 1809, the first building in the village, the first Centre Family Dwelling, now known as the Farm Deacon's Shop, was built. Of the 270 buildings erected over the ensuing century, 30 remain today.

The Shakers were active craftspeople. They produced brooms, cooper's wares, weaving implements, shoes, woolen goods, pressed cheese, medicinal products, seeds, and herbs. By 1816, they had begun to make trading trips to New Orleans to sell their surplus goods.

Pleasant Hill's membership had increased to nearly 500 by 1820. During the course of the century, 1,500 Shakers lived in this prosperous community. The society was divided into five communal families, each numbering from 50 to 100 members and governed by two elders and two eldresses.

Each family was a semi-autonomous unit, with its own dwelling, shops, barns, fields, and orchards. Together, their landholdings reached approximately 4,000 acres, and they grew wheat, rye, oats, flax, Indian corn, broomcorn, and potatoes. There were also extensive fruit orchards.

In 1825, a visitor to Pleasant Hill described the clothing of its members. The men wore suits made from light-colored domestic cloth, with coats and waistcoats of the long worsted fashion "with outer pockets in the former, half way down the leg, and those in the waistcoats resting on the hips." Their coarse cotton shirts were without ties.[1] The sisters wore dark-colored "long-waisted gowns," "long checked aprons" that extended to the neck, and "white long-eared caps." A white kerchief was worn over the shoulders and a checked handkerchief hung over the arm.[2]

When Charles Nordhoff visited in the 1870s, Pleasant Hill members did not eat pork, but they did drink coffee and tea and use tobacco. Reading materials were either their own publications or newspapers. They had no musical instruments.[3]

During the late 1850s, Pleasant Hill, like the other Shaker communities, began to experience the effects of the growing industrialization of the United States. Mass-produced items, manufactured on factory assembly lines, were cheaper than Shaker-made handicrafts. As their markets dwindled, so did Pleasant Hill's prosperity.

Mother Ann Lee's Shakers

Along with a declining economy, the Kentucky Shakers faced sectional issues generated by the Civil War. Although a border state with many Southern sympathizers, Kentucky remained loyal to the Union. The Shakers were pacifists and refused to fight. Elder Frederick Evans of Mount Lebanon persuaded President Abraham Lincoln to exempt Shakers on religious grounds. The Pleasant Hill Shakers, like their brothers and sisters elsewhere, generously fed, housed, and nursed both the Confederate and the Union troops that marched through their village. This impartiality angered their neighbors, who were also intolerant of the Shaker practice of buying and freeing slaves and accepting them into full membership in the society. The Shakers' stores of food, cattle, horses, wagons, and flatboats were often confiscated by the military. Nordhoff reported that "both armies foraged upon them, taking their horses and wagons; and they served thousands of meals to hungry soldiers of both sides."[4]

In 1898, the Trustees' Office and hundreds of acres were sold. By 1900, three of the families had disbanded, and their vacant buildings were rented out. On September 12, 1910, the last of the property was sold, and the society, four brothers and eight sisters, was dissolved. Between 1910 and 1960, the property was redivided and resold. The buildings, used for various purposes (including a bus station), were neglected, and two were destroyed by fire.

In the Trustees' Office a remarkably graceful spiral staircase winds up to the top floor. Photograph by Patricia A. Gutek.

Shaker Village of Pleasant Hill

In 1961, a group of people led by Earl D. Wallace of Lexington decided to restore Pleasant Hill. They formed a nonprofit educational corporation known as Shakertown at Pleasant Hill, Inc. James L. Cogar, a former curator of Colonial Williamsburg, became Pleasant Hill's first president, and the village opened to the public in the spring of 1968.

Cogar is responsible for restoring the thirty original buildings according to the principle of adaptive use. The three functional uses are exhibitions that tell the story of the life and customs of the Shaker society; education by means of seminars, symposia, and conferences; and hospitality, dining, and overnight accommodations. Pleasant Hill is the only museum village in which all overnight accommodations for guests are in restored buildings.

Tour

Begin your self-guided tour at the **Centre Family Dwelling**. The Centre, or First, family was the highest rank according to the spirituality of the members and was given the place of honor nearest the meetinghouse. The T-shaped Centre Family Dwelling was started in 1824 and completed in 1834. Master architect and carpenter Micajah Burnett laid out the plan of the village and designed the buildings, including this one.

The symmetry of the double doorways and two inside stairways to separate the men's quarters from the women's, along with the utter simplicity of the wide halls, white walls, high ceilings, arched doorways, wood trim, and plain wooden floors, contribute to the beauty of this outstanding building.

Burnett's design was based on an early New England Shaker building style with elements of Federal classicism. The roof has square gabled ends and three massive chimneys. There are forty rooms in this four-story Kentucky limestone building, the largest erected at Pleasant Hill; it housed 100 Shakers. It is now the major exhibition building.

All rooms contain authentic Shaker furniture from the early nineteenth century, much of it made at Pleasant Hill. There is a kitchen complete with cooking utensils, a dining room, a meeting room, and an infirmary. The sleeping rooms are simply furnished.

The **Meetinghouse** was the spiritual center of the community. The one at Pleasant Hill was built in 1820 and has the double doorways typical of Shaker architecture. The white frame building rests on a heavy limestone foundation. Roof and ceilings are supported by a series of interlocking cantilever-type trusses and overhead studdings and rafters; this construction made it possible to have a meeting room large enough to accommodate all the worshipers.

The **Farm Deacon's Shop**, built in 1809, was the first permanent structure in the village. Originally the dwelling house for the Centre family, it was used as a tavern after 1817 and, finally, as an office for the farm deacons. The two-foot-thick walls of this two-and-a-half-story structure are built of white limestone quarried from cliffs along the nearby Kentucky River. The ash floors are original. Artifacts relating to the Shakers' herb industry are displayed on the first floor; the second floor is used for guest lodgings.

In 1833, Micajah Burnett devised a water system that provided every house and barn in the village with running water. The yellow frame **Water House** contains the machinery and tanks for the first public waterworks in Kentucky.

Next to the water house is the small **Brethren's Bath House**, built in 1860. Each family was a self-sufficient unit with its own large dwelling for eating and sleeping; a craft shop for women; separate bathhouses for men, women, boys, and girls; a washhouse; and various other outbuildings.

On the first floor of the 1845 **East Family Brethren's Shop**, a broom maker works in his fully equipped shop. Across the hall, a carpenter uses traditional tools. The 1855 **East Family Sisters' Shop** houses spinning and weaving demonstrations on the first floor. The second floor of each shop now accommodates overnight guests.

The **Trustees' Office**, built in 1839 by Micajah Burnett, is one of the finest examples of Shaker architecture extant. It was used by the Shakers to conduct business with the outside world and to house and feed guests. Trustees were the people appointed to transact that business. The building is of Flemish-bond brick and has a single front door. As you enter it, you'll be struck by the impressive twin spiral staircases.

Today, the first floor is used as a restaurant and a registration office for overnight guests. Upstairs there are lodging rooms. The trundle beds for children are a delight.

Candle-making equipment used to demonstrate the traditional craft for museum visitors. Photograph by Patricia A. Gutek.

Shaker Village of Pleasant Hill

Coopering demonstrations are conducted in the **Cooper's Shop,** which was remodeled in 1847. The **East Family Washhouse** as its original cauldrons and parts of their washing apparatus. The 1848 **Post Office** and the 1815 **Carpenters' Shop** are craft shops, which sell many Shaker reproductions and Kentucky crafts. A **Research Library** is in the 1859 **Preserve Shop,** where Shaker sisters prepared jars of sweetmeats. The 1875 **Scale House** and the 1840 **Drying House** are undergoing restoration.

Pleasant Hill has two gardens: the **kitchen garden** by the Trustees' Office and the **herb garden** by the Centre Family Dwelling. You will also want to stroll over to the peaceful Shaker **graveyard.**

Special events at Shaker Village include demonstrations of flax working, beehive-oven baking, silk culturing, candle dipping, vegetal dyeing, basketry, cider making, and hearth cooking. There are also programs on Shaker songs.

You can take a one-hour ride on a paddlewheel riverboat, the *Dixie Belle,* from May through October. The rides on the Kentucky River leave from **Shaker Landing,** east of the village entrance.

SHAKERTOWN
AT SOUTH UNION
1807–1922, South Union, Kentucky
NR

ADDRESS: South Union, Kentucky 42283
TELEPHONE: (502) 542-4167, (502) 542-7734
LOCATION: In southwestern Kentucky, 10 miles west of Bowling Green, on US 68-80; from I- 65, take Exit 20, Natcher Parkway, to Exit 5, US 68-80, turn left and travel west 10 miles.
OPEN: Monday–Saturday, 9:00 a.m.–5:00 p.m., and Sunday, 1:00 –5:00 p.m., March 1–December 15; closed Thanksgiving weekend.
ADMISSION: Adults, $3; children, $1.
RESTAURANTS: Shaker Tavern, located on Highway 73, 1.5 miles from the museum; also has bed-and-breakfast facilities, (502) 542- 6801.
SHOPS: Museum Shop.
FACILITIES: Special events.

OVERVIEW

South Union was one of two Kentucky Shaker villages that resulted from missionary work by eastern Shakers. In 1805, three brethren traveled to the western frontier of the United States, which included Kentucky, only a state since 1792. Their work resulted in the founding of Shaker communities in Kentucky, Ohio, and Indiana.

Established in 1807 and disbanded in 1922, South Union Shaker Village endured for more than a century. Nine of the more than 220 buildings constructed by the Shakers still stand. Shakertown at South Union, Inc., owns four of these structures and maintains two of them as an outdoor museum. Another building is used as a restaurant and bed-and-breakfast, while the fourth one is a post office. The rest of the Shaker structures are privately owned.

As at Pleasant Hill, this site is in picturesque rural Kentucky and has well-landscaped grounds.

HISTORY

South Union Village founded in 1807, was home to Shaker sisters and brothers for more than a century until its dissolution in 1922. The community owned 6,000 acres of land and more than 220 buildings.

Shaker settlements were initially concentrated in the northeastern states. However, Mother Ann predicted that "The next opening of the gospel" would be at "a great distance" and "a great work of God."[1] She was right, as less than twenty years after missionary work was initiated in the western frontier, 1,700 people had been converted to Shakerism.

Shakertown at South Union

In the early nineteenth century, Mother Lucy Wright, the Shakers' lead eldress, authorized missionary activity on the western frontier. Her action was prompted by newspaper reports in the years 1801 to 1804 of great religious revivals occurring in Kentucky and the Ohio Valley. Methodist, Baptist, and Presbyterian preachers, including John Rankin, James McGready, and John and William McGee, attracted thousands of people. At these revivals, Shakers converted many people who were seeking spiritual renewal.

On January 1, 1805, three members of the gathering order left New Lebanon for the fertile fields of the Kentucky revival. Traveling 1,200 miles by sleigh and on foot, Issachar Bates, Benjamin Seth Youngs, and John Meacham reached Paint Lick, Kentucky, on March 3. The brethren then proceeded to the home of Malcolm Worley in Warren County, Ohio.

Worley was one of the "New Lights," a postrevival group consisting of several Presbyterian congregations in northern Kentucky and southern Ohio who rejected the Calvinist doctrine of divine election; that is, that God has arbitrarily and irrevocably chosen some people for salvation and some for damnation. The New Lights withdrew from the Synod of Kentucky and formed the Presbytery of Springfield, with headquarters at Cane Ridge, Kentucky.

Worley introduced the Shakers to Richard McNemar, the minister of the Turtle Creek Presbyterian Congregation of New Lights. In a short time, Worley, McNemar, and most of the Turtle Creek Congregation converted to Shakerism. By May, there were thirty new Believers in Warren County. In the process of making converts, the Shakers encountered local antagonism and occasional violence.

Still, the missionary work was going so well that the leadership at Mount Lebanon was solicited for reinforcements. Three additional brethren, David Darrow, Daniel Moseley, and Solomon King, arrived in Ohio at the end of July, and several sisters followed in the spring of 1806. The brethren lived with the Worley family, and the sisters stayed in a small log cabin nearby.

The Warren County, Ohio, Shaker community, called Union Village, became the governing society in the West. Father David Darrow was its leader. An elders' house at Turtle Creek was constructed in October 1807.

In 1805, Brother Issachar Bates and two of the western converts, Richard McNemar and Matthew Houston, converted twenty- three adults in Gasper, Logan County, in southern Kentucky. These twenty-three people were the nucleus of the South Union community situated on the property of Jesse McComb in Gasper Springs. The South Union meetinghouse was built in 1810. The following year, Benjamin Youngs was appointed to the ministry and served in that capacity for twenty-five years.

Life in Shaker frontier communities was demanding and harsh. During the War of 1812, pacifist brothers who refused to be drafted were each assessed a $100 fine. Soldiers frequently camped at their spring. In 1813, more than fifty South Union members died during an epidemic.

Families at South Union included the Center family, Church family, North family, and East family. Some of the people who joined the community were slaveholders, who, on becoming members, freed their slaves as the Shakers opposed slavery. About forty of the freed African Americans remained at South Union and formed their own family. When the number in that family diminished, members entered other families. Several English, German, and French people were also in the village.

As at other Shaker villages, agriculture was the primary enterprise at South Union. Corn, wheat, rye, and oats were raised. Kentucky pastures were excellent for raising cattle, which was a profitable business at South Union. Hogs, sheep, and chickens were also raised.

In addition to agriculture, Kentucky members manufactured products for sale to outside markets. Garden seeds were sold in Kentucky, Tennessee, Mississippi, and Arkansas. Brethren traveled down the Ohio and Mississippi Rivers as far as Louisiana to sell seeds and other produce. They sometimes complained that the seed salesmen from the Shaker community at Pleasant Hill, Kentucky, cut into their territory.

From about 1825 to 1875, silkworms were raised, and the sisters wove silk, which was made into women's kerchiefs. Whiskey was produced in their 1823 whiskey distillery. The industrious Shakers also marketed their preserved, canned, and dried fruit. In May 1872, the Church family put up 3,941 jars of cherries and strawberries. Cases of fruit were shipped by railroad to destinations as far away as Texas.

The 1819 meetinghouse, right, and the 1824 Centre Family Dwelling, left, with Shaker men, women, and children. The meetinghouse was torn down in the late 1920s. Photograph courtesy of The Western Reserve Historical Society, Cleveland, Ohio.

Shakertown at South Union

Although the Shakers sought isolation from outside events, they could not avoid the Civil War. Kentucky was a border state—in the Union but adjacent to Confederate states. Kentuckians were divided in their loyalties and viewed the neutrality of the Shakers with suspicion. Brethren were criticized for their refusal to fight and for their abolitionist position.

The Civil War negatively impacted the economy of the Shaker communities as their resources were rapidly depleted by the needs of the troops. Both Union and Confederate military units camped at the Kentucky villages and were routinely fed. Hay, fodder, horses, and wagons were confiscated by the military without remuneration. Twenty thousand Shaker oak fence rails were burned in federal campfires. In 1865, the South Union Shakers took in nineteen orphans from a Clarksville, Tennessee, refugee home that was closing.

Additional economic difficulties were caused by industrialization. Cheaply made mass- produced products, manufactured in factories, replaced handcrafted Shaker-made items. Declining populations in Shaker communities at the end of the nineteenth century necessitated the hiring of paid, outside workers. Peak population was reached in 1827 with about 350 members. When Charles Nordhoff visited South Union in the early 1870s, there were 230 members, of whom 40 were children. By 1880, there were 99 members and in 1900, only 55.

With a diminished labor force, the community sought financial diversity by speculating in stocks and bonds in the early decades of the twentieth century. They purchased stock in banks, the Terry Coal and Coke Company, Liberty Bonds, and Savings Stamps.

Unable to forestall the inevitable, South Union closed in 1922. It was the last remaining Shaker western community. South Union's land, buildings, and furnishings were sold at a public auction held September 26, 1922. Walter Shepard of Mount Lebanon and Arthur Bruce of Canterbury supervised the auction, which drew 5,000 people.

Shakertown at South Union, Inc., a nonprofit educational organization, has restored the site.

Tour

South Union Shaker Village is picturesquely set in a rural area. Construction on the 1824 **Center House**, a forty-room restored building that is used as a **museum** of Shaker furniture, photographs, and artifacts, was begun in 1822. Although it was not completed until 1833, the 1824 date indicates the year the outside stonework and brickwork were finished. It has four floors, center halls, dual staircases, wide doorways, and pegboards lining many walls.

On the first floor, both brethren's retiring rooms and sisters' retiring rooms are simply furnished with chests, beds, rocking chairs, and a stove.

An exhibit room focuses on the community's architectural style, which was rooted in the craftsmanship found in Virginia, Tennessee, and Kentucky. Doors, windows, railings, and cupboards from demolished South Union structures are displayed.

Interior hallway of the 1824 Centre Family Dwelling reveals the architectural symmetry designed to accommodate the separation of the sexes. Photograph by Patricia A. Gutek.

Documents, maps, and photographs from both South Union and other Shaker communities are exhibited in the meeting room. The emancipation of a slave is the subject of one legal document.

On the second floor is found furniture made at South Union. It tended to be more decorative than New England Shaker furniture. Three categories of chairs produced at South Union from 1813 until after the Civil War are high-lighted. Also exhibited is Kentucky-made furniture that was influenced by Shaker design.

A Victorian-style Shaker room features ornate furniture, kerosene lamps, and a Victrola. The Shakers were influenced by changing styles and adapted their decor over time.

A textile exhibit highlights coverlets, rugs, blankets, towels, and linens made by the sisters. A loom, spinning wheel, and skeins of yarn are displayed.

The sisters operated a gift shop stocked with their fancy goods from 1870 to 1920. In the replicated shop are sewing baskets, boxes, woolen cloaks, candy, and brooms.

Spirit drawings, artwork received through inspiration during periods of spiritualistic revivals, make a unique artistic display. Drawings often incorporate written religious messages as well as simple graphics.

An infirmary features containers of herbal medicines.

On the third floor are children's rooms and a primary school room.

Implements used in the family laundry include a wooden washtub, wringer, drying racks, and irons.

The long tables in the basement dining room have been set for dinner. A cast-iron stove purchased in the 1840s is in the kitchen.

Also restored is the 1835 **Smoke and Milk House**, which has butter- and cheese-making equipment and wooden dairy tools. Looms and spinning wheels are on the second floor.

Other original Shaker buildings adjacent to the museum are owned by a Roman Catholic religious order and are not restored nor open to the public.

Two Shaker buildings about one and one-half miles from the museum are also owned by Shakertown at South Union, Inc., the preservation organization that operates the museum. The 1869 **Shaker Tavern** faces the railroad and served train passengers for many years. Now it is operated as a restaurant and bed-and-breakfast. It has a Victorian decor with wallpaper, frosted light fixtures, cornices over the windows, and a tiled fireplace.

Across the street from the Tavern is a functioning 1917 **Post Office** in an original Shaker structure.

SHAKER MUSEUM AND LIBRARY
Old Chatham, New York

ADDRESS: Shaker Museum, Shaker Museum Road, Old Chatham, NY 12136

TELEPHONE: (518) 794-9100

LOCATION: The Shaker Museum is located off of the Taconic Parkway and the New York State Thruway, 1 mile south of Old Chatham, off County 13, on Shaker Museum Road.

From New York City, take the Taconic Parkway north to Route 295, left at East Chatham Post Office. In Old Chatham, follow County 13 1 mile south to Shaker Museum Road.

From Albany and New York State Thruway, take Interstate 90 to Exit 11E, right on US 20, right on Route 66 South, near Brainard. At Malden Bridge, turn left onto Shaker Museum Road.

From Boston, take Massachusetts Pike to B2 Exit, left on Route 295, left at East Chatham Post Office. In Old Chatham, follow County 13 1 mile south to Shaker Museum Road.

OPEN: Daily, 10 a.m.–5 p.m., May 1–October 31.

ADMISSION: Adults, $3.50; reduced for senior citizens and children; family rate, $8.50; members, free. Reservations required for groups and special rates available.

RESTAURANTS: Snacks available in Museum Shop.

SHOPS: Museum Shop and Bookstore.

FACILITIES: There is limited access for disabled visitors; direct inquiries to receptionist. Picnic area.

OVERVIEW

The Shaker Museum is a nonprofit educational organization chartered by the New York State Board of Regents. It is one of the nation's outstanding collections of Shaker furniture and artifacts.

HISTORY

Using outstanding representative items, the Shaker Museum seeks to offer visitors a comprehensive view of Shaker life and culture. While other sections of our book treat individual Shaker communities, the Shaker Museum is an assemblage of furniture, tools, and other items from the various Shaker communities. Unlike the other sites in the book, the Shaker Museum is a conventional indoor rather than an outdoor museum village. It contains an outstanding collection of Shaker artifacts that portrays the artistic skills and craftsmanship of the religious group founded by Mother Ann Lee.

John S. Williams acquired the majority of the museum's collections between 1935 and 1965 with the help of the Shaker leadership. Today, the Shaker Museum is recognized as the premier Shaker collection in the United States.

Members of a unique American religion, the Shakers were, in addition, among the most inventive and creative craftspeople of the nineteenth century. Among their innovations were collapsible dining tables, rocking chairs with

80

drawers under the seat, double desks that could accommodate two writers at the same time, and a wrinkle-proof cloth that anticipated modern permanent press. Among their useful inventions were the more efficient flat broom, which eventually replaced the old circular broom, and clothespins.

Today, Shaker furniture, much admired for its functional simplicity, has captured the attention of antique collectors and students of design. In the nineteenth-century Victorian Era, when furniture was ornate and formal, Shaker pieces were considered plain and drab, however. Now, they are highly prized and expensive collectors' items.

In addition to the outstanding furniture collection, the museum's exhibits include wood and iron working tools, farm equipment, machinery, sewing implements, looms, furniture, oval boxes, baskets, buckets, and stoves. The collections represent all the major Shaker industries, such as broom and chair manufacturing, cloak making, herbal pharmaceutical, and garden seeds.

The Shaker Museum illustrates many examples of Shaker inventiveness. There is an 1820 seven-ton double trip-hammer from Mount Lebanon, New York; a horse-drawn fire engine from Canterbury, New Hampshire; the first tongue and groove machine invented in 1828; and the patented washing machine from Canterbury.

Tour

The tour of the Shaker Museum is self-guided. The **Room of Shaker Furniture** features an assemblage of pieces from the various Shaker sites. Among the many items, the following are extraordinary for their simplicity of design: an 11-foot, cherry trestle table used in the Dwelling House dining room at Hancock in Massachusetts; a red-painted case of drawers from the North family at Mount Lebanon in New York; a pine and maple, yellow-painted case of drawers from the Church family at Mount Lebanon; a three-sectioned drying rack from Sabbathday Lake in Maine; a counter that originally was built into a room in the 1792 meetinghouse at Canterbury in New Hampshire; a domed chest from the Church family at Mount Lebanon; side chairs from Canterbury and Enfield; a yellow-painted pine cupboard from Hancock; a pine tailor's counter from the North family at Mount Lebanon; and a yellow-painted wheelchair and large rocking chair from the South family at Mount Lebanon.

Other rooms feature the well-made Shaker baskets, which followed the design of Native Americans; cast-iron Shaker stoves; and various tools and utensils.

Special events are the Antiques Festival, held on the first Saturday in August, and the Harvest Festival and Crafts Fair, held on the third Saturday in September.

George Rapp's Harmony Society

Portrait of Father George Rapp (1757–1847), founder of the Harmony Society. This portrait has been attributed to Phineas Stanton. Photo courtesy of the Old Economy Village, Pennsylvania Historical and Museum Commission.

OLD ECONOMY VILLAGE
1824–1905, Ambridge, Pennsylvania
NR, NHL

ADDRESS: Fourteenth and Church Streets, Ambridge, PA 15003
TELEPHONE: (412) 266-4500
LOCATION: Ambridge is in west central Pennsylvania, 15 miles northwest of Pittsburgh.
OPEN: Tuesday–Saturday, 9:00 a.m.–3:00 p.m.; Sunday, 12:00 noon–3:00 p.m.; closed holidays, except Memorial Day, July 4, and Labor Day.
ADMISSION: Adults, $5; senior citizens, $4; children 6–17, $3.
RESTAURANTS: No.
SHOPS: Gift Shop.
FACILITIES: Special events.

OVERVIEW

George Rapp (1757–1847) was the patriarchal founder of the Harmonist Society, a group of German Pietists who immigrated to the United States in 1804. The Harmonist Society survived 100 years, 1805–1905, and founded three sites, which they lived in successively—the first at Harmony, Pennsylvania, in 1806; the second at New Harmony, Indiana, in 1814; and the third at Economy, located in the present-day Pittsburgh suburb of Ambridge, Pennsylvania, in 1824.

George Rapp, the charismatic founder of the Harmonists, rejected Lutheranism, the official religion of his native Württemberg, especially its formal rituals. Rapp adopted Pietism, which stressed a personal relationship with God and a simple form of Christianity based on the Bible. His preaching resulted in repeated clashes with the civil and religious authorities of Württemberg.

In 1803, Rapp led an advance party to the United States, searching for freedom for himself and his many followers to practice their religious beliefs. Hundreds of Rapp's disciples soon followed. These Germans purchased land in Pennsylvania and began building a town, which they named Harmonie

Formally, the Harmony Society was established in 1805 and included a communal economy from its inception. In 1807, celibacy became a tenet of the society, but it was encouraged rather than mandatory.

Harmony Society members were hard working and industrious and the society became prosperous. It owned large farms, built towns with impressively large buildings, and produced goods for markets. In later years, they used their capital for investments and were quite wealthy.

New Harmony, Indiana, the Harmonists' second location, was sold by the society to Robert Owen, the utopian visionary, in 1824. A tour of New Harmony can be found in the section on the Owenites at New Harmony.

This section focuses on the history of the Harmonists and their leader,

George Rapp, at all three sites and provides a tour of the well-restored museum village of Old Economy, the third Harmonist site.

The first Harmonist site, Harmony, Pennsylvania, has one museum building and a few other buildings that may be viewed from the exterior only.

HISTORY

Johann George Rapp was born November 1, 1757, in Iptingen, a village in the German province of Württemberg. He was the second of five children of Rosina Berger and Hans Adam Rapp, a farmer and vine planter. George attended a traditional Lutheran school and was confirmed in the Lutheran Church in 1771 when he was fourteen years old. That year, George's father died.

As a young man, George learned the weaver's trade. He had also studied vinedressing with his father. He married Christine Benzinger of Fiolzheimin 1783. The couple had a son, Johannes, born in 1783 and a daughter, Rosina, born in 1786.

Rapp, a religious man, was highly critical of the Lutheran Church, the official religion of Württemburg, its clergy, and its rituals. He separated from the Lutheran Church and embraced the tenets of Pietism, which stressed a return to simpler, less ritualized forms of Christianity as outlined in the Bible and a personal relationship with God. Rapp, who was a student of the Bible and of the works of Jacob Boehme, a seventeenth-century mystic, and Jacob Spener, founder of the Pietists, began preaching from his home.

In 1785, Rapp was summoned before the Iptingen Church Council to explain his absence from Lutheran Church services. This confrontation between government authorities and Rapp was the first in a series that continued for two decades. Because religious and civil matters were intertwined in Germany, a religious transgression was also a civil offense. During questioning by officials at Maulbronn in 1792, Rapp declared, "I am a prophet and am called to be one." Rapp was imprisoned briefly and threatened with exile if he persisted in preaching, which he did.

Rapp's eloquent preaching attracted a group of followers who shared his aversion to the Lutheran Church. These Separatists refused to have their children baptized in the Lutheran Church or to have them educated in the Lutheran schools. By 1791, Rapp's followers numbered between 3,000 and 4,000; a decade later they had grown to over 10,000. Clearly, Rapp was a charismatic figure, like other leaders of religious groups referred to in this book.

In 1798, in answer to an inquiry by the Reform Legislature of Württemberg, Rapp and his associates provided a written statement of their Articles of Faith. It included conducting religious meetings in their own homes in imitation of the early Christians, educating their children themselves, opposition to infant baptism and to confirmation, refusal to take oaths or bear arms, and conducting Communion service for the righteous following confession of sins. In addition to the stated Articles of Faith, sharing of assets was a practice that evolved among Rapp and his followers. Communalism was formally adopted by the

Harmony Society in Pennsylvania in 1805.

Millennialism, the Kingdom of God on earth following the Second Coming of Christ, was a foundation of Rapp's beliefs. Based on his interpretation of the Book of Revelation, Rapp asserted the Second Coming of Christ would occur during his lifetime. Rapp saw Napoleon's wars in Europe as a fulfillment of biblical prophesies foreshadowing the Second Coming.

Rapp believed that he and his disciples personified Saint John's vision of the Sunwoman, referred to in the twelfth chapter of the Book of Revelation, who "fled into the wilderness, where she hath a place prepared of God." Because of their recurrent conflicts with the Württemberg government, Rapp's group decided to prepare for the Second Coming in a more hospitable place. Relocation sites they considered included Louisiana and Russia, both of which were rejected in favor of a settlement in Pennsylvania.

Leaving his congregation in the care of his associate Frederick Reichert, a stonemason and architect from Endersback, Rapp left for the United States accompanied by his son, Johannes, Dr. Christopher Mueller, and Dr. Frederick Conrad Haller. They arrived in Philadelphia aboard the ship *Canton* on October 7, 1803. The mission of this advance party was to purchase land for their community. Three hundred of Rapp's followers arrived on the *Aurora* July 4, 1804. Two hundred sixty-nine believers led by Frederick Reichert, who had coordinated the emigration, landed at Philadelphia on the *Atlantic* on September 15, 1804, succeeded by another 70 aboard the *Margaret* on September 19, 1804. Despite estimates as high as 20,000 of Rapp's followers in Germany, approximately 1,200 German immigrants actually joined Rapp's colonies in America.

A Harmonist woman in costume. Photograph courtesy of the Old Economy Village, Pennsylvania Historical and Museum Commission.

Old Economy Village

Although almost 650 of Rapp's followers had arrived in Pennsylvania by early fall 1804, it was not until December that Rapp purchased 5,000 acres at three dollars per acre on Connoquenessing Creek in Butler County, Pennsylvania. The vine planter Rapp was not totally satisfied with this land, which he described as "too small, too brocken too cold for to raise Vine."

Before proceeding with building a town, Rapp personally inquired of President Thomas Jefferson in early 1804 about purchasing government land in Ohio. Jefferson indicated that this request must be made to Congress. In early 1806, George Rapp and the Harmony Society presented Congress with their petition to purchase 30,000 acres of land in the western country.

Written rather awkwardly in English, the petition, or memorial as they termed it, describes the background and goals of the Harmony Society. The document records that the petitioners were natives of Würtemberg who, enlightened by God's grace, following "the Way of Piety," formed a "proper Community" of "Two thousand men." Because of persecution in their native land, they sought "a place where is liberty of Conscience," where they could practice their religion. Based on their understanding of the history of the United States, the society "unanimously resolved" to relocate to America. Their number of "about fourteen hundred men" consisted primarily of "Tradesmen, Farmers and chiefly cultevators of the Vine, which last occupation they contemplate as their primary Object."[1]

Rapp went to Washington, D.C., where, on January 29, 1806, the bill passed the Senate but was narrowly defeated in the House of Representatives on February 18. Despite the failure of their petition, Rapp's followers began to develop their town of Harmonie. The term "harmony" referred to the relationship between God and man, which, after the Second Coming of Christ, would be restored to its original state before Adam's fall.

Not every Harmonist who emigrated from Germany joined the community at Harmonie. Balking at communalism in which all property, including cash, land, cattle, and possessions, would be vested in the common treasury, some people preferred an association based on private property with a fund for assistance to those in need. The majority of the immigrants who had sailed on the *Margaret* followed Dr. Frederick Conrad Haller, a member of Rapp's advance party, who established the Blooming Grove colony in Lycoming County, Pennsylvania. Haller's colony was not communal. Still others purchased individual farms at Bull Creek in Columbiana County, Ohio.

The formal beginning of the Harmony Society was February 15, 1805, when the Articles of Association for George Rapp and Associates were drawn up and signed by 500 charter members. Communalism was officially established in the articles. In addition to contributing all their property to the society, members relinquished their right to compensation for their services if they should leave. They also pledged to submit to the laws and regulations of the congregation, and to obey its leaders. In return, the Harmony Society promised to provide lodging, food, clothing, medical care, education, spiritual guidance, and the right to attend all religious meetings. It also pledged to return to those who left in an orderly fashion the value of their original property without interest or a cash donation to those who had been unable to make a contribution on joining.

George Rapp, a commanding presence and a powerful speaker, was the temporal and religious leader of the newly formed Harmony Society. At forty-eight years old, he was six feet tall and had blue eyes and a full beard. He was kindly, healthy, and hardworking.

Frederick Reichert, Rapp's associate and close friend, was adopted by George Rapp in 1805 and thereafter used the name Rapp. Frederick Rapp, the business leader of the Harmonists, was credited with the community's financial success. A man of many talents, Frederick was skilled in masonry, architecture, drafting, accounting, and, most importantly for the Harmonists' future success, town planning.

To establish their first village in Pennsylvania, the Harmonists pooled their money to purchase land, livestock, food, and building materials. They were not wealthy people but were very industrious and frugal. The first year at Harmonie, 150 acres of land were cleared, crops were planted, and a church, a mill, a large barn, and several log houses were built. After five years, the community had 2,000 acres of cultivated land. Soon, their land was productive enough to not only provide for their own needs but also produce surplus products for market. Families lived in houses on quarter-acre lots, where they tended gardens and kept chickens, pigs, and cows. Merino sheep were raised for the production of woolen cloth.

Harmonie eventually grew to include 150 dwellings most of which were brick. Among the buildings were six large brick houses, a store, a weaving shop, a dye plant, a woolen factory, a meetinghouse, a granary, and various shops. The society operated several mills, a brewery, a tannery, and a hotel. Barns, stables, and a large warehouse were located on the river away from the town.

During a period of religious renewal in 1807, the Harmonists gave up the use of tobacco and adopted celibacy even among married people. George and Christine Rapp had abstained from sexual relations since 1786. However, they continued to live together in the same house until Christina's death; little is known of this virtually invisible woman.

Based both on his interpretation of the Book of Genesis and the writings of Jacob Boehme, Rapp held that God had originally created man, Adam, with a dual nature combining female and male elements. This conclusion was based on Genesis 1:26–27: "And God said, let us make man in our own image, after our own likeness, and let them have dominion. So God created man in his own image, in the image of God created he him: male and female created he them." Rapp interpreted this passage to mean that both the creator and the created possessed this dual nature, and had Adam been allowed to remain in his original state, he would have begotten offspring without the aid of a female. But Adam became discontented, and God separated from his body the female part.

Based on the Harmonist interpretation of the fall of man, Rapp concluded that celibacy is more pleasing to God, and in the "renewed" world man would be restored to his original "Adamic condition."[2]

Unlike the Shakers, the Harmonists' celibacy pledge appears to have been voluntary, at least in earlier years. Children continued to be born into the society after 1807. Between 1803 and 1813, 262 births were recorded in the Harmony Society. From 1814 to 1824, there were 69; and from 1825 to 1830, there were 25.[3]

Responding to a letter in the Harrisburg *Morgenrothe* on September 13, 1819, that accused the Harmony Society of not producing children, Frederick Rapp wrote to the editor, John S. Wiestling denying that "the begetting of children or sexual intercourse of married people is forbidden in the Harmonie." As proof, Rapp reported that the Harmonist school had consistently enrolled from 80 to 100 children between the ages of six and twelve. He added that a small number of Harmonists had chosen celibacy to advance their "sanctification." Of their "own free will," they "have given up carnal intercourse" to prepare for the coming of "Christ and His Kingdom."[4]

After ten years of growth and prosperity at Harmonie, the Harmonists were in an economic position to relocate the community. They had never been satisfied with their situation in Pennsylvania. Not only was it not conducive to wine making, there was no nearby waterway for transporting goods to market. In the spring of 1814, Father Rapp, John L. Baker, and Ludwick Shriver began a serious search for a more suitable location.

The Harmonists selected property in the Indiana Territory on the banks of the Wabash River and purchased almost 2,500 acres in May 9, 1814, and another 5,370 acres that year. Over 6,000 acres were added in the following three years so that by 1817, they owned over 14,000 acres. The town of Harmonie was sold for $100,000 to Abraham Ziegler on May 6, 1815. By that time, over 800 Harmonists, their livestock, supplies, and equipment had relocated to Indiana.

The town in Indiana was also named Harmonie or Neu Harmonie to distinguish it from their settlement in Pennsylvania. Rapp and about 100 men moved there in June 1814 to make preparations for the community. The initial work parties were greeted by heat, humidity, mosquitoes, and swampy land. A malaria epidemic caused many deaths—forty-nine in 1814 and seventy in 1815. In the spring of 1817, about 130 people from Württemberg joined the Indiana community. The population of Rapp's Harmonist community remained between 700 and 800 people.

The skilled adopted son of George Rapp, Frederick, planned the new community. On June 6, 1814, Frederick forwarded the town plan to the register of the Vincennes Land Office, asking that the plots be laid out according to his specifications.[5] New Harmony was surveyed and laid out August 8, 1814, in a grid pattern with Main and Church its principal intersecting streets.

The years the Harmonists lived on the Wabash were hardworking, productive, and prosperous ones during which a large town was built. The Harmonists engaged in agriculture, expanded industrially, planted extensive vineyards and orchards, and raised large herds of stock. They operated stores in Vincennes, Indiana, and Shawneetown, Illinois, and contracted with agents to handle their goods in Pittsburgh, St. Louis, Louisville, and New Orleans. They sold whiskey, rope, shoes, leather goods, woolen cloth, linen, cotton cloth, seed, hops, hemp, tobacco, sugar, cheese, butter, wax, cattle, sheep, horses, hogs, furs, hides, beer, wine, cider, pottery, lard, bacon, and feathers.

On February 15, 1818, at the suggestion of George Rapp, the book that contained the record of each member's contributions to the Harmonist common treasury was burned in the presence of the congregation. From that time on, society members who withdrew had no proof of their original contribution. This action improved the financial security of the society and fortified Father Rapp's authority.

The Harmonist presence in Indiana was now well established. Frederick Rapp was an elected delegate to the Indiana Constitutional Convention in 1816 and was appointed to a commission to select a permanent seat of government for Indiana in 1820.

Interested in education, the society subscribed to eleven newspapers and owned a library of 360 books. Christopher Mueller, a man of many talents, operated the printing press, which was acquired in 1824. That year, it was used to publish the German edition of George Rapp's only book, *Thoughts on the Destiny of Man, Particularly with Reference to the Present Times*, in which Rapp articulated his religious and social theories. The English version was published in 1825.

The Harmonists created a total community that included education, art, and music as well as work. Children attended school until age fourteen. Older children attended classes in the morning and worked in the afternoon. Instruction was bilingual, though German was preferred. The curriculum included reading, writing, arithmetic, geography, history, and music. Children were taught singing and the fundamentals of music.

Music was very important in the Harmonist community. The society purchased musical scores and instruments, including a piano. Even at Harmonie, Christopher Mueller had organized an orchestra. He also composed and arranged music. The society's first hymnbook, *Harmonisches-Gesangbuch*, was published in 1820. The musicians and the music they played and composed became more sophisticated over time and included religious and secular pieces. The orchestra frequently gave public concerts for their neighbors. Children who wanted to learn an instrument could apprentice with an experienced performer.[6]

Ten years after New Harmony was established, 2,000 of their 20,000 acres were cultivated, 15 in vineyards and 35 in apple and pear orchards. Structures in the comprehensive community included forty two-story brick and frame houses, eighty-six log houses, six two-story brick dormitories, a frame church and a brick church, two granaries, two distilleries, a brewery, a three-story merchant mill, a cotton and wool factory, two saw mills, a dye works, a two-story brick store and stone warehouse, a tavern, three frame barns, three sheep stables, a doctor's office, a hospital, a brick kiln, two greenhouses, and a tannery. Some building materials were standardized and mass-produced. Houses were well designed, insulated, centrally heated, and fire resistant. Many of these carefully designed and constructed buildings, which were later used by the Owenites, are still standing.

Gabriel's Rock, one of the more curious Harmonist acquisitions, can still be seen at New Harmony. Actually two slabs that were originally one stone, the first of two limestone slabs has a square figure, and the other contains the imprints of two feet. The stone was discovered along the Mississippi River near St. Louis. In a letter dated December 5, 1818, from Frederick Rapp to John L. Baker, Rapp urged Baker to purchase it for between $50 to $100.[7] The rock was bought and placed near the Rapp house. According to an undocumented anecdote, Father Rapp allegedly told his people that the footprints were those of the angel Gabriel. However, there is no evidence that Rapp ever made this statement.

After a decade on the Indiana frontier, Rapp decided that the Harmonists should return to Pennsylvania. His decision had a religious basis. According to Rapp's interpretation of Revelation, the Sunwoman would move into her era of glory, called the era of the golden rose, after 1822. The golden rose was an important Harmonist religious symbol. According to Father Rapp, the era of the golden rose would be fulfilled at Economy.

Father Rapp had received a detailed design for a church in a dream. This cruciform brick church was built at New Harmony in 1822. The entrance to the church was regarded as the door of promise referred to in Micah 4:8, which reads "your era of the golden rose will come, namely your earlier dominion, the Kingdom of the daughter of Jerusalem."[8] Over the church door was a stone lintel with a golden rose carved in it.

A Harmonist rose decorated the ceiling of the grotto of the labyrinth at Economy. Labyrinths of flowering shrubs, vines, and trees with grottoes in the center were constructed at each of the three Harmonist sites and were intended for meditation. A rose is on the newel posts of the Great House in Economy and on the only tombstone in the graveyard at Harmony, Pennsylvania. The golden rose became the society's trademark.

In 1824, Father Rapp asked David Shields of Pennsylvania to locate property suitable for the group resettlement. Shields identified a 3,000-acre tract of land on the Ohio River, which the society purchased. The new Harmonist location, Economy, was in Beaver County, Pennsylvania, close to Pittsburgh. It was home to the society until it was dissolved in 1905.

Richard Flower, a prominent resident of the English Prairie community in Illinois, was asked to find a buyer in England for New Harmony. In early 1825, Flower negotiated a deal with Robert Owen for $150,000 for the property and

$40,000 for the stock and equipment. (The Owenite period is discussed in the section on New Harmony.)

Economy, the Harmonists' third location, was laid out in a grid arrangement of streets with houses at the center. A formal garden was surrounded by the principal buildings. Factories and farm buildings were located on the outskirts, and fields ringed the town.

The Harmonists were millennialists, who believed that Christ would come again during George Rapp's life. They believed this long-awaited event would occur in 1829. Coincidentally, in 1829, Rapp received a letter from a self-proclaimed Messiah named Count Leon, Archduke Maximilian of the Stem of Judah and the Root of David, announcing that he was coming to Economy. Because this coincided with their expectations, the Harmonists anticipated Count Leon's timely visit as the long-awaited Second Coming of Christ. In fact, Bernhard Muller, Leon's real name, had notified many European heads of state and religious leaders of his identity as the Messiah. While Muller had received very few interested replies, the Harmonists extended an enthusiastic invitation.

Arriving in Economy in October 1831 by horse and carriage and accompanied by forty followers, Count Leon was dressed in full uniform with epaulets and swords. In addition to being the Messiah, Count Leon claimed to possess the "Philosopher's Stone" and the secret formulas of alchemy, which could turn base metal into gold. George Rapp, a believer in alchemy, had been searching for this knowledge without success for years.

In a matter of months, Rapp and Count Leon had several disagreements, the most serious of which revolved around celibacy. Some Harmonists had begun to feel that Rapp's position on sexual relations was hypocritical, as he displayed great partiality to one young woman in the community. She was Hildegarde Mutschler, the daughter of Frederika Bentel and John Mutschler, whom George Rapp had married in 1805. Hildegarde was born April 29, 1806. During the 1820s, Father Rapp chose Hildegarde as his laboratory assistant when he conducted chemical experiments and brewed medicines. Their relationship caused gossip and indignation among some members.[9] In 1829, Hildegarde eloped with Dr. Conrad Feucht. Father Rapp, in a very controversial decision, sent for the couple and accepted them back into the community even though they refused to practice celibacy. They had four children.

Many Harmonists supported Count Leon's opposition to celibacy. The community became hopelessly divided over leadership as many welcomed a change from what they considered the absolute and despotic rule of Rapp. Father Rapp now concluded that Count Leon was an imposter.

In March 1832, Muller and 175 Harmonists left for Philipsburg, Pennsylvania, to form their own, more liberal New Philadelphia Society. This devastating schism claimed one-third of the Harmony Society membership and caused severe financial damage. After negotiations with the Rapps, the dissenters agreed to accept a payment of $105,000 as well as their personal and household belongings. One of the worst losses was that of Christopher Mueller, the multi-talented musician, physician, schoolmaster, and printer. After a year, Count Leon's communal settlement at Philipsburg dissolved with some people following him to Louisiana and others joining Dr. William Keil, who founded a communal colony at Bethel, Missouri.

Despite these losses of people and property, the Harmony Society continued to be very successful. They bought tons of cotton for their cloth mills from the South and textile machinery from Lowell, Massachusetts. They owned stock in the Second Bank of the United States. They lent money for a water system to Pittsburgh. Their fine silk, produced under the direction of George Rapp's granddaughter, Gertrude, won awards from the Franklin Institute of Philadelphia in 1838 and the Boston Fair and American Institute in New York in 1844. Father Rapp accumulated gold and silver coins that he kept in a vault in his home. The church fund, which grew to a half million dollars by 1846, was intended for the reconstruction of the temple in Jerusalem when the millennium began.

George Rapp never wavered from his belief that the Second Coming of Christ would occur during his lifetime. He lived ninety years and never abandoned hope. On his deathbed, he declared, "If I did not so fully believe that the Lord has designed me to place our Society before His presence in the land of Canaan, I would consider this my last."[10] Then Rapp died on August 7, 1848.

After Rapp's death, the society was governed by a board of nine elders with Romelius L. Baker and Jacob Henrici as trustees to manage its business affairs. In the subsequent two decades, the society became a financial power as it changed its emphasis from agriculture to investments. Concurrently, membership from the late 1840s to the mid-1860s dropped from 288 to 146. Hired laborers did most of the manual labor. The cotton and wool factories closed in 1864. Silk production had already ended.

Coal was an area of investment. The society owned coal mines near Darlington, Pennsylvania, and sold coal in Chicago, New York, and Cleveland. The Harmonists also became involved in the emerging oil industry. By 1862, the Economy Oil Company was operating four producing oil wells. They also refined oil and laid an oil pipeline. They made real estate investments, developed the town of Beaver Falls, and backed many local businesses.

During the Civil War, Jacob Henrici was a U.S. Deputy Marshal in Harmony Township and was required to draw up the militia lists and notify those eligible for military service. Only five Harmonists were young enough to serve, and being pacifists, they were able to obtain releases by paying substitutes.

In 1868, R. L. Baker died and was replaced as trustee by Jonathan Lenz. At that time the society had 140 members.

The Harmony Society invested heavily in railroads and was a major factor in their development in Pennsylvania. Henrici was president of the Pittsburgh and Lake Erie Railroad and its subsidiary, the Pittsburgh, Chartiers, & Youghiogheny Railway, from January 12, 1881, to January 14, 1884. At that time, the Harmonists sold their interests to the Vanderbilts for $1,150,000.

Simultaneously, the Harmonists were growing older. The average age of the membership was about seventy in 1880 and was almost entirely composed of immigrants who had been adherents of Rapp in Germany. The Harmonists did not engage in missionary activities in America and accepted few members after the 1832 schism. These factors combined with a low birth rate led to the demise of the society. Although it lasted 100 years, its later years were characterized by reduced productivity.

Gertrude Rapp died December 29, 1889, and trustee Jacob Henrici died December 25, 1892. Gertrude Rapp was the beloved only grandchild of George Rapp. After her father's early death, she and her mother lived with her grandparents, her Aunt Rosina, and her Uncle Frederick. She was a gifted and talented woman who had been tutored particularly in music by Christopher Mueller. After his defection with Count Leon, Gertrude shunned Mueller, with whom she had a loving relationship. She managed the society's award-winning silk industry. She and Jacob Henrici were in love with each other but, because of their commitment to Harmonist principles, remained celibate and never married.

By the time of Gertrude Rapp's death, there were fewer than twenty members in the Society. Less than a month later, January 21, 1890, Jonathan Lenz, the junior trustee, died. Because there was no legal provision for the disposition of the wealthy society's assets, nor were there any legal heirs, at this time many people with questionable motives sought membership. On January 24, 1890, four new members were admitted to the society. They were Moritz J. Friedrichs, J. Jacob Niclaus, Hermann Fischern, and John S. Duss. The next month, sixteen new members were admitted, including Susie C. Duss, John Duss's wife, as well as Henry and Benjamin Feucht and their wives.

John S. Duss was born in Cincinnati February 22, 1860. His mother, Caroline Duss, came to Economy in March 1862 and was employed as a nurse; she was not a member of the society. His father was wounded at the Battle of Gettysburg and died in 1863. Until age thirteen, John was educated at the common district school at Economy and then attended the Soldier's Orphan School at Philipsburg until he was sixteen. For a short time, he was a tailor's apprentice and a German teacher in the Economy school after which he attended Mount Union College, Ohio. In 1882, he married Susie C. Creese and bought a farm in Nebraska, which was unsuccessful.

John Duss, accompanied by his wife and two children, returned to Economy in July 1888 as a teacher. His mother had become a member of the society the previous year, and John and Susie became members in early 1890. When a trustee, Ernest Woelfel, died suddenly in July 1890, John Duss replaced him. Henrici, the senior trustee, was about ninety years old and near death.

Duss drew up a document, a Statement of Membership in the Harmony Society and Definition of Rights and Powers of Trustees of Society, which gave legal title of the society's assets to Henrici and him. The notarized document was recorded December 22, three days prior to Henrici's death on December 25. From that date, Duss, the only living trustee, held total legal power and control of the Economy fortune. He proceeded to liquidate its capitalist ventures while encouraging members to leave the society.[11]

Duss was a bandleader who had grandiose notions about a musical career. He diverted substantial amounts of society funds to publicizing his band. In 1902, the New York *Herald* announced "MILLIONAIRE MAKES HIS DEBUT WITH BAND. DUSS, OWNER OF THE TOWN OF ECONOMY, IS ORIGINAL, AND HIS MUSICIANS MAKE LOTS OF NOISE."

His self-proclaimed status as a millionaire attracted more attention than his military band, which was judged mediocre at best. In 1903, a replica of Venice was recreated in Madison Square Garden at a cost of $100,000 for a single performance of the Duss band.

In May 1903, John Duss resigned as trustee and withdrew from the society. He was replaced by his wife, Susie, who awarded him a leaving present of $500,000. One hundred five acres of the Economy property had been sold to the American Bridge Company in 1902. In December 1905, the last two living members, Susie C. Duss and Franz Gillmann, dissolved the 100-year-old group. The two agreed to equally divide the society assets. Immediately thereafter, Gillmann, who was described as an imbecile, gave his share to Mrs. Duss.

In 1919, the Commonwealth of Pennsylvania took over the 6 acres of land that constitute the present historic site and turned it over to the Pennsylvania Historical and Museum Commission. In 1937, architects Charles Stotz and Edward Stotz Jr. began restoration work; they were later aided by the Works Progress Administration.

Today, Old Economy is a carefully restored and well-maintained outdoor museum.

TOUR

The **Museum Building**, probably designed by Frederick Rapp, blends traditional German and Georgian architecture. When completed in December 1827, a museum was to be housed on its first floor while its second floor contained a large room for community gatherings, concerts, and religious festivities. This sizable Harmonist structure is one of the earliest buildings constructed as a museum in the United States. A receipt indicates that Frederick Rapp purchased twenty- eight boxes of "natural curiosities" as well as paintings for $4,000 in 1826.

Exhibits of art, American Indian relics, botanical specimens, and stuffed animals were used for teaching purposes. The museum curator was Dr. Mueller, who was a botanist, naturalist, and musician. There was also a library and possibly a schoolroom on the first floor.

The second floor of the building is entirely occupied by a room that could hold 500 people and was used for ceremonial occasions. On most religious holidays, all the members of the society gathered in the room for a feast, with

The Feast Hall as it appeared 1900. Photograph courtesy of the Old Economy Village, Pennsylvania Historical and Museum Commission.

men on the right and women on the left. After a meal of stew, noodles, bread, fruit, salad, beer, and wine, a religious service that included music was held.

The museum in the Museum Building is being restored as it was in early Harmonist days.

Fearing fire, the Harmonists did not permit a kitchen in the Museum Building. Cooking was done nearby in the **Community Kitchen**, a separate one-story frame building. Meals for as many as 500 people at a time were prepared here; the large-scale functional design of this kitchen included twelve large kettles sunk in ovens.

A series of shops produced necessities for the community. The **Cabinet Shop** is a one- story building; this is where the furniture, doors, moldings, and mantels for society buildings were made.

The large **Granary** held a year's supply of grain on the upper three and one-half floors; the first floor was used for stockpiling food. Although the Harmonists were expecting the millennium, they were well prepared for the fire, disease, and starvation that were to precede it. The granary is constructed of huge chestnut beams, and the first floor is half-timbered.

The first floor of the large two-story brick **Mechanics Building** houses a **shoemaker's shop**, a **tailor's shop,** and a **hat shop**. The tailor and the shoemaker were responsible for the appearance of the members, who wore clothes supplied by the society. As members filed into church each Sunday, the tailor and shoemaker would check their attire; if they noted signs of wear or shabbiness, the craftsmen would ask that person to come to the shop to be measured for a replacement.

A Ramage Press, acquired by the society in 1822, is displayed in the **Print Shop** of the Mechanics Building. Dr. Muller who was also the community's printer, used the press to print several books, including the society's hymns, a speller, a school singing book, a book of pietistic maxims, and George Rapp's *Thoughts on the Destiny of Man* published in German and English.

Underneath the Mechanics Building is a large vaulted stone **wine cellar**, where the homemade wine was aged in large casks both for the Harmonists' own use and for sale.

The **Blacksmith Shop** is located in a 1905 auto garage.

The society sold shoes, hats, flour, whiskey, farm products, and cloth to the public. Distribution of goods to the 120 households that made up the Harmony Society was also handled at the 1826 **store**. During the community's most prosperous years, from 1825 to 1850, the store took in $100,000—brisk business by nineteenth-century standards.

The store, in addition to several other functional rooms, includes the **doctor's office**, furnished with some pieces that belonged to Dr. Christopher Mueller. Mueller was also the town's pharmacist, taught school, conducted the orchestra, was in charge of the museum, operated the printing press, and tended the botanical garden. What a loss when this jack-of-all-trades left in the 1832 schism!

Harmonists lived in groups of three to seven people; they ate, cooked, and slept in the houses they shared. Love feasts were the only meals taken communally. The houses followed uniform design. The necessary doors, windows, sashes, precut lumber, and bricks were delivered to each building site and quickly assembled. A man headed each household, and the house was known by his name.

Baker House is a typical Harmonist household. The first floor has a large living room, where the members ate and relaxed. It is simply furnished with Harmonist-made tables, chairs, and a corner cupboard containing Harmonist pottery. It also has a kitchen and bedrooms with rope beds and large wardrobes.

Each house also had a shed. The **Family Shed** has been reconstructed on its original site. Its four rooms were used for food storage, tool and wood storage, a chicken house, and an outhouse.

All food was drawn from the store except vegetables, which were grown in each household's kitchen garden. The **Baker House Garden** has been restored with appropriate vegetables, flowers, and herbs based upon a Harmonist girl's list of 1825.

Economy's restored **formal George Rapp garden** at the center of town has boxwood- edged intersecting paths dividing it into quarters. The garden, which has the same kind of flowers as those planted by the Harmonists, has been recreated based on planting lists maintained by the Harmonists. Using historically correct, nonhybrid seeds, the garden display includes a colorful profusion

The garden of the Baker house is planted with old varieties of plants and vegetables. Photograph by Patricia A. Gutek.

of old-fashioned peonies, lilies, and a large variety of columbines.

The **large pavilion** and **grotto** were designed by Frederick Rapp. The orchestra played in the pavilion while villagers strolled through the garden admiring the flowers. A thatched-roofed grotto made of rough stones stands in the southwest corner. The interior is decorated like a Roman temple, and under a large dome is a gold lily, said to have had religious significance for the Harmonists.

The **Rapp House** consists of two separate, but connected, structures: the **George Rapp House**, built in 1826, and the **Frederick Rapp House**, which dates from 1828. The central structure and two wings of George Rapp's house have twenty-five rooms. It is furnished more elegantly than other Harmonist homes. Although equality was one of the tenets of the religion, the Harmonists wanted their leader, whom they considered a prophet, to live in a house appropriate to his position. The great house faced the main street so that visitors could see "what a united brethren could do," according to George Rapp.

Frederick Rapp's two-story house is a separate structure, but connected. Here, too, the furniture and decorations are elegant. There are both American and Harmonist pieces, carpeting, and wallpaper. Some of Frederick Rapp's possessions, including his surveyor's compass, a microscope, musical instruments, and books, are displayed.

The **Carriage House** contains the 1826 fire engine pumper built by the society, a Seneca Falls, New York, suction-hose engine purchased in 1836, a carriage made for George Rapp in 1843, and the Harmony Society hearse.

Old Economy Village

Outside the museum grounds are sixteen square blocks containing eighty privately owned Harmonist buildings. Notable is the **Harmonist Church**, built in 1828. Now named **Saint John's Lutheran Church**, it is located on Church Street across from the George Rapp House. Six hundred Harmonists are buried in unmarked graves in the **Harmonist Cemetery** at Church and 11th Streets.

SIDE TRIPS

Harmonie was the first town built by the Harmonists in 1804. On 4,000 acres of land purchased from Dettmar Basse, 130 houses, craft shops, and agricultural buildings were constructed in a ten-year period. The town was sold to Abraham Ziegler for $100,000 in 1814, and the Harmonists moved to Indiana, where they founded New Harmony.

About a dozen original Harmonist structures are located around or near the central square of the contemporary town named Harmony, including the **Frederick Rapp House** and the **church**. The **Harmonist Cemetery** has 100 people buried in it, but there is only one gravestone, that of Johannes Rapp, George's son.

The **Harmony Museum** is in an 1809 Harmonist washhouse and contains objects made or owned by the society's members, including a one-handed clock, tables, beds, chairs, and a stove. There is also a **wine cellar**.

Harmony is located twenty-five miles north of Old Economy, on Routes 19 and 68. Open daily 1:00 to 4:00 p.m., June 1–October 1. Main and Mercer Streets, Harmony PA; telephone (412) 452-7341. Admission is charged.

Joseph Bimeler's Separatists

A Zoar house faces the community's large formal garden. Photograph by Patricia A. Gutek.

ZOAR VILLAGE STATE MEMORIAL
1817–1898, Zoar, Ohio
NR, HABS

ADDRESS: P.O. Box 404, State Route 212, Zoar, OH 44697
TELEPHONE: (216) 874-3011
LOCATION: Zoar is in east central Ohio between New Philadelphia and Canton; it is 3 miles southeast of I-77 Exit 93 on Ohio 212.
OPEN: Wednesday–Saturday, 9:30 a.m.–5:00 p.m., and Sunday and holidays, noon–5:00 p.m., Memorial Day weekend–Labor Day; Saturday, 9:30 a.m.–5:00 p.m., and Sunday, noon–5:00 p.m., April–mid- May and September–October.
ADMISSION: Adults, $4.00; seniors, $3.20; children 6–12, $1.00.
RESTAURANTS: Zoar Tavern; Inn on the River Restaurant.
SHOPS: Zoar Store; antique, book, candle, and gift shops are in the town of Zoar.
FACILITIES: Special events; demonstrations; orientation video; guided tours.

OVERVIEW

Zoar Village State Memorial is a museum complex of ten restored buildings maintained by the Ohio Historical Society within the very small nineteenth-century town of Zoar founded in 1817. It is the location of a community established by a group of German Separatists headed by Joseph Bimeler (1778–1853), originally called Bäumler. Persecuted in their homeland for their religious beliefs, 300 men, women, and children from Württemburg reached Philadelphia in August 1817. There they hoped to practice their religion in peace. The pietistic Separatists, who left the Lutheran Church, did not believe in sacraments and refused to enter military service, pay taxes, or send their children to state schools.

In Philadelphia, the Quakers warmly received Joseph Bimeler and his group. The Separatists purchased 5,500 acres along the Tuscarawas River in Ohio, and the first log cabin in the town called Zoar was completed in December 1817.

Due to harsh winters and poor harvests, the Zoarites adopted a communal economy in 1819. Private property was eliminated, and work and assets were shared in exchange for food, lodging, and clothing. Hard work and skilled business practices resulted in a prosperous community, which owned large tracts of land, herds of cattle, and successful industries. The Zoar Society lasted until 1898, when it disbanded due to declining membership.

The Ohio Historical Society acquired several Zoar buildings in the 1940s and 1960s. The buildings have been faithfully restored to their appearance in the 1830s, the period of Zoar's greatest prosperity.

Because of its relatively isolated location and peaceful setting in Ohio's

Zoar Village State Memorial

Tuscarawas Valley, Zoar has retained much of its simplicity and charm. In addition to the restored buildings, preserved by the Ohio Historical Society, other Zoarite buildings are privately owned and used as residences, bed-and-breakfasts, and shops. Zoar is an outstanding museum village because of its historical significance, its fine restoration, and its exquisite setting.

HISTORY

Barbara Grubermann was the original leader of a German group of Christian Pietists who eventually settled at Zoar, Ohio. This Swiss woman was an "inspired one," or medium, who received messages while in a trance, similar to the inspired ones among the people who founded Amana in Iowa. After Grubermann's death in Germany, Joseph Michael Bimeler assumed her leadership role. He brought his people to America in 1817 and served as their spiritual leader, business manager, and physician until his death in 1853.

Joseph Michael Bimeler was born in 1778, the son of a farmer. He was trained as a weaver and worked as a teacher. By all accounts, he was not an imposing figure. He had an oversized head, different-sized protruding eyes, and walked with a limp. Bimeler had a profound religious conversion experience after which he separated from the Lutheran Church. He was known for his great preaching skills.

Bimeler and his Separatist followers were Christian Pietists who preferred a simple form of Christianity to the rituals of the state Lutheran Church. While still in Germany, Bimeler's people codified their beliefs into twelve key principles. They believed in the Holy Trinity, the fall of Adam, and the Holy Scriptures as the basis of religious beliefs. They regarded sacramental rituals, including baptism, confirmation, and Communion, as useless and divisive. They rejected sectarian religion, an ordained clergy, ecclesiastical authority, and rituals and regulations imposed by established churches. They refused to send their children to schools operated under clerical auspices.

The Separatists were pacifists who refused to serve as soldiers "because a Christian can not murder his enemy, much less his friend." Except in their refusal to adhere to the officially established church, they were law- abiding citizens who regarded government as necessary "to maintain order, and to protect the good and honest and punish the wrong-doers; and no one can prove us to be untrue to the constituted authorities."[1]

Because of their principles, both the civil and ecclesiastical authorities in Württemberg levied fines and imprisonment on these Separatists. After years of enduring persecution, they decided to leave their homeland.

Three hundred German Separatists left Württemberg for the United States in search of religious freedom, sailing from Antwerp in April 1817. Joseph Michael Bimeler and his followers landed in Philadelphia August 14, 1817. Looking for help in relocating, the religious refugees had appealed to the English Society of Friends, Quakers, who shared many religious beliefs. The

Württemburgers were met at the dock by members of the Philadelphia Society of Friends. The Quakers provided the immigrants with money, food, medical care, and housing in a hospital wing.

Two sisters in the group, Catharine and Christina Zellerin, wrote a letter dated August 26, 1817, from Philadelphia to their aunt at Harmony, Pennsylvania, which expressed their joy and proclaimed their thanks at being in the United States. They praised the warm welcome they received from the Quakers, who, they said, had "almost the same religion as ours. . . . As soon as we arrived in Philadelphia, the Quakers gave us food and shelter . . . as if we were their children."[2]

The Separatists' initial concern in America was to locate good land to establish a settlement. The Quakers used their business contacts to help the Separatists locate a suitable property, but Bimeler was dissatisfied with these tracts of land.

In 1817, with a loan from the Quakers, Bimeler purchased land in Tuscarawas County, Ohio, from Godfrey Haga, a Moravian businessman who frequently acted as an agent for the Harmonists. Bimeler wrote Frederick Rapp that, dissatisfied with the land offered by the Quakers, "we decided without delay to go to the western provinces and to look for land ourselves." Bimeler negotiated a transaction with Godfrey Haga for 5,500 acres of land in Ohio on the Tuscarawas River for the price of $15,000.[3]

Bimeler and the Separatists were pleased with the land purchased from Haga. It had heavily wooded hills, fertile plains, and several good springs. An advance party laid out the town on the eastern bank of the Tuscarawas and began building log houses. They named their village after Lot's biblical city, called Zoar, which means "a place of refuge" and "a sanctuary from evil." Bimeler wrote to Rapp that despite "a very hard winter," the Separatists were living in "fair comfort."[4]

The remainder of the Württemberg people gradually moved from Philadelphia to Ohio in the spring of 1818. Some were forced to seek employment on neighboring farms to augment their limited financial resources.

Zoar's early years found the community hard-pressed economically. Displeased that the Separatists had left Pennsylvania for Ohio, the relationship between the Quakers and Bimeler soured. The Quakers refused to lend money to the Zoarites for building mills. They questioned the wisdom of having Bimeler hold sole title to the land, and he refused to change the land title. For financial rather than religious reasons, the Separatists decided to establish a communal economy. Their religious beliefs did not oppose private ownership and profit.

In April 1819, the German Pietists formally organized as the Society of Separatists of Zoar. Two classes of membership were established: permanent associates, called second class, and novitiates, called first class. Those in the probationary class, which included children until the age of eighteen, did not turn over their property but worked and obeyed society rules for a year before applying for full membership.

Zoar Village State Memorial

Second class members signed a covenant in which they gave their entire real and personal property, including future inheritances and gifts, to the Society of Separatists forever, even after death. In the covenant, they promised and bound themselves "to obey all the commands and orders of the trustees and their subordinates, with the utmost zeal and diligence, without opposition or grumbling; and to devote all our strength, good-will, diligence, and skill, during our whole lives, to the common service of the society and for the satisfaction of its trustees."[5]

When questions arose about the legal ramifications of the communal covenant, Bimeler turned to Frederick Rapp of the Harmony Society for advice. The Rapps, George, the founder, and Frederick, his adopted son, both had experience with communalism and common property, including the thorny issue of the property rights of those who left the society. Bimeler inquired about the need for a charter of incorporation from the state. He especially wanted to know if the Harmony Society's property was held by the collective membership or by George Rapp, its leader. The practical Bimeler asked if those who left the society would be compensated for their labor and if the membership could force the dissolution of the society.[6]

The Society of Separatists of Zoar adopted a constitution that provided for the election of officers by majority vote; both men and women could vote. Three elected trustees would manage the economic affairs, appoint supervisors of industries, and supply housing, clothing, food, and medical care for each member. All money would be turned over to the cashier, who was the treasurer and bookkeeper. An agent would conduct all business transactions outside of the society; Bimeler held this position until his death. A standing committee of five provided general council to the other administrators and arbitrated disputes.

The communal economy coupled with German habits of thrift and hard work and the wise business sense of Bimeler resulted in prosperity for the Zoarites. Agriculture was the primary pursuit at Zoar; wheat, oats, rye, and barley were raised. Apple and pear orchards and vineyards for wine production were planted. In addition, cattle, sheep, chickens, pigs, and horses were raised. The community operated a flour mill, woolen mill, sawmill, and planing mill. It also had a saddlery and hay wagon, cooper, and tin shops.

The building of the Ohio-Erie Canal, which commenced in 1825, proved to be an economic windfall. In 1827, the Zoarites contracted to build a seven-mile section of the Ohio-Erie Canal, which crossed their land, for $21,000. They also sold their produce to other contractors. This unanticipated cash enabled them to pay off their land debt and acquire more land. The canal opened new markets for Zoar products, and the community acquired and operated four canal boats. Two blast furnaces, the Zoar furnace in 1834 followed by the Fairfield Furnace in 1835, were built on the canal. Subsequently, pig iron and castings were shipped to eastern and midwestern cities.

105

By the mid-1830s, the community was prosperous and self-sufficient. They owned over 7,000 acres of land, had a woolen factory, looms for weaving linen, a dye house, a foundry, a distillery, and a cider press. They had their own tailors, dressmakers, shoemakers, carpenters, and wagon makers.

William Hinds, a nineteenth-century visitor to America's utopian communities, wrote:

> Zoar was a little world by itself. It had small use for outside society, and limited communication with it. For many years its people wove their own linen and woolen cloths from flax and wool of their own growing, and made their own simple garments; they tanned the hides of their own cattle, and made their own shoes; they made their own castings and pottery; ground their own flour and feed; repaired their own tools and agricultural implements; had their own church and their own preacher; their own school and their own teacher; their own physician, Bimeler caring for the bodies of his flock as well as their souls, so long as he lived; they had no lockup, and needed none, for no member of Zoar, they proudly boast, was ever charged with crime; they had no use for courts and lawyers, having no disputes they could not settle without their aid; no divorces, no social scandals, no controversy over property matters. It was indeed a haven of peace and rest, such as the world has too rarely seen.[7]

Zoar reached its highest population, 500, in 1832 after more German immigrants arrived. In 1834, cholera killed nearly one-third of the members. After that, outside laborers were hired.[8]

The Separatists operated a country store for non-Zoarites, where their crafts, iron stoves, and produce were sold, and a tavern serving the needs of the travelers on the canal. They built a large hotel, which attracted summer visitors.

The Zoarites lived in family units with more than one family sharing a house. Families cooked their own meals using produce from their own gardens and chickens and eggs they raised. Meat, excluding pork, which Zoarites did not eat, salt, coffee, and tea were obtained from the Magazine. Bread was baked in a central bakery and distributed daily. These hardworking people got up at 6:00 a.m., ate breakfast at 7:00 a.m., dinner at noon, and supper at 6:00 p.m. Although they drank cider and beer, they did not use tobacco.

Charles Nordhoff, who visited Zoar in 1874, described the Zoarites as unintellectual German peasants who did not value beauty but achieved comfort and wealth. He called them "sober, quiet and orderly, very industrious, economical and the amount of ingenuity and business skill which they have developed is quite remarkable." He added that "they are not great readers, except of the Bible and the few pious books which they brought over from Germany."[9]

Nordhoff found that the community's views on sexuality and marriage were addressed in the original twelve principles of the Separatists printed in Bimeler's

Zoar was known for its 1835 greenhouse, where oranges and lemons were grown. Photograph by Patricia A. Gutek.

first volume, which stated, "All intercourse of the sexes, except what is necessary to the perpetuation of the species, we hold to be sinful and contrary to the order and command of God. Complete virginity or entire cessation of sexual commerce is more commendable than marriage."[10] Celibacy was adopted in 1822 while the Zoarites were still struggling financially, and was abandoned in 1830 when the community had grown more prosperous economically. Joseph Bimeler, himself, married and had a family.

Children lived with their parents until they were three years old. For the next twelve years, they lived together in children's dormitories. In 1840, placing children in the dormitories became optional, and in 1860, the dormitories were abandoned. Children attended school for eight grades and were taught bilingually in both English and German.

Sunday was observed with three religious meetings; no services were held on weekdays. Men sat on one side of the church and women on the other. At meetings, Bimeler spoke extemporaneously on a variety of religious topics. The congregation also sang hymns. Marriages were performed very simply by a justice of the peace. Funerals consisted of a procession to the graveyard, where the body was buried in an unmarked grave. There was no baptism, confirmation, Communion, or ordained clergy.

Joseph Bimeler died on August 27, 1853. Consistent with the Zoarite absence of religious rituals, there was no funeral service, and his grave was unmarked. After Bimeler's death, Jacob Sylvan was appointed leader. After Sylvan's death in 1862, he was succeeded by Christian Weebel, who was replaced by Jacob Ackermann in 1871.

Bimeler was an able preacher, and his addresses, which the Zoarites called meeting speeches rather than sermons, held his listeners in awe. Although Bimeler did not write or publish his meeting speeches, a Separatist member named Neef had taken notes for his father, who was deaf. After Bimeler's death, the notes were transcribed and published and read during Sunday services for the next forty years. No other Separatist leader possessed Bimeler's power of speech.

An outstanding feature of Zoar was its 2.5-acre garden that was designed to symbolize a New Jerusalem as described in the Book of Revelation. A Norway spruce planted in the center represented everlasting life, and an arbor vitae hedge circling it represented heaven. Another circle of twelve juniper trees connoted the twelve apostles. Twelve narrow pathways, which led from the center, exemplified the paths to heaven. Flowerbeds included zinnias, roses, lilies, pansies, dahlias, and morning glories. There were pomegranate and lemon trees and salvia, as well as strawberries, blackberries, and herbs. A gardener's house and a greenhouse were on the edge of the garden.

At Zoar, as at Amana, Ephrata, and Economy, Pietism based on the ideas of mystic Jakob Boehme was fundamental to the German communal settlements. Boehme said that nature's laws "are God's commandments; he who lives according to them needs no other commandments, for he fulfills God's will."[11] Boehme's writing may have inspired the planting of the "elaborate symbolic gardens" by the Harmonists and the Zoarites.

In 1876, the community at Zoar consisted of 250 members and 170 hired workers and their families. Its assets were estimated to be worth one million dollars.[12] By 1898, membership had declined. The first generation of Zoarites had died. For their children, who lacked their religious zeal, the religious commitment was no longer dynamic. No charismatic leader had ever replaced Bimeler. The communal impulse had dissipated. In spite of the Separatist commitment to pacifism, fourteen young men from Zoar had enlisted during the Civil War. Outside laborers were needed for both farm and factory work, which increased expenses and introduced noncommunal values. Industries, failing to keep pace with the nineteenth century's technological innovations, no longer were profitable. Poor investments resulted in heavy financial losses.

The Zoar Hotel was a disruptive factor in the community. Although hotel business was vigorously pursued because it earned income, the hotel's guests brought with them different beliefs to Zoar. Hotel employees received cash tips, which they pocketed against society regulations. Many Zoar families, individually, sold produce and craft items for cash to the increasing number of tourists.

One frequent hotel visitor, Alexander Gunn, a retired businessman from Cleveland, liked Zoar so much that he purchased a log cabin there. He was not a member of the society nor even a German, a prerequisite for membership. Moreover, he used the cabin to entertain the society's leaders, alienating the envious membership from their leaders.

In January 1898, a meeting was held to discuss dissolution of the society, which then had 222 members, including 11 members in the first or probationary class as well as 86 children. An appraisal of the society's assets indicated holdings of 7,300 acres of land valued at $340,820 and personal property valued at $16,250. The church, school, town hall and cemetery were not assessed, as they would revert to the town. A division of property occurred in September 1898. Second class members received about 50 acres of land, a home, and $200, while the eleven first-class members received half shares. Those involved in the society's industries received a share of those businesses.

Tour

Begin your visit to Zoar at the 1833 **Store,** which also serves as a **Reception Center**. The store was the center for the community's commercial dealings with the outside world. It stocked items made in the community and other necessary goods. Society members could take what they needed from the store free. Today, the store has been restored to its original appearance. Visitors may purchase reproduction pottery, baskets, tinware and other craft items.

After watching the orientation video, begin your guided tour with a costumed interpreter. Behind the store is the restored **Community Dairy**. Zoarites came to the dairy daily to get milk. Zoarites were noted for their cheese making skill.

The **Number One House**, built in 1835, was the home of Joseph Bimeler and the administrative center of the community. It was originally intended to be a home for the community's aged but was never really used for that purpose. A two-and-a-half-story red brick Georgian colonial mansion, the house contained three separate living quarters for the Bimeler family and two of the trustees and their families.

Some of the furnishings are Zoarite pieces, which are simple and Germanic; some are more elegant Empire-style pieces. Bimeler conducted business from his office in the Number One House, and his desk, which was designed specifically for him, is displayed.

A deep cellar, where the temperature is an even fifty degrees Fahrenheit, was used for storing fruits and vegetables.

A **Greenhouse** and a large **garden** are special features of the community. The formal garden, which occupies an entire block, contains beautiful annuals, perennials, shrubs, and herbs, reflecting the Separatists' love of flowers. The gardens of Zoar became well known and spawned a thriving business in the sale of plants and bulbs.

The greenhouse, with its attached **Gardener's Residence**, dates from 1835. The Zoarites raised oranges and lemons, regarded as exotic fruits for Ohio. The greenhouse was heated by a system of pipes under the floor that brought in warm air from an outside charcoal furnace. Seedlings for the garden were raised in the greenhouse, and people from Cleveland sent their best plants to Zoar for the winter.

The simple gardener's residence has been restored and is decorated with Zoar furniture. There is a parlor downstairs and a bedroom upstairs; the kitchen was outside.

The **Bakery**, built in 1835, provided daily bread for the residents of Zoar. Bread was baked in two brick ovens that could hold fifteen loaves each. The baker lived upstairs in the two- story stone and clapboard building.

Several craft shops, which required some reconstruction, are open and operative at Zoar. The **Tin Shop**, which was built in 1825, was torn down in the 1940s. Now rebuilt on its original foundation, the small two-room structure is of brick and timber. The building is a good example of the Zoar method of construction called *nogging*; soft bricks or sandstone were placed between framing timbers. The inside of the building was then covered with plaster, and the outside was covered with clapboards, brick, or stucco.

The tinsmith produced household products such as basins, cups, buckets, sconces, and milk pails. Similar items are produced in the restored shop; traditional tools and methods are used.

Buggies and farm wagons were built in the restored **wagon shop**, which dates from 1840. The nearby **blacksmith shop** produced any metal tools or parts required by the society. The charcoal- fired forge, with its huge bellows, is going again, demonstrating traditional methods.

The **Bimeler Museum** was the residence of Joseph's great-grandson, William. It is furnished as it would have looked in the 1890s, at the end of the communal experience.

The **Magazine/Dining Room/Kitchen** complex behind Number One House is currently undergoing restoration.

Many other Zoarite buildings that are privately owned and used as residences or businesses can be seen on a leisurely stroll around the town.

The **Zoar Hotel**, built in the 1830s as a popular resort hotel, was visited by distinguished Ohioans, including President William McKinley. The hotel is now closed.

Special events at Zoar include the Quilt and Needlework Show, which alternates with a Toy Show, and the Strawberry Social in June, the Candlelight Dinner Tour in July, the Harvest Festival, Wine tasting, and Volkswalk in August, the Apfelfest in October, and Christmas in Zoar in December.

The sundial clock is on the side of Dormitory Number Two.
Photograph by Patricia A. Gutek.

Robert Owen Owenites

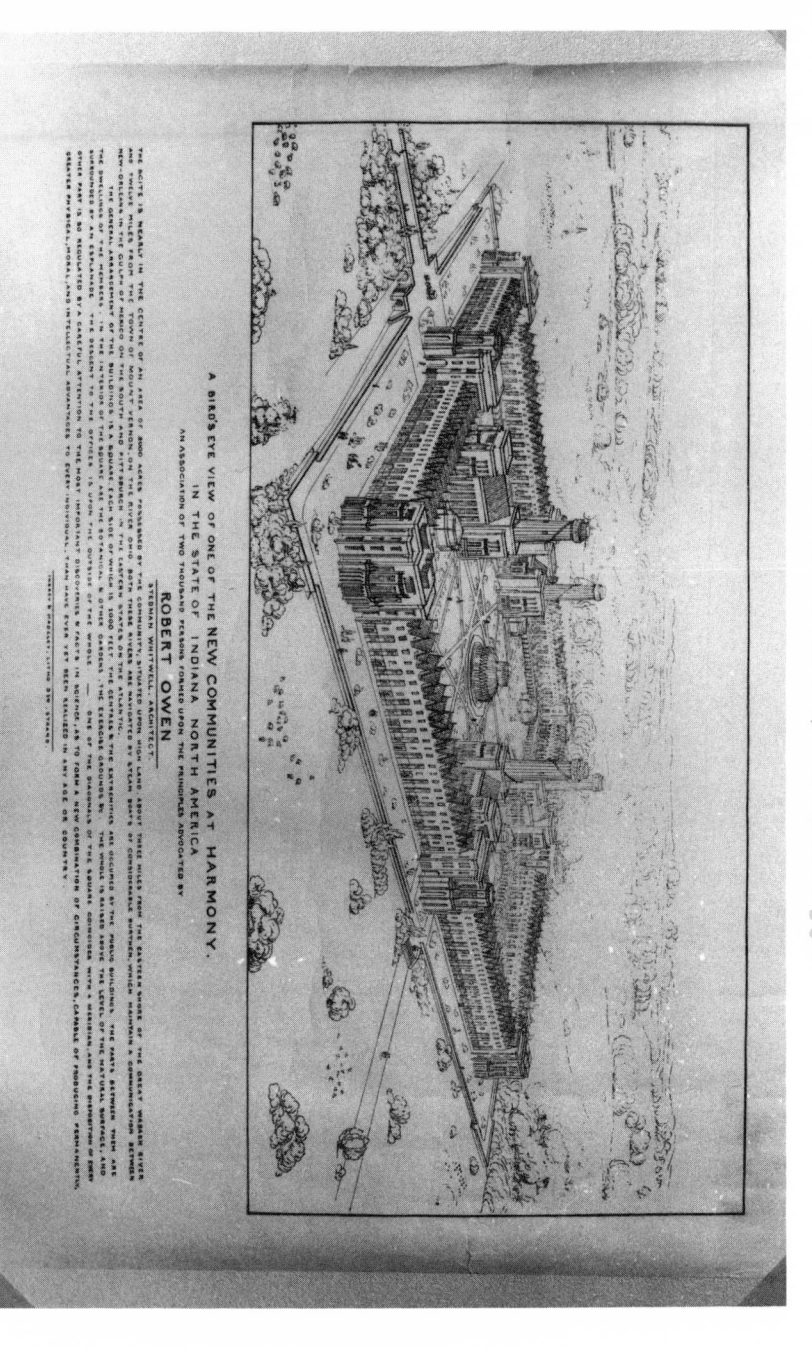

Robert Owen's conception of a utopian community. Photograph courtesy of the Library of Congress.

HISTORIC NEW HARMONY
An 1814–1860 Harmonist Religious Community
and an 1825–1830 Owenite Utopian Community
STATE HISTORIC SITE, NR, NHL

ADDRESS: P.O. Box 579, New Harmony, IN 47631

TELEPHONE: (812) 682-4482, (812) 682-4488

LOCATION: In the southwest corner of Indiana, near the Illinois and Kentucky borders, on the Wabash River, at the intersection of IN 66 and IN 68.

OPEN: Daily, 9:00 a.m.–5:00 p.m., April–October and weekends in March, November, and December; Atheneum open, but no tours given in January and February and on weekdays in March, November, and December.

ADMISSION: Introduction Tour: $3.00. Story Tour: adults, $8.00; seniors, $7.00; children, $4.50. Short Story Tour: adults, $6.00; children, $4.50. Arts and Sciences Tour: adults, $6.00; children, $4.50.

RESTAURANTS: Red Geranium; Bayou Grill; Country Cottage Restaurant & Confectionery; Main Café; Yellow Tavern.

SHOPS: Museum Shop in the Atheneum; Red Geranium Bookstore Antique Showrooms; Golden Raintree Books; Harmony Pottery; Weathervane Shop; Harmonie Haus; mudpies; earthcare at the depot Harmonie Weaving Institute.

FACILITIES: Atheneum, a visitors' center with orientation film; guided tours; partially wheelchair accessible; New Harmony Inn.

OVERVIEW

New Harmony is distinctive as the location of two communitarian groups: the Harmonists and the Owenites. It illustrates both the religious communitarianism of the Harmonists and the secular communitarianism of the Owenites.

New Harmony was the location of a utopian, communitarian experiment inaugurated by Robert Owen (1771–1858), a British utopian socialist, industrialist, social planner, and educational innovator. By creating perfectly planned and organized communities of equality, Owen believed he could shape the character and behavior of their residents.

Before coming to Indiana, Owen had developed the mill town of New Lanark in Scotland into a model community. Owen's utopian experiment at New Harmony linked two continents, Europe and North America, two countries, the United Kingdom and the United States, and two cities, New Lanark in Scotland and New Harmony in Indiana.

Owen predicted that his utopian experiment at New Harmony would end material scarcity, poverty, unemployment, and crime. Using the metaphor, "the machine in the garden," Owen envisioned New Harmony as a model city of mutual cooperation in which the inhabitants' work would be balanced between agriculture and industry.

Owen purchased the village of New Harmony from George Rapp's Harmonist Society in 1825 and then began his American utopian experiment.

Portrait of Robert Owen (1771–1858), the British industrialist and utopian socialist and founder of New Harmony. Photograph courtesy of the Library of Congress.

Today, a visit to New Harmony captures the life and times of two distinctive communal groups—the religious Harmonists and the secular Owenites. Buildings, artifacts, and exhibits of both groups can be viewed at this carefully restored and maintained site.

HISTORY

Robert Owen was born May 14, 1771 in Newtown, a small town in North Wales, in the United Kingdom. In his autobiography, Owen, who identified his father as an ironmonger and saddler, claimed he inherited his parents' habits of hard work, industriousness, and thrift.[1] Owen's own self-appraisal shows a strong sense of self-esteem that his critics often saw as an overbearing egotism. Owen was a man who delighted in hearing his own voice and reading his own words. Owen's childhood reminiscence reveals a confident self-made and mostly self-educated man. He was, he asserts, Newtown's fastest runner, most skilled dancer, most popular boy, and most gifted scholar. Because of his academic accomplishments, Owen claimed the village schoolmaster relied on him to teach other pupils in the school. Owen's self-generated enthusiasm for his own ideas, words, and plans often caused him to operate in a reality of his own making. Perpetually optimistic, Owen had difficulty distinguishing between successes and failures.

At age ten, young Robert Owen left Newtown to win fame and fortune. His journey to utopia would take him on a seventy-seven-year quest, and he would not return to the town of his birth until the eve of his death in 1858.

Owen found employment as an apprentice in a draper's shop of James McGuffug at Stamford. Later, he worked in Manchester, a rapidly growing British industrial city.[2] In 1789, the ambitious Owen, now eighteen, had saved enough money to invest in a firm that manufactured cotton-spinning machinery. His next business venture, in 1792, saw him managing a mechanized cotton mill. Commenting on his success in business, Owen noted that he had improved the technique of cotton manufacturing, knew how to supervise employees, and was involved socially with Manchester's leading entrepreneurs and intellectuals.[3]

In 1799, Owen and several associates formed the Chorlton Twist Company, which then purchased David Dale's New Lanark cotton mills. Cotton manufacturing was a leading British industry, and Dale's mills, situated in the Clyde Valley, near the falls of the River Clyde, at New Lanark, Scotland, were among the most prosperous. While negotiating for the properties, Owen met Dale's daughter, Anne Caroline, fell in love, and married her. Owen had not only entered a profitable business arrangement but had also married into one of nineteenth-century Britain's leading industrial families.

New Lanark, located halfway between Scotland's large cities of Glasgow and Edinburgh, was the locale of Owen's social and educational experimentation from 1799 to 1824. A factory town, New Lanark consisted of mill buildings where cotton cloth was manufactured by water power-driven machinery, several large apartment or row houses for the workers, a company store, and the owner's mansion. Assuming control of the mills in 1799, Owen found he was responsible for managing more than a thousand workers, including men, women, and children. Surveying New Lanark's living and working conditions, Owen was depressed by what he found—a town ridden with delinquency, vice, drunkenness, theft, and vermin. His direct encounter with these conditions moved the self-made, young businessman down the path to utopianism, communitarianism, and a life dedicated to social reform.

Owen based his reform program on what he claimed was his great philosophical discovery that "Man's character is made for and not by him."[4] Rejecting the traditional belief that poverty and vice were caused by human sinfulness, Owen argued that human behavior was shaped by the social environment in which people lived. Better housing, food, clothing, and education would improve the social environment and reform human character. Still committed to private property, Owen believed he could make a profit without exploiting his workers.

Owen initiated reforms at New Lanark. He improved working conditions and reduced the hours of labor. Children under age ten were not permitted to work in the mills. He introduced a system whereby every employee's efficiency was rated daily. He then set about improving living conditions. The streets were swept and trash removed. Workers' apartments were inspected for cleanliness. The company store was stocked with fairly priced items.

Owen stressed education. He established an infant school for the early education of children from ages two to six and a general school for those from six to twelve. Owen also founded an Institute for the Formation of Character, which featured adult education, after work lectures, and concerts.

The story of Owen's reforms at New Lanark traveled throughout Europe and the Americas, and a steady stream of visitors came to New Lanark to see the famous reformer's achievements. Owen spent more time guiding visiting notables around New Lanark than on managing the mills. He began to write tracts describing his reforms and was a frequent speaker to groups throughout England.

Thoroughly enjoying his reputation as a philanthropic social reformer, Owen decided that his plans for reform should be diffused throughout the British Isles, Europe, the Americas, and even perhaps the world. Owen, now a full-fledged communitarian socialist, called for the creation of self-supporting "villages of unity and mutual cooperation," for all classes and all persons. In these villages, where all property would be owned communally, residential accommodations would be arranged in a parallelogram of connected buildings, which would also house schools, apartments, factories, libraries, kitchens, hospitals, dining rooms, and lecture halls. His concept of the "village of unity" developed into a comprehensive communitarian ideology that he tried to implement at New Harmony, Indiana, from 1825 to 1828. The Scottish factory town of New Lanark and the American frontier village in Indiana were linked by the transatlantic bonds of Owen's communitarian ideology.

Attracted to the United States as an open society, Owen saw America's frontier as the ideal locale for his utopia. The United States, the "new world," free of Europe's class conscious prejudices and irrational traditions, would be the place for Owen's "new moral world." From 1824 to 1828, he sought to establish his new communitarian society in the southern Indiana village of New Harmony, which he purchased from the Harmonists, a sect of German religious Pietists who, too, lived a communitarian lifestyle.

The Harmonists, led by George Rapp, had migrated in 1814 from Harmonie Pennsylvania, to southwestern Indiana to establish a religious communitarian settlement. The Harmonist community of New Harmony, located near the confluence of the Wabash and Ohio Rivers, was a large holding of 30,000 acres. Motivated by religious zeal and instilled with a Germanic sense of industry, the Harmonists created a prosperous settlement at New Harmony, which included textile and grist mills, wineries, a granary, brewery, and distillery. They constructed large buildings, some of which were used as dormitories. Despite their prosperity, George Rapp, the authoritarian leader of the Harmonists, determined that they should return to Pennsylvania. In 1825, after selling New Harmony to Owen, they returned to Pennsylvania to create still another prosperous communitarian settlement, Economy. (For the Harmonists at Harmonie, New Harmony, and Economy, see the section on Old Economy Village).

When Owen came to the United States, he possessed a ready-made village oriented to a communitarian lifestyle. However, unlike the Harmonists, Owen was a thoroughgoing secular communitarian who regarded the established churches as obstacles to reform.

Before going west to Indiana, Owen, who was a famous personage, spoke to joint sessions of the U.S. Congress, which were attended by the Supreme Court and the president. Everywhere he went Owen enthusiastically extended an open invitation to all interested parties to join him forthwith at New Harmony. One thousand people came.

It was an odd and uneven assortment of humanity that came to the Indiana frontier town. Some were inspired by Owen's vision of a new society in a new land. Others had continually failed and were looking for one last chance to begin anew. Still others were opportunists who saw Owen as a naive dogooder whom they could divest of funds.

117

Robert Owen's Owenites

Significant historically, Owen's utopia on the Wabash attracted some of America's leading scientists and educators, the most famous of whom was William Maclure (1763–1840). A self-made man of wealth like Owen, Maclure had left his native Scotland to become an American citizen. A man of repute, Maclure had produced a geological map of the United States and had been president of such learned American societies as the Academy of Natural Sciences, the American Geological Society, and the American Philosophical Society.

While traveling in Europe, Maclure had visited Johann Heinrich Pestalozzi's educational institute at Yverdon in Switzerland and decided to introduce Pestalozzi's educational method to the United States. Committed to developing science and education in the United States, Maclure funded his own geological expeditions, supported scientific research, and subsidized Pestalozzian schools.[5]

Maclure was initially reluctant to join forces with the enthusiastic but visionary Owen at New Harmony. Persuaded by Madame Marie Duclos Fretageot, a Pestalozzian teacher who was his longtime associate, Maclure put aside his doubts and decided to join Owen in what proved to be an ill-defined and eventually contentious partnership.

Maclure had several motives for relocating his scientific and educational associates from Philadelphia to New Harmony. A convinced egalitarian, he believed the diffusion of useful knowledge would break what he claimed was the upper-class monopoly over education. Using New Harmony as a scientific and educational outpost, he hoped to diffuse practical knowledge throughout the country. At New Harmony, his team of scientists would conduct basic research on the frontier region's minerals, plants, and animals.

Maclure firmly believed that scientific education, taught by the Pestalozzian method, would move the United States to a more productive and egalitarian economy. At a time when science was absent from the school curriculum, Maclure wanted it included in the education of the working agricultural and industrial classes. This practical knowledge, contrasted with what he regarded as "useless" classical Latin and Greek studies, would be taught in New Harmony's Pestalozzian schools by his educational associates, Joseph Neef, Marie Duclos Fretageot, and Phiquepal d'Arusmont. Pestalozzian education was unique at the time in that it emphasized teaching by using actual physical objects and field trips rather than rote memorization.

Maclure sponsored three schools at New Harmony: the infant school for children until age four conducted by Marie Duclos Fretageot; the higher school for children ages five through twelve conducted by Joseph Neef; and the vocational school for older pupils and adults conducted by Phiquepal d'Arusmont. Along with Owen and Maclure, Marie Duclos Fretageot was a principal character in New Harmony's history. Maclure had supported Fretageot in establishing a Pestalozzian girls' school in Philadelphia and later entrusted management of his enterprises at New Harmony to her during his frequent long absences from the community.

Maclure brought with him to New Harmony several of his associates in the

Historic New Harmony

American Academy of Science in Philadelphia, including Thomas Say, Charles-Alexandre Lesueur, Gerard Troost, (1776–1850) and Constantine Rafinesque. The group of scientific and educational notables came with Maclure to New Harmony on a flatboat, the *Philanthropist*, which was dubbed the "boatload of knowledge."

Thomas Say (1787–1834) a naturalist, conducted meticulous research on insects, mollusks, crustaceans, and reptiles. In 1817–18, he had accompanied Maclure to explore the Sea Islands off the coasts of Georgia and Florida.[6] Say, the official zoologist on Major Long's 1819 expedition to the Rocky Mountains, had traveled extensively in North America. His book on insects, *American Entomology*, was a pioneering work in American natural science. The New Harmony School Press published Say's seven-volume *American Conchology* from 1830 to 1837.

The press, supported by Maclure and supervised by Madame Fretageot, published scientific books long after Owen's communitarian experiment had ended. The press was noted for its meticulously executed engravings and carefully edited printed texts.

Charles-Alexandre Lesueur (1778–1846) was known for his zoological studies, especially his study of the fish of the Great Lakes.[7] Lesueur accompanied Maclure on his geological explorations of New York's Finger Lakes region and the Connecticut Valley. In addition to his research in natural science, he was skilled in art, drawing, engraving, and printing. Because of his skills, he taught at the community school and engraved plates for several works published by the school press.

Constantine Samuel Rafinesque (1783–1840), a European botanist who was a professor at Transylvania University in Kentucky, was an expert on American plants and trees. He developed a theory of evolution that anticipated Darwin's.

Gerard Troost, first president of the Academy of Natural Sciences was trained in crystallography, mineralogy, and geology. After leaving New Harmony in 1827, Troost established the Natural History Museum in Nashville, Tennessee.

For Maclure, Owen's communitarian experiment at New Harmony gave him an opportunity to implement his scientific and educational theories. Maclure's efforts at New Harmony in the Education Society and the School of Industry brought about a merger of scientists, teachers, scientific laboratories, library collections, and a press in what anticipated a twentieth-century "think tank."

A key provision in the New Harmony plan was ending private ownership of property, which Owen had identified as the primary cause of human misery and social ills. At New Harmony, common property supported by common education, as the "great equalizers," would end class conflict. On May 1, 1825, the "Preliminary Society of New Harmony" was organized "to improve the character and conditions of its own members, and to prepare them to become associates in independent communities, having common property."[8] Ten months later, on February 5, 1826, an overly optimistic Owen proclaimed New Harmony as a "Community of Equality." New Harmony's constitution committed its members to "equality of rights" and "equality of duties" within a society of "cooperative union" and a "community of property." Based on Owen's principle of character formation, the constitution proclaimed that "man's character, mental, moral, and physical, is the result of his formation, his location, and . . . the circumstances within which he exists."[9]

The constitution heralded that "all members of the community" were "one family" with "similar food, clothing, and education," and they would "live in similar houses" and "be accommodated alike." Restating the importance of education, the document pronounced, "It shall always remain a primary object of the community to give the best physical, moral, and intellectual education to all its members."[10]

Unfortunately for Owen, his ambitious plan for creating a new social order that was to begin at New Harmony did not succeed. Displaying a chronic tendency to disharmony, New Harmony's communitarians endlessly debated constitutional revisions, quarreled over the division of property, which Owen continually postponed, and disputed over social and educational theories and practices.

With the community in the throes of disintegration, Owen and his chief associate, William Maclure, quarreled. After litigation, they divided what was left of the community. In 1828, Owen left New Harmony to return to England, remaining confident that his prophesied new world had been merely postponed. Convinced of the inevitability of the new world order, Owen continued to work for cooperatives, women's rights, improvement of working conditions, and universal education until his death in 1858.

Maclure, who left New Harmony to locate in Mexico, entrusted management of his property and the school press to Thomas Say and Marie Duclos Fretageot. It was Madame Fretageot's efforts that continued to implement Maclure's plans for a scientific and educational press and school of industry at New Harmony during the important, but often neglected, period from 1828 through 1831. That period, while less dramatic than the Owenite experiment, was highly significant for the history of natural science and education in America.

A remote and enigmatic character, Maclure preferred to remain a comfortable distance from his New Harmony enterprises. While consistently committed to diffusing useful knowledge, he preferred that Fretageot act as on-site administrator of New Harmony's school press and the School of Industry. Receiving detailed instructions from Maclure in Mexico, Fretageot faced the challenge of managing affairs at New Harmony and fending off intrigues by Maclure's relatives.

After some efforts to establish Pestalozzian schools in Ohio, Joseph Neef returned to New Harmony.

Owen's sons—Robert Dale, David Dale, and Richard—remained in Indiana and played a significant role in the state's history. Robert Dale Owen (1801–77) was active in Indiana politics. He served in the Indiana House of Representatives from 1836 to 1839, the U.S. Congress from 1844 to 1847, and again in the Indiana House of Representatives from 1851 to 1852. While in Congress, he drafted the bill establishing the Smithsonian Institution and actively opposed the extension of slavery. He was a supporter of public education and women's rights.

Though educated as a physician, David Dale Owen (1807–60), Robert Owen's third son, followed Maclure's interest in geology and conducted geological surveys, using his laboratory at New Harmony as a base. At various times in his life, he was the state geologist of Indiana, Kentucky, and Arkansas. He married Caroline Neef, daughter of Joseph Neef, the Pestalozzian educator.

Richard Owen (1810–1890), interested in education like his father, was a professor of geology at the University at Nashville, Tennessee, and a professor of natural science at Indiana University. In 1872, he became the first president of Purdue University, serving for two years.

Tour

Today, New Harmony, with a population less than a thousand, is both a living rural Indiana small town as well as a historic site. The historic locations are interspersed among private homes and businesses. Begin your tour at the **Atheneum**, which houses the **Visitors' Center**, where guided tours originate.

The Atheneum, a gleaming white modern structure designed by architect Richard Meier, was completed in 1979. It contains exhibit areas, conference facilities, a display of publications, a scale model of the 1824 town, and an orientation film.

New Harmony was the location of two communitarian groups: George Rapp's Harmonists and the Owenites. While a few buildings are unique to each community, the Owenites occupied many of the Harmonist buildings. The Harmonist period is portrayed in the 1822 **David Lenz House,** a frame home, which illustrates the sturdy Germanic-influenced architecture of the Harmonists. It has been restored and furnished with Harmonist artifacts by the National Society of Colonial Dames of America.

Harmonist building frames, with self-supporting rafters, were fastened with mortise and tenon joints and locked in place with wooden pegs. The energy-conscious and frugal Harmonists insulated their homes with *Dutch biscuits*, a wooden board wrapped with mud and straw. Note the centrally located chimney, which was used for both cooking and heating, and the small window-panes, which resisted wind while providing a source of light. Of interest is the Christian door, a symbol of the Harmonists' religious faith; the upper panels form the cross, and the lower ones represent an open Bible. Among the furnishings are Harmonist-style chairs; a pie safe typical of southern Indiana; a small Shaker table; and a Harmonist-style bed and chest.

The **West Street Log Cabins** are replicas of early Harmonist buildings built between 1814 and 1819. In the **Potter's Shop** is a broom-making machine. The **Eigner Cabin** is furnished as an early Harmonist home.

Robert Fauntleroy House, a Harmonist frame home, represents a building that was constructed by the Harmonists in 1822 and then enlarged by Robert Fauntleroy, the husband of Robert Owen's daughter, Jane, in 1840. Their daughter, Constance Fauntleroy, organized the Minerva Society, a women's literary association, in 1859. The house's appointments are Victorian in style.

The **Workingmen's Institute and Library**, built in 1894, has archives and collections on both the Harmonists and Owenites that attract scholars and authors from around the world. In its archives are extensive collections on William

Maclure and his scientific and educational associates. The building also houses the **New Harmony Public Library**, a small **art gallery**, and a local **history museum**.

The **Institute** established in 1838 by William Maclure, was designed as an educational center for the diffusion of useful knowledge to working men and women. From 1826 to 1860, the institute's **school press** published pioneering scientific books by several of Maclure's scientific associates, such as Thomas Say and Charles-Alexandre Lesueur. Be sure to see the portraits of William Maclure and Joseph Neef, a Pestalozzian pioneer educator and author.

Murphy Auditorium, built in 1913, was extensively restored and renovated in 1975. Funds for its original construction were provided by Dr. Edward Murphy (1813–1900), a New Harmony physician. Today, it is used for lectures, concerts, and other educational and artistic performances and professional summer theater.

Lichtenberger Store, built in 1901, now houses the Maximilian-Bodmer collection of hand-colored lithographs called *Travels in the Interior of North America, 1832–1834*. These drawings and sketches were made by the Swiss artist Karl Bodmer (1809–93), who accompanied the German nobleman Prince Alexander Philip Maximilian on an expedition through the American frontier wilderness. Especially noteworthy are Bodmer's drawings of Indians, animals, and frontier scenes.

George Keppler House, a Harmonist residence built in 1822, contains exhibits on New Harmony as a geological research center. William Maclure brought his dedication to geological research to New Harmony. Among the displays are exhibits on the geological surveys of Robert Owen's third son, David Dale Owen, who conducted geological surveys in Iowa, Wisconsin, Nebraska, Kentucky, Indiana, and Arkansas.

In the 1830 **Owen House** is a decorative arts display of the 1830s and 1840s, which includes Chippendale, Sheraton, and Empire furniture. The Jaquess parlor and entry are stenciled, and there are folk art works by Jacob Maentel.

The 1829 **John Beal House** is a one-story frame building of waddle and daub construction. Exhibits here focus on Owenite educational and scientific figures, including William Maclure, Gerard Troost, Joseph Neef, Thomas Say, Charles-Alexandre Lesueur, and Marie Fretageot.

The 1822 **Scholle House**, a brick residence, was the home of Harmonist shoemaker Mattias Scholle. It houses changing exhibits of regional art and history.

The Victorian period **Doctor's Office** displays a collection of medical equipment and tools donated by the Mead Johnson Foundation. There is also an **apothecary shop**.

Thrall's Opera House, restored in 1969 by the state of Indiana, is used for theatrical performances, conferences, and lectures. Originally a Harmonist dormitory built in 1824, it was converted into an opera house in 1856.

Solomon Wolf House, a Harmonist brick residence built in 1823, now houses an electronic scale model of New Harmony in 1824, the year of the Harmonist departure and the Owenite arrival. The model's sound and light show provides an excellent overview of New Harmony's rich and intriguing history.

Dormitory Number 2, one of New Harmony's earliest restorations, is a fine example of Harmonist architecture. Built in 1822, it was put to significant use by both Harmonists and Owenites. The Harmonists used it as a dormitory for single persons. In the Owenite period, it was the location of Joseph Neef's Pestalozzian School. Neef, once a noncommissioned officer in Napoleon's army in Italy, was trained by Pestalozzi, the Swiss educational reformer, at Burgdorf in Switzerland. Neef came to the United States under Maclure's patronage to introduce the Pestalozzian educational method, which was based on object lessons. Dormitory Number 2 contains exhibits on education and printing.

Roofless Church, built in 1959 and maintained by the Robert Lee Blaffer Trust, commemorates New Harmony's spiritual meaning. Although a contemporary structure, the Roofless Church, which was designed by architect Philip Cortelyou Johnson, incorporates many symbols of New Harmony's religious past, especially from the Harmonist period. The concept of rooflessness unites earth and sky; the rectangular brick wall (130 feet wide by 230 feet long) recalls the egalitarian spirit of the Harmonist cemetery. Within the 50-foot dome tabernacle is the sculpture *Descent of the Holy Spirit* by Jacques Lipschitz.

The Roofless Church and the nearby **Tillich Park,** which is a memorial to and the burial place of the theologian Paul Johannes Tillich, were projects of Jane Blaffer Owen, the wife of an Owen descendent. Dr. Tillich spoke at the dedication of the park on June 2, 1963, on the subject of "Estranged and Reunited: the New Being."

The **New Harmony Inn**, which offers lodging, and the **Red Geranium Restaurant**, both built in a compatible style to the historic buildings, are part of the New Harmony revival as a historical and cultural center.

The graves in the **Harmonist cemetery** are unmarked, exemplifying the Harmonist principle of equality. Members of Rapp's society would remain equal in death as they had been in life. The wall surrounding the cemetery was built with bricks from the Harmonist Church, which was taken down in the 1870s.

The hedge **labyrinth**, a fascinating maze located eight blocks south of the town, is a recreation of the one designed by the Harmonists. **Maple Hill Cemetery**, half a mile south of New Harmony, contains the burial sites and monuments of many New Harmony notables, including David Dale Owen and Joseph Neef.

Lining New Harmony's streets are golden rain trees (*Koelreuteria paniculata*), supposedly introduced to the area by the naturalist Thomas Say. The trees bear bright yellow flowers in June that become long seedpods by fall.

Several buildings of historical significance are privately owned and not open to the public. However, visitors will want to take note of them.

Rapp-Maclure-Owen Mansion, the town's dominating 1844 structure, located prominently on the corner of Church and Main streets, was restyled and rebuilt by Alexander Maclure, the brother of William Maclure. The white one-story Greek Revival residence was built on the foundation of the residence of New Harmony's founder, George Rapp. From 1850 to 1860, it was David Dale Owen's residence. On the grounds is the tomb of Thomas Say, called the founding father of American zoology, who died in New Harmony in 1834, and **Gabriel's**

rock, a limestone rock with indentations resembling footprints. The unusual rock was discovered along the Mississippi River and purchased by Frederick Rapp. According to legend, Father Rapp said the limestone slab contained an angel's footprints, but there is no evidence that Rapp ever made that claim.

The vine-covered **granary**, a large stone and brick building, was erected in 1819 by the Harmonists to store grain and supplies. In 1843, David Dale Owen housed his third geological laboratory there.

The **Owen Geological Laboratory** is an imposing stone building with a turret. It was designed and built by David Dale Owen in 1859.

Joseph Neef House, a Harmonist frame and brick family dwelling built in 1822, became the home of Joseph Neef.

John Humphrey Noyes's Perfectionists

Getting ready to wash floors is a young Perfectionist woman with short hair and an Oneida female bloomer dress. Photograph courtesy of Oneida Community Records, Syracuse University Library, Department of Special Collections.

ONEIDA COMMUNITY
1841–1880, Oneida, New York

ADDRESS: 170 Kenwood Avenue, Oneida, NY 13421
TELEPHONE: (315) 363-0745
LOCATION: In New York, halfway between Syracuse and Utica; Exit 33 off New York
   State Thruway I-90; 1.2 miles south of NY 5 at Sherrill (the Mansion House is
   actually in Sherrill, not Oneida).
OPEN: Wednesday–Saturday, tours at 10:00 a.m. and 2:00 p.m.; Sunday, tour at 2:00
   p.m.
ADMISSION: $3.
RESTAURANTS: Dining room, by reservation.
SHOPS: Museum Bookstore.
FACILITIES: Guest rooms.

OVERVIEW

Oneida, Ltd., an eminent American silverware company, has its roots in a
nineteenth-century religious commune whose leader held unconventional social views on marriage and sexuality.

John Humphrey Noyes (1811–86), from Vermont, was the charismatic
religious and social leader of several hundred New Englanders who formed a
communal family that extended from the 1840s to late 1880. Because of its
longevity, the Oneida Perfectionists are considered successful compared to other
communal groups.

Like other leaders of utopian religious groups, Noyes clearly deviated from
the accepted theological teachings of the established churches, thus necessi-
tating establishment of a separate denomination. Noyes was an evangelical
Protestant who, after a conversion experience at age twenty, studied for the
ministry at Andover Theological Seminary and Yale Divinity School and earned
a license to preach. That license was revoked two years later when Noyes refused to recant his position on perfectionism. Noyes declared that man alone,
without divine intervention, was capable of perfection if he had a right attitude and an inner sense of salvation from sin. This doctrine opposed the orthodox Christian position that man's nature was sinful.

Noyes's religious beliefs were eventually overshadowed by his unorthodox
social views on communalism, marriage, sexual relations, and procreation, all
of which were implemented in the Oneida Community. Oneidans adopted
what they referred to as Bible communism in which property was jointly owned.
Communalism at Oneida included not only sharing money and property, but
also spouses and children. Monogamous marriage was abandoned and replaced
with another arrangement called complex marriage in which each man was a
husband to all wives and each woman a wife to all husbands. Children belonged to the community rather than to their parents. The right to bear a child

was not an individual right but one bestowed by the community.

Complex marriage, one of the cornerstones upon which the Oneida Community rested, was the most unique aspect of this nineteenth-century experiment and generates the most interest. For thirty years of the nineteenth century, a group of 250 Americans practiced radically unconventional sexual arrangements.

Given the sexual practices of its members, restricting pregnancies was a concern. The Oneidans practiced a unique, but successful, form of birth control devised by the man who planned all aspects of life at Oneida—John Humphrey Noyes. The community also implemented a eugenics program called stirpiculture, which produced fifty-eight children from 1869 to 1879.

Noyes's first attempts to form a community were at Putney, Vermont, from 1837 to 1847. The Perfectionists, in 1848, moved to Oneida, New York, where they lived in a large home called the Mansion House until late 1880. After the community's breakup, precipitated in part by questions of succession to the aging Noyes, property was divided among the members. One of the communal businesses was Oneida Silverware, which continued to be operated successfully by many of the former communitarians. The Mansion House in which the entire Oneida family resided remains and many of its rooms may be seen on a tour.

HISTORY

John Humphrey Noyes was born in Brattleboro, Vermont, on September 11, 1811, the eldest son of the eight children of Polly Hayes and John Noyes. The Noyeses were an upper middle-class, intellectual, and politically prominent family. Rutherford B. Hayes, the nineteenth president of the United States, was a nephew of Polly Hayes Noyes. John Noyes was a successful storekeeper and a member of the U.S. House of Representatives.

John H. Noyes attended private schools in Putney, Vermont, where the family had moved, until age fifteen when he entered Dartmouth. Noyes was a good student and graduated Phi Beta Kappa in 1830, but his social life was handicapped by severe shyness. After Dartmouth, Noyes attempted a career in law for a year but decided to become a minister after a conversion experience during the Finney Revival. Initially, he studied at Andover, then at Yale. Upon completion of his divinity studies at Yale in 1833, Noyes received his license to preach.

While a student, Noyes had joined the New Haven Free Church, whose members questioned orthodox teachings and practices and emphasized emotional revival services. Soon, Noyes came to some religious conclusions of his own, which were more radical than any beliefs held by members of the New Haven Free Church.

Noyes believed in perfectionism, which was not a clearly defined set of beliefs but a loosely defined rejection of human sinfulness and the then-prevalent Calvinist doctrine of predestination which stated that humans are depraved, sinful, and incapable of attaining salvation without divine election.

John Humphrey Noyes's Perfectionists

Portrait of John Humphrey Noyes (1811–1886), founder of the Oneida Perfectionists. Photograph courtesy of Oneida Community Records, Syracuse University Library, Department of Special Collections.

Perfectionism stressed the doctrine of holiness—that a person, alone and without help, was capable of attaining a state of perfect love between himself and God.

The revivalists who preached this doctrine became known as Perfectionists. Considered radicals, they did not form a single, cohesive group or congregation. There is a history of perfectionism within Christianity. The leader of the communal religious group at Bishop Hill, Illinois, Erik Jansson, was a Perfectionist who encountered strong opposition in Sweden.

Noyes dedicated himself to spreading Perfectionist beliefs throughout New York and New England. His preaching, particularly in regard to his own perfection, was met with distrust and disapproval by religious authorities. His license to preach was revoked. Even the New Haven Free Church asked Noyes to leave.

Noyes developed a strong attachment to a young woman named Abigail Merwin, who became one of his first converts. Later, Abigail spurned Noyes as a suitor, married another man, and rejected his religious beliefs. In January 1837, Noyes wrote a letter to David Harrison stating his unorthodox views on marriage, including forsaking monogamy. Parts of this letter were published a few months later in the *Battle-Ax and Weapons of War*, a free-love and antiestablishment newspaper.

Noyes's social views eventually made him unique among Perfectionists. His rejection of monogamous marriage caused a furor. Despite widespread disapproval of his beliefs, Noyes began attracting a small core of followers. Originally, they consisted of his sisters and their husbands, his brother, and his mother.

Another disciple was Harriet A. Holton, whom he married in 1838. Harriet was three years older than Noyes, an only child who was orphaned young and was raised by her grandfather, Mark Richards. Richards was a member of an illustrious New England family. He had been lieutenant governor of Vermont and a member of Congress. Harriet, like Noyes, was a shy child, but became engaged at age eighteen to a young lawyer of whom her grandfather disapproved because of political differences. The couple did not marry.

When Harriet was twenty-three, she left the Unitarian Church and became committed to revivalism. A few years later, in 1834, a friend of Harriet's, Maria Clark, who was a follower of John Noyes, sent her some of his writings. After studying them, Harriet became a Perfectionist, a follower of Noyes, and a financial contributor to his cause. John Noyes and Harriet began corresponding.

By 1838, Noyes had accepted Abigail Merwin's rejection. He had also come to believe strongly in his divine commission to spread his Perfectionist beliefs. Noyes wrote Harriet a letter containing a marriage proposal in June 1838.[1] The letter, neither passionate nor romantic, informed Harriet of Noyes's unique definition of marriage. He explained to Harriet that their marriage was not to "limit the range" nor "to monopolize" their affections but to enlarge them "in the free fellowship of God's universal family."[2] Harriet happily accepted Noyes's proposal, and within three weeks, they were married in a ceremony conducted by Larkin G. Mead, Noyes's brother-in-law, in Chesterfield, New Hampshire. The couple settled in Putney, where Harriet provided money to build a house and to purchase a printing office with press and type.

Within three weeks of his marriage, Noyes resumed printing the *Witness*, a newspaper whose publication had been suspended because of canceled subscriptions following announcement of his views on marriage in the *Battle-Ax*. He felt that periodicals were the best way to disseminate his theological doctrines and obtain converts to perfectionism. The *Witness* was replaced by the *Perfectionist*, which later was replaced by the *Spiritual Magazine*.

With John Humphrey Noyes as its spiritual leader, the Putney group included his sisters, Harriet and Charlotte, for whom he would arrange marriages to his followers, John L. Skinner and John R. Miller, his brother George, his mother, and his wife. Male members served as an informal governing board to assist Noyes.

As more disciples joined the Putney group, steps to formalize the organization were taken. On February 22, 1841, a Society of Inquiry was officially established. At about the same time, Noyes's father divided his estate among his children, four of whom belonged to the Society of Inquiry, and their inheritances were its financial basis.

Noyes was now able to economically support a larger community. By 1843, approximately thirty-five men, women, and children lived in three houses owned by the Noyeses. These Perfectionists considered themselves an enlarged family who accepted and adopted the religious and social views of its autocratic leader.

The foundation of Noyes's religious theory was Christian perfectionism, a belief prevalent among revivalists but rejected by the established churches. Noyes maintained that God expected Christians to have a "right attitude and inner sense of assurance of salvation from sin." By perfection, Noyes did not mean that a person could not improve, but "so long as one's attitude and motivation were right, one's acts would follow a pattern acceptable to God."[3]

John Humphrey Noyes's Perfectionists

Based on his interpretation of a theory of an Andover instructor, Moses Stuart, who argued that Christ had predicted his Second Coming during the lifetime of his then-living followers, Noyes believed that Christ's Second Coming had already occurred. Noyes claimed that the Second Coming had taken place in A.D. 70 when the Temple of Jerusalem was destroyed. A primary resurrection and judgment had occurred in the spiritual world, establishing God's Kingdom in heaven. A second resurrection and judgment was imminent and would establish the Kingdom of God on earth. Once having attained salvation, the human being could not fall from grace, and should not allow his or her inner convictions to be overruled by church authority.[4]

Derived from his religious doctrines, Noyes's social theories were implemented in the Oneida Community. Complex marriage was his most controversial social principle. Noyes claimed that when the heavenly kingdom was established on earth, there would be no monogamous marriages. Sexual intercourse would not be restricted to exclusive arrangements but would be free to everyone. He compared the "marriage supper of the Lamb" to a "feast" in which "every dish is free to every guest."[5]

Noyes, who held strong opinions on sexual relations and reproduction, saw sexuality as having two aspects: the social and the propagative. The social aspect involved communication and expression of affection between a couple, while the propagative function was to produce children. He felt that the propagative aspect of sexual relations was less important than the social aspect. Noyes based his conclusion on a biblical passage from Genesis 2:18, which holds that God created woman because it was not good for man to be alone.

Noyes felt the procreative function of sexuality needed to be controlled. This view was partially based on his experiences as a husband. Harriet Noyes had given birth five times in her first six years of marriage and only one child had lived. Noyes wanted to spare his wife further suffering.

Noyes read a pamphlet entitled *Moral Physiology* written by Robert Dale Owen, son of the founder of the New Harmony utopian community, which concerned sexuality and outlined a method of birth control. Noyes did not accept Owen's method of birth control, *coitus interruptus*, or withdrawal before ejaculation. He felt that the "useless expenditure of seed certainly is not natural."[6] Noyes designed his own method of birth control, called male continence or *coitus reservatus*, in which the man exerted such control that he never ejaculated, even after withdrawal as in the *coitus interruptus* method. Noyes considered this method of controlling propagation natural, healthy, effective, and contributing to affection in lovemaking.

Complex marriage, then, the social system in which no one man was married to any one woman, but in which all men and all women were married to each other, and in which all had sexual access to each other without any exclusive relationships, relied on the practice of male continence. This method of birth control involved a great deal of male self-control and took much practice. Because accidents during the learning process could result in unintentional pregnancies, young men in the Oneida Community were initiated sexually and taught the method of male continence by older, postmenopausal women in the community. It was also the custom for Father Noyes or another older man to be the first lover of the female virgins of the community.

Noyes introduced complex marriage to the Putney community in 1846. Initially, Noyes proposed it to only one other couple, George and Mary Cragin. Noyes was very attracted to Mary, but solicited her husband's consent along with the consent of his wife, Harriet, before he would pursue a sexual relationship with Mary. After a good deal of initial resistance from Mr. Cragin, the two couples agreed to have full sexual access to each other. Gradually, other couples from the Putney community were added to the group.

Noyes and his followers began moving toward communalism in the early 1840s. In February 1844, a Contract of Partnership introduced a joint-stock principle of property ownership. A constitution issued in March 1845 made the terms of communal property more explicit. Oneidans practiced what they termed "Bible communism." New members contributed their property to the community. This was one of the primary sources of the community's income.

A declaration of principles, signed in November 1846 by the Noyes, Cragin, Skinner, and Miller families, stated that communalism extended to persons as well as property. "All individual proprietorship of either persons or things is surrendered, and absolute community of interests takes the place of the laws and fashions which preside over property and family relations in the world."[7] The ownership of persons and property belonged to God, who appointed John Humphrey Noyes as the father and overseer of the family. Noyes was the sole leader in both temporal and spiritual matters, and members would defer to all of his decisions.

Because of legal suits from seceders, by 1864 the community issued to new members contracts in which they accepted support and sustenance in lieu of wages. The community also pledged to refund property or its value if members seceded.[8]

In October 1847, John Humphrey Noyes was charged with adultery after word about the unique sexual practices of Noyes's group reached the townspeople of Putney. Warrants were issued in Brattleboro for the arrest of George and Mary Cragin on similar charges. Larkin G. Mead, Noyes's brother-in-law and a lawyer, advised the group to leave Putney. The group disbanded and the Noyeses and Cragins went to New York City.

Noyes had attended a Perfectionist convention in Oneida County, New York, in September 1847. There he expounded on the beliefs and practices of the Putney group and several persons enthusiastically adopted Noyes's theories. Soon afterwards, these converts started a new community, based on Noyes's principles, at Oneida Reserve. After leaving Putney, Noyes visited these converts on Jonathan Burt's sawmill property at Oneida Creek, New York, and became convinced that it should be the new site of his community.

Subsequently, Noyes purchased a property of 160 acres on which were two small farmhouses, two log cabins, and a shed. A dormitory for young men was quickly erected. Since the Oneidans were one family living communally, they needed a facility designed to their needs. In the summer of 1848, construction of a home under the supervision of Erastus Hamilton, a builder and architect, began. The Mansion House, completed in 1848, was a three-story frame building containing a kitchen, dining room, meeting room, sitting rooms, and many small sleeping rooms. Additions were made to the first Mansion House in 1849, 1850, and 1851.

The Second Mansion House, built of red brick in 1861–62, was situated on high ground on a bend of the Oneida Creek. The house was designed to combine large rooms like the hall, where the entire community gathered daily, sitting rooms, libraries, and workshops with small bedrooms. A main access road separated the house from barns and service buildings. Kitchens and dining rooms were in a separate building. A third wing was added in 1878. Eventually, the house and its additions enclosed a landscaped courtyard.

Resettlement at Oneida, in a Perfectionist region of the state, increased the membership of Noyes's community. By January 1849, there were 87 members; a year later, there were 172, and the following year, there were 205 members. The Oneida Community would stabilize at approximately 250.[9]

In addition to living in one house, members ate together, worked together, and practiced complex marriage. Children, who were considered to belong to the larger family rather than to their birth parents, were raised and educated communally.

New members pledged their loyalty to Christ and Father Noyes. A central committee, consisting of men and women appointed by Noyes, carried out his orders and ran the community during his absence. The basis for Noyes's religious leadership was divine inspiration, which he received through the "link and chain"—from God to Christ, from Christ to Paul, and from Paul to John Humphrey Noyes.[10]

According to Oneida's system of ascending and descending fellowship, which was based on spirituality, Noyes, who was the most spiritual, held the highest rank. Central committee members ranked the highest after Noyes, with the men being more spiritual, and thus of a higher rank, than the women. Next in rank were groups of men of lesser spirituality, and so on.

Economically, the Oneida Community developed into a self-supporting unit that became impressively profitable. Farming and publishing were the earliest economic activities at Oneida, and originally Noyes expected agriculture to make the community self-sufficient. The Oneidans also ran a sawmill, a flour mill, a machine shop, and a large orchard. They sewed carpetbags and lunch bags designed by Noyes. A member who was a blacksmith and hunter, Sewell Newhouse, developed a hunting trap that, in 1855, the community began manufacturing successfully. Trap production became the main source of income. Tableware manufacture began at the Wallingford branch commune in 1877.

Although the group was founded on unorthodox religious beliefs that caused them to seek isolation, curiously enough the Oneidans held no formal religious services, nor did they build a church, attend church services, or have any special reverence for the Sabbath. There was no clergy other than Noyes, whose license to preach had been revoked. What could be termed a religious practice was the group's habit of assembling every evening at 7:30 or 8:00 in the large hall of the Mansion House for informal meetings that combined business and religion. In an article in the *Circular*, November 30, 1851, the evening meetings are described as "devoted to religious conversation and reading though business and other topics are not excluded."[11] If Noyes were present, he would speak to the assemblage; if not, one of his articles from *Home Talks* would be read. Hymns were often sung.

Oneidans also studied the Bible, and many of Noyes's views on women were based on the biblical account of creation. Since Adam was created first, and Eve was to be his helpmate, Noyes reasoned that women were on a lower level than were men. Despite this inequality, Oneida women had more opportunities for self-fulfillment than in the larger society because Noyes felt that they should be free from the burdens of childbearing and child care to develop themselves. Male continence was a better solution to freeing women from that burden, Noyes believed, than the Shaker reliance on celibacy.

Noyes felt that women's long dresses were cumbersome and interfered with their activities. In 1848, he ordered women to wear costumes similar to that which children wore: knee-length skirts with long pantalets under them. Because long hair was time consuming to take care of, Oneida ladies bobbed their hair. The appearance of Oneida women was much different than other women of their day and was always commented on by visitors.

Work at Oneida was not assigned strictly by gender although in practice, men and women's work roles were often traditional. Any person of either sex could be trained for a particular job if they were interested in it. Jobs were rotated to prevent boredom. Particularly onerous tasks were often performed at a bee consisting of a large number of men and women who would quickly get the job done. Women were assigned administrative duties and appointed members of the powerful central committee.

As in any community, differences between Oneida Community members developed. Noyes, an autocratic leader, implemented a procedure, which he called mutual criticism, to resolve interpersonal and organizational differences. Noyes first became aware of this method of social control when he was a theological student at Andover. He belonged to a secret society called "The Brethren," a group of Congregationalist theological students who intended to become foreign missionaries. The society had originated at Williams College in 1808. The Brethren were expected to submit to criticism of their character and enumeration of their faults by the other members. John Noyes introduced mutual criticism to his followers in 1846, and they greeted it with enthusiasm.[12]

Mutual criticism, seen as an essential aspect of communal life, used interpersonal feedback for the members' personal development. Although criticism could theoretically be positive or negative, a member's negative qualities were usually pointed out. Critics were admonished to give criticism with love, respect, and simplicity. The object of criticism should not resist or object but accept and even join in and be a self-critic. "The great secret of going through the judgment comfortably is to help judge ourselves."[13]

Criticism was an important means of maintaining the Oneidan's unique sexual arrangements. Complex marriage was a controlled system in which men approached an intermediary about having sexual relations with a woman. The intermediary approached the woman and returned with her answer. Detailed records were kept of sexual encounters so that instances of special love did not develop. Oneidans who developed an exclusive love for each other were severely criticized, and one party was often sent away to a branch commune.

Oneidans were not against having children but believed that adults should be able to choose if and when they would produce children. Male continence gave adults this power. For the twenty-one-year period, 1848 to 1869, not more than thirty-one children were accidentally conceived in the Oneida Community, which consisted of approximately 200 sexually active adults.[14] Male continence was such a successful method of birth control, particularly among the first generation of men, that in 1869, there were no children in the Oneida Children's House from any of the original Putney group of men, with one deliberate exception.

Since its beginnings, the Oneida Community had a procreation program as one of its goals but felt that economic security was a prerequisite. Many women in the community were anxious to have children. In 1869, Oneida began the human breeding program called stirpiculture, a term coined at Oneida that combined stirpes, the Latin word for race, and culture, in the sense of cultivation with a view to improvement. The eugenics experiment carried out at Oneida during the years 1869–79 is one of the most unusual aspects of this or any other communal group.

When the stirpiculture experiment began, the community decided not to admit any more new members except those born into it. Fifty-three women who wished to volunteer for motherhood signed a statement acknowledging Noyes's right to select women for childbearing and to combine them with men as he deemed appropriate. They pledged to "become martyrs to science, and cheerfully renounce all desire to become mothers, if for any reason Mr. Noyes deem us unfit material for propagation."[15] Thirty-eight men interested in becoming fathers volunteered themselves to Father Noyes for scientific propagation in any combination he wished. They referred to themselves as "your true soldiers."[16]

A Stirpicultural Committee of six men and six women made the decisions about parenthood, but because it deferred to John Humphrey Noyes in all things, in effect he alone made most of the decisions. The committee approved or rejected each couple who applied to become parents. If a particular couple was turned down, the individuals might be paired with someone else.

One hundred community men and women participated in the ten-year stirpiculture experiment and eighty-one of them became parents. Fifty-eight live children were born, and there were four stillbirths. On the average, fathers of the children were twelve years older than mothers and were heavily weighted in favor of original Putney-era members. It was felt that the choice of the father was more significant than that of the mother. John Humphrey Noyes himself fathered nine of the stirpiculs.

Noyes asserted that Bible communism brought people to such a degree of perfection that they could found a line of superior humans. It was the duty of communistic societies to discover the laws of breeding. For Noyes, there was "no reason why . . . every child . . . should not be a 'genius,' fitted to supply to society, in some of the multifarious chords of which its music is composed, the harmonies of a celestial nature."[17]

Were the stirpiculs geniuses? It's hard to say. Oneida's experiment in procreation ended in 1880 when the Oneida Community ended. At that time, the oldest stirpiculs were only ten years old. Constance Noyes Robertson said that the experiment produced fine, healthy children with above average intelligence.[18] Robertson notes that the fifty-eight stirpiculs appeared to outlive their contemporaries in that only six deaths had occurred by September 1921, when the stirpiculs' ages ranged from forty-two to fifty-two. "According to actuarial computation based on the Elliott tables for 1870, the deaths of forty-five out of these fifty-eight would have been nearer normal."[19] Other factors that could have contributed to that statistic, according to Robertson, were the "hardy New England stock" in the stirpicultural matings and the exceptional "domestic and personal hygiene in the Community house."[20]

Although the Oneidans called stirpiculture a "scientific experiment," this term had a very loose definition. The anticipated results of this breeding experiment are unclear, and the hypothesis being tested was never stated. The criteria for selecting parent couples are not known. What is remarkable is that people willingly gave up their right to select their own partner with whom to have children.

Stirpiculs, like other Oneida children, were cared for by their mothers for their first year, until they were weaned. After that, they were cared for by those assigned to child care. Children lived in the Children's House until adolescence. Although the Children's House had formerly been a separate building, in 1869–70, a new wing called the Children's House was added to the Second Mansion House for the stirpiculs. Children were raised communally so the mothers would not develop a special love for their offspring. They had frequent contact with their parents but were considered the entire community's responsibility.

The endurance of the Oneida Perfectionist community revolved around its strong, charismatic leader. Oneidans accepted John Humphrey Noyes as their inspired leader. As Noyes entered old age, serious fissures developed in the group. When in 1875, Noyes, nearly deaf, able only to speak in a weak voice, and becoming increasingly remote from day-to-day responsibilities, proposed his oldest son, Theodore, as his successor, agreement was not unanimous. Noyes appeared to be violating one of the basic taboos of the community—that of "special love."

Thirty-six-year-old Theodore Noyes was a Yale graduate in medicine and an agnostic who openly questioned Perfectionism. As leader, he would not be guided by divine inspiration like his father. After much discussion, the community rejected Theodore, and John Humphrey Noyes remained its leader. Two years later, in 1877, Noyes appointed a committee to govern the community with Theodore as its head. Thus, Theodore became the de facto leader of the Oneida Community much to the displeasure of some members.

Other issues besides succession troubled the community. The stirpiculture program created ill will among those not accepted for parenthood. Special relationships developed in couples who were having a child. Younger members who had grown up at Oneida did not have the same degree of commitment to the community's religious and social values as their parents, who had chosen to become members.

In 1879, internal dissension erupted over the issue of initiating virgins into the sexual life at Oneida. Girls normally had their first sexual experience shortly after menstruation began. The average age for the onset of menstruation in the community was thirteen, but it ranged from ten to eighteen. John Humphrey Noyes reserved for himself the right of "first husband" to these young women, or he appointed an older man from the central committee.

In 1879, two Oneida men questioned Noyes's right to decide who was to introduce young women into the sexual life of the community. These men were James Towner, an 1874 convert from a free love community at Berlin Heights, Ohio, and William A. Hinds, a founding member of Oneida. Members of the community became divided on this subject, which amounted to a challenge to Noyes's leadership. The Townerites, composed of friends and relatives of Towner who had joined the community with Towner as well as a large number of long-term members, implied that those who sexually introduced the young women at Oneida could be legally guilty of statutory rape.

Outside of the community, clergy led by Professor Mears of Hamilton College and Bishop Huntington launched a concerted attack on the moral irregularities of the Oneida Community. Newspaper articles regularly condemned the community and its leader.

Pressure from Mears and Huntington, fear of legal action against him, and Towner's leadership challenge led John Humphrey Noyes, without the community's knowledge, to leave Oneida during the night of June 22, 1879, and flee to Canada. Communication with Noyes continued, but the community was, in effect, leaderless.

Although some members remained neutral, at this point Oneida was divided into two opposing parties: the dissident Townerites and the loyal Noyesites. Shortly after Noyes's departure, the two parties met to consider the recommendations of the Townerites, which included governance of the community by an administrative council. In addition, they recommended "that the sexual relations of those under age be the concern of the young people and their parents and guardians."[21] Noyes yielded on these proposals, which then received unanimous community support. The administrative council consisted of people from both parties.

Complex marriage and community reorganization were other issues before the new council. On August 20, 1879, the community received a document from John Humphrey Noyes in which he proposed that Oneidans abandon the practice of complex marriage. Noyes recommended that the Oneidans follow "Paul's plan, which allows marriage but prefers singleness." Noyes now argued that the Perfectionists recognize only "marriage and celibacy," obey the state law on fornication and adultery, and not be "responsible as a community for what individuals chose to do outside these forms."[22] Noyes explained that his rationale for his startling reversal of Oneida's religious and social principles was to halt the negative campaign waged by the clergy against the Oneida Community. Noyes's proposal urged that all other aspects of communal living be retained at Oneida, including male continence and the stirpiculture program.

The Oneida Community voted to end their practice of complex marriage as of August 28, 1879. Soon after, couples began requesting and received permission to marry. Couples who had produced a stirpicult usually married. There were thirty-seven marriages performed at this time. However, there were women, like Harriet Worden, whose children had been fathered by married men. Her son, Pierrepont, was a son of John H. Noyes, and another son, Ormond, was the son of Abram Burt, also married. Twelve young women with children remained single.

Oneida's social structure had been based on complex marriage. With the introduction of traditional marriage and the recognition of nuclear family rights and needs, the commitment to communal goals eroded. Noyes's absence hastened this process. In September 1880, the Oneida Community decided to abandon communism and become a joint-stock company.

Oneida Community, Ltd., was founded January 1, 1881. Dividends were to be paid on the shares of stock that each community member was issued based on their years of membership. Employment in Oneida's industries was to be provided to those who wanted it. Economically, the early years of the Oneida Company were not notably successful. About half of the 300 members left to seek other employment by the late 1880s.[23] People who wished to leave the community were free to do so, while those who stayed could continue to live in the Mansion House and pay for their room and board.

Friction between the Towner and Noyes parties continued, and eventually, the Townerites, outvoted and powerless on the company board, left the community. Some of the elderly loyalists decided to join Noyes at Niagara Falls, Canada, when he refused invitations to rejoin Oneida. Noyes never returned to Oneida and died in 1886 at age seventy-four. His body was brought back to Oneida for burial, and those people who had lived with him in Canada returned to live in the Mansion House.

One of John Humphrey Noyes's sons, Pierrepont B. Noyes, a stirpicult who was only ten years old when the community break-up occurred, emerged as a successful leader of the Oneida Company. His youthful enthusiasm and innovative ideas brought the company, which eventually concentrated on silverware production, in line with contemporary American industries. He used new production techniques, large-scale distribution methods, and effective advertising programs.

Pierrepont attracted many of his fellow stirpicults, with whom he felt a very strong bond, back to Oneida to work for the company. In the mid-1930s, thirty-one of them lived at Oneida or worked for the company and were the core of Oneida Community, Ltd.[24] Remnants of the communal spirit lived on in the descendants of the Oneida Community. In addition to those who continued living in the Mansion House, a community called Kenwood, where Oneida Company executives built large homes, was carved out of former Oneida Community acreage.

TOUR

According to Dolores Hayden, an expert on communal architecture, the Oneida **Mansion House** had "the facade of a Victorian country house and the corridors, bedrooms and sitting rooms designed to facilitate complex marriage." The Oneidans built "a structure with a conventional bourgeois, exterior form concealing an unusual arrangement of interior spaces suited to their sexual revolution."[25] Commenting on the wedding of architecture and communalism, Noyes said, "The organic principle of Communism in industry and domestic life, is seen in the common roof, the common table, and the daily meetings of all the members."[26]

In 1987, the Mansion House, in an agreement with Oneida, Ltd., was deeded to Oneida Community Mansion House, a nonprofit corporation. The Oneida Mansion House is both a museum building and a residence for people, some of whom are descended from community members.

The Mansion House, an 1860 brick, three-story, U-shaped building with over 400 rooms, exhibits elements of both high Victorian Italianate and Second Empire styles. Architectural features include an open hipped central cupola, a one-story balustraded porch and balcony, and four-story projecting end towers. The well-landscaped grounds contain several flower gardens. Guided tours of the 1860 Oneida Mansion House include restored spaces such as the **Big Hall, Upper Sitting Room, Outer Library**, and **Nursery Kitchen**. Other parts of the building that may be visited include the **Lounge, Dining Room** and **Visitor Center,** and **History Room**.

Tours begin in the Visitor Center room, which also serves as a museum. Displayed are photographs and artifacts from the community. Other items of interest include a painting of John Humphrey Noyes, his wife Harriet, and

Oneida Community

Luncheon party on the lawn of the Oneida Mansion House. Photograph courtesy of Oneida Community Records, Syracuse University Library, Department of Special Collections.

their son Theodore; an 1870s quilt made by Noyes's mother and others depicting scenes from their life; architectural drawings of community buildings; a small chest used to store a woman's personal possessions; silk thread; an example of the successful animal traps; a small 1835 buckboard; silverware; bibles; a woman's short dress with pantaloons; a large desk; chairs; and many examples of community publications.

The **Children's House**, a wing added to the building in 1869, was the location where community children ate, slept, and went to school under the care of people assigned as their caretakers. There is an original cupboard that was used to store children's clothing. The **Nursery Kitchen** has its original iron stove and white enamel sink with three taps.

The **Big Hall** is a large room with a stage and a balcony where, each evening, the membership would gather to listen to their leader, Noyes. Musical, dramatic, and cultural performances both by community members and professional entertainers were presented here. The Big Hall is painted a cream color with blue trim. Murals on themes of astronomy, music, art, and history decorate the ceiling. Original deacon's benches remain.

In the hallway outside of the Big Hall are portraits done from photographs of prominent Oneidans. Walnut display cases contain memorabilia that belonged to the extended family.

The **Upper Sitting Room** is a large room decorated with late Victorian furniture in which members could read or converse. There are paintings of Noyes's parents and unique religious pictures constructed of silk braid. On two sides of the two-story room are galleries off which are small bedrooms. Members slept in individual bedrooms, which were deliberately quite small so they could not be used for social purposes. Typically, they were furnished with a single bed, a dresser, and two chairs. Although the women's rooms were used for sexual interaction, beds were small so that men would return to their own quarters to sleep.

John Humphrey Noyes's Perfectionists

The **Library** is a comfortable room lined with bookshelves. It had formerly served as a schoolroom. In the Old Library are beautiful built-in book cabinets with glass doors.

The upstairs **Lounge** was added in 1914 and serves as a recreation room. There is a portrait of Pierrepont Noyes.

Bronson Alcott's Consociate Family

A. BRONSON ALCOTT AT THE AGE OF 53

From the portrait by Mrs. Hildreth

Portrait of Bronson Alcott, transcendental author and educator and founder of
Fruitlands. Photograph courtesy of the Library of Congress.

FRUITLANDS
June 1843–January 1844, Harvard, Massachusetts

ADDRESS: 102 Prospect Hill Road, Harvard, MA 01451
TELEPHONE: (508) 456-3924
LOCATION: Thirty miles west of Boston, approximately 6 miles from the junction of
 Routes 495 and 2; take Route 2 Exit 38A to Old Shirley Road, then right on Old
 Shirley Road for 2 miles.
OPEN: Tuesday–Sunday and Monday holidays, 10:00 a.m.–5:00 p.m., from mid-May to
 mid-October.
ADMISSION: Adults, $6; senior citizens, $5; children 4-17, $3.
RESTAURANTS: Tea Room; picnic area.
SHOPS: Museum Shop.
FACILITIES: Research library open by appointment; nature trails.

OVERVIEW

Fruitlands was a short-lived (June 1843–January 1844) spiritual utopian community conducted by Amos Bronson Alcott (1799–1888), the transcendentalist author and educator, and Charles Lane, an English educator, on a farm in Harvard, Massachusetts.

Bronson Alcott was an intellectual, a creative educator, a writer, and a mystic. His controversial educational ideas were not well received in conservative New England, which resulted in his chronic unemployment. Married and the father of four daughters, Bronson, his capable wife, Abigail, and his four daughters led an impoverished, itinerant lifestyle funded primarily by Abigail Alcott's relatives.

Alcott was the father of Louisa May Alcott, author of *Little Women*, who was ten years old when Fruitlands was established. Louisa's fictionalized satirical account of the communal experiment called *Transcendental Wild Oats* was published thirty years later.

The farmhouse where Alcott and his companions conducted their experiment has been restored and contains many artifacts belonging to the Alcott family.

HISTORY

Amos Bronson Alcott, the educator, transcendentalist philosopher, father of author Louisa May Alcott, and cofounder of Fruitlands was born November 29, 1799, on a farm in Wolcott, Connecticut. He was the oldest of the eight children of Joseph Chatfield Alcox and Anna Bronson, both descendants of families that had been in America since 1635. Around 1820, Bronson and his cousin William decided to change the spelling of their last name to "Alcott." Records indicate that the family name had also been spelled "Alcock," "Alcocke," and then "Alcox."

Alcott received little formal education. He and his cousin William at-

142

tended a local district school from age six to age ten, yet both of them ultimately became well-known educators. After his schooling ended, Bronson helped his father with farm work.

Alcott's mother and her family were Episcopalians. Anna's father, Amos Bronson, for whom she named her son, was a member of the Protestant Episcopal Church, and her brother, Reverend Tillotson Bronson, was a Yale graduate, the editor of an Episcopal magazine, and the principal of Cheshire Academy. Although the Alcoxes were Congregationalists, Bronson was confirmed as an Episcopalian when he was sixteen.

At age seventeen, Bronson traveled to Norfolk, Virginia, looking for employment as a teacher. Finding no openings, he became a peddler, or traveling salesman, selling combs, thimbles, needles, thread, buttons, razors, spectacles, scissors, and children's books throughout the small towns and plantations of the Carolinas and Virginia. For the next four years, Alcott made annual peddling trips on foot in the South. Although he initially made money, his later trips were unsuccessful, and he returned home owing money to a Norfolk merchant for peddler's goods. His father sold part of his land to pay Bronson's debt.

On his final peddling trip in 1822, young Alcott visited a Quaker community on Albermarle Sound in North Carolina and was captivated by the Quaker doctrine of the "inner light" in every person. He agreed with many Quaker beliefs—that God speaks directly to the soul of a person, that true religious experience is inward, personal, and spiritual, and that individual souls are illuminated by the divine spirit.

In his mid-twenties, Bronson began a career in education. From 1823 to 1828, he held a variety of teaching positions in Connecticut schools, including the Fall Mountain District in Bristol, a penmanship school in Wolcott, and the West Street School in Bristol. From November 1825 to June 1827, he served as schoolmaster at the Centre District School in Cheshire, which was also known as the Cheshire Pestalozzian School and the Cheshire Philosophical School.

In 1828, Alcott moved to Boston, where he resided for the following decade. In 1830, he married Abigail May, sister of the abolitionist minister Samuel J. May. They had four daughters: Anna, born in 1831; Louisa, born in 1832; Elizabeth, born in 1835; and Abby, born in 1840. Their only son, born in 1839, died shortly after birth. The four sisters served as the models for the March sisters in Louisa May Alcott's *Little Women*.

In Boston, Alcott became involved in an intellectual and philosophical movement called transcendentalism. Transcendentalism was an American version of idealism, a philosophy that asserted the spiritual nature of ultimate reality. Transcendentalists believed that by overcoming the material world of appearance, a person could arrive at the truth, which was universal and enduring.

Many transcendentalists were young New Englanders, the majority of whom were Unitarians, middle class, and Harvard educated. The philosophy was adopted by such famous Americans as Ralph Waldo Emerson, Amos Bronson Alcott, Theodore Parker, Henry David Thoreau, Margaret Fuller, George Ripley,

Bronson Alcott's Consociate Family

James Freeman Clarke, Frederic Henry Hedge, Convers Francis, William H. Furness, Orestes Brownson, Elizabeth Palmer Peabody, William Henry Channing, Jones Very, and William Ellery Channing. Ralph Waldo Emerson was the leader of the movement and its most gifted writer. Amos Bronson Alcott voiced its mystical tendencies.

The term "transcendental" was used by Immanuel Kant to refer to ideas acquired by intuition rather than through the senses. Critics, who derisively applied the term to the Boston movement, said that in their enthusiasm for German philosophic idealism, these young people walked with their heads in the clouds while their feet barely touched the ground.

Transcendentalists believed that the Creator was a spiritual force, an oversoul, and people were endowed with an inner spiritual power that allows them to intuitively know the truth, which was interior to them. Further, this intuitive knowledge was superior to sensory knowledge. Interested in social reform, they believed that effective reformation originated with individuals and worked outward toward society. Because of their commitment to social reform, the transcendentalists supported causes for human improvement, such as the abolition of slavery, the prohibition of alcoholic drinks, women's rights, and common or public schooling.

The transcendentalists were only loosely organized, but in 1836, they formed a club whose first meeting was held September 19 of that year. At club meetings, they discussed a variety of topics, including law, truth, property, worship, genius, and education. Beginning in July 1840 and continuing for four years, they published the *Dial*, a journal of philosophical opinion.

In 1841, George Ripley founded a transcendentalist utopian experiment called Brook Farm. Ripley's project combined transcendentalist philosophy with the communitarianism of Charles Fourier, the French theorist whose ideas were then popular in the United States. In its six-year life, it had a membership of over a hundred. A goal of Brook Farm was to combine body and mind, laborer and intellectual into one. Members of all ages engaged in educational and cultural pursuits. Alcott was involved in the planning stages of Brook Farm but decided not to join.

Alcott's most significant educational experiment in Boston was the 1834 Temple School, which was conducted in a Masonic temple. Alcott saw education as a religious and moral endeavor in which latent knowledge was brought to consciousness. Teachers were to draw knowledge from children that they already possessed intuitively. "Spirit Culture," a term coined by Alcott, referred to the process of exposing the God-like nature of humans. For Alcott, education was a process of drawing out the truths that God had placed in the children's minds. Through skillful, almost Socratic questioning and conversing, he sought to awaken the child's mind and bring the ideas that were latently present to consciousness. At Temple School, Alcott's teaching style was to engage his students, ages six to twelve, in probing, analytical conversations. An important subject was the New Testament Gospels.

Fruitlands

Elizabeth Palmer Peabody, a transcendentalist, was Alcott's assistant at Temple School. She lived with the Alcott family, and their third child, Elizabeth Peabody Alcott, was named for her. Peabody recorded Alcott's conversations for future publication.

Alcott conversed with the Temple School children on the subject of the conception and birth of John the Baptist and the birth of Christ. He was providing sex education in early- nineteenth-century New England at a time when sexual information was withheld from young children.

Some conversations related to birth were recorded by Sophia Peabody, a younger sister of Elizabeth, who had replaced her for a few weeks. On her return, Elizabeth found certain passages objectionable even for Sophia's ears and entreated Bronson to remove them from his manuscript, but he refused. Anticipating the condemnation Boston critics would heap on Temple School and its headmaster, Elizabeth resigned from the school in August 1836. Peabody would remain interested in education, however, and would found the first English language kindergarten in the United States.

In December 1836, James Munroe and Company published the first volume of Alcott's *Conversations with Children on the Gospels* at a cost of $741. Peabody's worst fears were realized. A two-page attack by Nathan Hale on *Conversations* appeared in the *Daily Advertiser*. Joseph Tinker Buckingham wrote a series of highly critical articles in the *Courier*. Alcott was called insane, half-witted, ignorant, blasphemous, and a charlatan. Reverend Andrews Norton, a Unitarian minister who deplored the transcendental movement, called the book "one-third absurd, one-third blasphemous, and one-third obscene."[1]

Transcendentalists including Emerson, James Freeman Clarke, Margaret Fuller, who had replaced Elizabeth Peabody as Alcott's recorder, and Elizabeth herself rallied to Alcott's defense. They wrote articles praising his innovative educational practices. A second volume of *Conversations* was published in February 1837.

At that time, Boston was in the throes of the financial panic of 1837 during which all of Boston's banks suspended specie payments and business ground to a halt. Bronson had borrowed heavily to buy books, furnishings, and equipment for the school, and now his creditors demanded payment of loans amounting to $6,000. To raise money, Alcott sold the entire school library and equipment at auction but realized only a few hundred dollars.

By the spring of 1837, ten students remained at Temple School, which had moved to a single room in the basement. The Alcotts, who were chronically impoverished and frequently survived on the largess of relatives, moved from their comfortable home to a very small house in Boston's South End.

In 1838, Temple School closed. Elizabeth Peabody, who was unable to secure a teaching position in Boston because of her connection to Alcott, returned to her home in Salem. Abigail Alcott, who viewed Elizabeth as disloyal, changed her daughter Lizzie's name to Elizabeth Sewell Alcott.

Unable to find employment, Alcott began a school in his home. One of his students was Susan Robinson, a black child. The parents of the other students demanded that Bronson dismiss Susan; he refused. Most of the children were withdrawn.

Emerson encouraged the Alcotts to move to Concord, which they did in 1840. James Pierrepont Greaves, who had read and admired Alcott's *Conversations*, invited Alcott to England. Greaves, who had worked with the Swiss educator Johann Heinrich Pestalozzi in Yverdon, had established a school that he named for Alcott. Ralph Waldo Emerson funded the trip abroad, and Alcott sailed for England in May 1842.

Greaves had died two months earlier, leaving Henry Gardiner Wright, William Oldham, and Charles Lane administering Alcott House School. Alcott and these three educators developed the idea of founding a community, a New Eden, in America. When Alcott returned home in October 1842, Wright, Lane, and Lane's son, William, accompanied him.

Lane cofounded the utopian community named Fruitlands with Alcott. The Englishman paid Alcott's Concord debts and, in May 1843, purchased a 90-acre farm in Harvard, Massachusetts, for $1,800. The agreement included one year's rent-free use of the farmhouse on Prospect Hill, overlooking Nashaway Valley. Because Lane's funds were somewhat inadequate, Sam May, Abigail's brother, acted as trustee for the purchase and signed a note for $300, which he agreed to pay in two equal installments within a year.

Lane and his son, William, and Alcott and his wife, Abigail, along with their four daughters, moved to the red farmhouse named Fruitlands in June 1843. Members of Fruitlands formed the Consociate family. Original family members also included twenty- year-old Samuel Larned, who had been a member of Brook Farm; twenty-year-old Wood Abram, who had transposed his name from Abram Wood; Abraham Everett, a cooper who had once been committed to an insane asylum; and Samuel Bower, an English wool comber, writer, and nudist. Joseph Palmer, a neighbor, was highly involved with Fruitlands but not an official member. He was well known for his long beard, for which he had endured ridicule and imprisonment. Henry Wright had lost interest in the project and returned to England. Ann Page joined later but soon left because she and Abigail did not get along.

Fruitlands was a spiritual and religious community that was not tied to any institutional religion. Governance was democratic. Money was forsaken as the members intended to live off the land. There was no formal constitution. Education of the children was a high priority.

Lane and Alcott's plans for Fruitlands, published in a letter in the July 1843 issue of the *Dial*, announced that they were taking possession of 100 acres on which they planned "to initiate a Family in harmony with the primitive instincts in man." Rather than engage in ordinary farming, they were going to cultivate "[f]ruit, grain, pulse, herbs, flax, and other vegetable products, . . . will afford ample manual occupation, and chaste supplies for the bodily needs." The founders of Fruitlands announced that they anticipated "no hasty" enrollment of members because their peaceable kingdom could be "entered only through the gates of self-denial."[2]

The two-story red farmhouse that housed the Consociate Family required cleaning and repairs to make it habitable. Abby Alcott and her older daughters did most of this work. Eleven acres were plowed and planted with maize, rye, oats, barley, potatoes, beans, peas, melons, and squash. Although named Fruitlands, only ten apple trees were on the property. Fruit, bread, and water were staples of the family's vegetarian diet, as meat, alcohol, tea, coffee, butter, and milk as well as vegetables that did not grow toward the sun, like carrots, were prohibited.

Because the founders of Fruitlands believed that living animals should not serve human needs, no animals were kept, whale oil was not used in lamps, and manure was not used to fertilize the land. Cotton and woolen garments were forbidden, as cotton was produced through the labor of enslaved black people and wool was taken from sheep, thus depriving them of their coat. The Consociates wore simple, brown linen garments of their own design, which included bloomers for the women. Alcott planted mulberry trees near the house for the cultivation of silkworms.

Visiting the Consociate family in July, Emerson was impressed with Fruitlands' serenity. Prophetically, he commented that while all looked well in July, he wondered how they would appear in December. In fact, Wood Abram and Sam Larned left after only a short stay. Isaac Thomas Hecker arrived from Brook Farm in July and remained only two weeks. When Alcott asked him why he was leaving, he pointed out Alcott's lack of frankness, the shortage of fruit, the dilapidated buildings, and the preoccupation with literature and writing rather than farming even though the Consociate family claimed to be a self-sufficient vegetarian community. Hecker did comment that Fruitlands was far more ascetic than was Brook Farm. Hecker became a Roman Catholic priest and founded the Paulist order of priests.

Lane and Alcott continued to publicize their project at Fruitlands. Their letter in the *Herald of Freedom* on September 8, 1843, described their daily regimen at Fruitlands. Rising with the sun, they commenced their day with "cold bathing, followed by music, and then a chaste repast." Each family member pursued their own interest until after lunch when they engaged in "deep-searching conversation." This was followed by individual occupations and then the evening meal. Once again, the group gathered for more intellectual conversation. At sunset, they retired "to sweet repose, ready for the next day's activity."[3]

In *Transcendental Wild Oats*, Louisa May Alcott paints a different picture of Fruitlands and its leaders, who were often absent seeking new members. Since they abjured money as the source of all evil, she recalled that the leaders believed that they could live off produce they raised. What could not grow, they planned to obtain through barter. While this caused inconvenience, it was praised in the name of self-denial. Furthermore, she recounted, the leaders, who were great spokesmen for reforms of all sorts, "said many wise things and did many foolish ones." Unfortunately, their frequent travels and intellectual discussions caused them to neglect farming. Following the inclinations of their inner spirits, they simply trusted to "Providence and went a-reaping in wider and . . . more fruitful fields than their own."[4]

Bronson and Abigail Alcott were the only married couple at Fruitlands. At Alcott House School in England, Greaves and his associates had advocated celibacy, although Wright later married. The question of celibacy became an issue at Fruitlands with Lane exerting pressure on Alcott to abandon the married state. Abigail Alcott strongly resented Lane's attempts to break up her marriage.

Only the Lanes and Alcotts remained at Fruitlands by November. Shortly after Abigail visited her brother in late November, a letter from Samuel May informed the Consociate family that he would not pay the next installment on the Fruitlands debt. Since the Lanes and Alcotts were penniless, this move clearly meant the end of the Fruitlands experiment.

Writing about her father and Fruitlands, Louisa May Alcott, reminisced, that "The world was not ready for Utopia yet, and those who attempted to found it only got laughed at for their pains." In the past, holy poverty and almsgiving were honored but in modern times were ridiculed. "To live for one's principles, . . . is a dangerous" undertaking. She concluded "the failure of an ideal, no matter how humane and noble, is harder for the world to forgive and forget than bank robbery or the grand swindles of corrupt politicians."[5]

On January 6, 1844, Charles and William Lane left to join the Shakers, and Alcott, in a fit of depression over the failure of the experiment, lay in his bed without food and water for several days. On January 11, the Alcotts, with

The red farmhouse in Harvard which was the site of Alcott's communal experiment. Photograph by Patricia A. Gutek.

no food or firewood remaining, left Fruitlands. Kind neighbors, the Lovejoys, gave them shelter in their farmhouse.

After two years of moving from one New England communal situation to another, Lane returned to his teaching position at Alcott House School in England. His son, William, remained with the Shakers until 1848 when Emerson and the Alcotts removed him and sent him to his father in England. Years later, the advocate of celibacy, Charles Lane, married and had six more children.[6]

In late 1844, the Alcotts returned to Concord and their ongoing financial struggle. Bronson did not seek work, as he disapproved of working for hire. With funds from Emerson and an inheritance from Abigail's father, they bought a house called Hillside. Abigail and their daughters found employment wherever they could, and long-suffering relatives and friends helped out. Economic stability finally occurred when Louisa took over the support of her family after publication of her successful book *Little Women*. In his later years, Bronson Alcott presented lectures on spiritual culture and progressive education. He served as superintendent of the Concord Public Schools from 1859 through 1864. In the last decade of his life, with William Torrey Harris, Franklin B. Sanborn, and others, he founded the Concord School of Philosophy. The school met for nine successive summers, until Alcott's death in 1888.

Before Lane left Fruitlands, he asked Emerson to act as its trustee. Joseph Palmer bought the property from Emerson, renamed it Freelands, and used it as a hostel for homeless people. Clara Endicott Sears restored the farmhouse and opened it to the public in 1914.

TOUR

Fruitlands Museums refers to the four museums founded by Clara Endicott Sears on the site of the Alcott-Lane utopian experiment. Included are the restored **Fruitlands Farmhouse** that was home to the Consociate family, the restored **Shaker House** that was moved from nearby Harvard Shaker Village, an **American Indian Museum**, and a **Picture Gallery,** all picturesquely located on the top of Prospect Hill, overlooking Nashaway Valley and far-away Mount Wachusett. Nineteenth-century visitors to Fruitlands never failed to comment on the site's exceptional natural beauty. Today, the museum site is comprised of 200 acres of woodlands, meadows, and pine trees, with a series of winding nature trails.

Fruitlands Farmhouse is a 1740 ochre-red, two-story frame farmhouse used by Amos Bronson Alcott and the Consociate family in 1843 as the center of their utopian adventure. Restoration of the farmhouse by Clara Endicott Sears began in 1914. The weatherboarded house is a modified rectangle of from one to two and a half stories, with gabled and shed roof sections. It has a central chimney, a rear granary, kitchen, and storage sheds. Its front entrance is slightly off-center and has a transom.

On the first floor are a small dining room, a study, a library, and a kitchen.

Bronson Alcott's Consociate Family

Much of the furniture in the house belonged to Joseph Palmer, who was involved with Fruitlands and later purchased the property. The Alcotts took their furniture with them.

Pictures of Bronson Alcott, Charles Lane, Abigail Alcott, Ralph Waldo Emerson, Nathaniel Hawthorne, and Henry Thoreau adorn the walls of the dining room. In the study is a bust of Socrates, which accompanied the Alcotts through their many moves. A long, narrow back kitchen runs the width of the house.

On the second floor are Bronson and Abigail Alcott's bedroom, Charles Lane's bedroom, and a hallway between the bedrooms where William Lane slept. A large room over the kitchen was used as a dormitory for other family members. The Alcott girls slept in the attic.

Throughout the house are exhibited numerous items and documents relating to the Alcotts and other transcendentalists.

The **Shaker House**, built in 1794 by the Harvard Shakers, was used as an office. Its exhibits focus on their community industries.

The **American Indian Museum** exhibits contain several dioramas depicting Indian encampments in the Nashaway Valley, the Sun Dance of the Plains Indians, and the redemption of Mary Rowlandson, an Indian captive. Artifacts from North American tribes are displayed.

The **Picture Gallery** displays a collection of early-nineteenth-century portraits by itinerant artists in its west galleries, while its east galleries hold a collection of Hudson River School landscapes.

Wilhelm Keil's Keilites

Born in 1812 in Erfurt, Prussia, Dr. William Keil founded and led the Aurora Colony. He died in Aurora Oregon, in 1877. Photograph courtesy of Aurora Colony Historical Society, Aurora, Oregon.

HISTORIC BETHEL GERMAN COLONY AND OLD AURORA COLONY MUSEUM

Historic Bethel German Colony
1844–1883, Bethel, Missouri
NR

ADDRESS: P.O. Box 127, Bethel, MO 63434
TELEPHONE: (816) 284-6493
LOCATION: Bethel is located on Route 15.
OPEN: Self-guided tours; other tours may be arranged by appointment.
ADMISSION: Free
RESTAURANTS: Fest Hall.
SHOPS: B.G.C.C. Shop with crafts and books; inquire here for information about Bethel and tours.

Old Aurora Colony Museum
1856–1883, Aurora, Oregon

ADDRESS: P.O. Box 202, Aurora, OR 97002
TELEPHONE: (503) 678-5754
LOCATION: Aurora National Historic District is located 24 miles north of Salem and 30 miles south of Portland off of Highway 99E. Southbound on I-5, take Canby Hubbard Exit 282; northbound on I-5, take Aurora Exit 278.
OPEN: Tuesday–Saturday, 10:00 a.m.–4:00 p.m., Sunday, noon–4:00 p.m., June–August.
ADMISSION: Adults, $3.50; senior citizens, $3.00; children 6–18, $1.50.
RESTAURANTS: No
SHOPS: Gift Shop; Wilhelm Keil and Company Gift Shop.
FACILITIES: Orientation slide show; guided tours; living history programs; special events.

OVERVIEW

One consistent theme emerges when examining communal groups: their founders were anything but boring. For instance, Wilhelm Keil (1812–77), a German immigrant who established colonies in Missouri and Oregon was a self-proclaimed *hexendoktor* whose cures emanated from a secret volume written in blood. Also known for his charisma and dynamic speaking style, Keil attracted hundreds of followers who willingly donated all their property and possessions to a community he founded.

Keil immigrated to the United States when he was twenty-five and became a Methodist minister after a conversion experience. He left the ministry to build a successful communal settlement in Missouri in 1844. In 1856, Keil and some of the Bethelites established a second colony in Oregon. Wilhelm Keil was the charismatic leader of both communities, which flourished until his death in 1877. With no successor to Keil, the colonies dissolved.

HISTORY

Wilhelm Keil was born in Ehrfurth, Prussia, March 6, 1812. He received an elementary education, showed some interest in going on the stage, and was trained as a tailor. He was a self- taught physician whose medical procedures were based on botany and on mysterious secret remedies.

Keil carried out botanical experiments in an attempt to discover the hidden laws of nature, hoping to find a universal medicine to cure all human ills. (A Boehmist belief held that if one discovered God's Truth, he would also find a cure for all diseases.) In Germany, Keil was given secret remedies by a woman who enjoyed a reputation from the success of her treatments. She shared her remedies with Keil on the condition that he emigrate and not practice medicine in Germany.[1]

Keil married Luise Ritter, and the young couple immigrated to the United States in 1836. In Pittsburgh, Keil established an apothecary shop and practiced medicine, becoming known as the "*Hexendoktor*." Described as a mystic, Keil is alleged to have "used animal magnetism and a book of prescriptions . . . written in human blood."[2]

In 1838, Keil experienced a powerful religious conversion at a revival led by Wilhelm Nast, a Methodist preacher from Stuttgart, Germany. Subsequently, Nast ceremoniously burned, at Keil's request, the book of secret remedies from Germany, thus ending his career as the *Hexendoktor*. However, Keil practiced medicine and used the title doctor throughout his life.

Keil became a probationary preacher for the German congregation of the Episcopal Methodist Church at Deer Creek, near Pittsburgh but soon became dissatisfied. He was especially critical of ministers accepting salaries. He and his congregation joined the Protestant Methodist Church, but he was expelled due to a conflict over authority.[3]

In 1842, Keil condemned all denominational religions, including Methodism, and became an independent preacher who stressed noninstitutionalized, simple, pietistic Christianity based on the Bible, especially the books of Daniel and Revelation. His set of beliefs fell into the category of Radical Pietism, a form of Pietism known for millennial expectation, asceticism, celibacy, mysticism, and charismatic, prophetic leaders.[4] A gifted and charismatic preacher, Keil's missionary journeys through Kentucky, Ohio, and Pennsylvania made many converts. Among them were some former Harmonists from George Rapp's community at Economy, Pennsylvania, who had defected in the 1832 schism led by Count Leon, Archduke Maximilian. Leon's colony at Philipsburg was short-lived, and while some adherents accompanied him to Louisiana, others later became disciples of Wilhelm Keil.

Wilhelm Keil's Keilites

Keil, a millennialist, prophesying that judgment day would occur Easter 1843, foretold "the death of the two heralds of the apocalypse." Identifying a fellow preacher Michael Schaefer and himself as the two witnesses in the prophecy, Keil and Schaefer commenced a forty-day fast.[5] When the event did not occur, Keil revised the judgment date to Easter 1844.

Keil's dates for the Second Coming of Christ closely paralleled those of William Miller, a well-known millennialist and founder of the religious movement known as Millerism, which swept the northeastern United States between 1840 and 1844. Both the Millerites and Keilites suffered disappointment when their predictions were not realized.

Influenced by his spiritual mentor, Reverend J. Martin Hartmann, who was interested in the concept of a Christian communal society, as well as his own observation of communalism at Rapp's Economy, Keil decided that he and his followers should establish a communal community. An advance party sent out by Keil located 2,500 acres of land on the banks of the North River in Shelby County, Missouri. Keil, his family, and a few others traveled to Missouri in the fall of 1844 and founded a settlement at Bethel, Missouri. Many others came in the spring of 1845.

Bethel participants sold their property and deposited their funds in a common treasury. Originally, there was no constitution, but after a legal suit by a former member, the remaining members signed a written constitution in 1847. The Keilite communitarians did not keep records or accounts of work done or supplies provided within the community. Food was distributed on Saturday, and clothing was provided in spring and fall.[6]

Everyone labored for the common good, and many were skilled craftsmen. Through hard work, Bethel developed rapidly and became economically successful. Keil was the religious, legal, and social head of the community, and his decisions were final. Day-to-day activities were administered by supervisors and managers appointed by Keil. In 1850, the Bethel community had 476 members, and in 1855, 650.

William Hinds, a nineteenth-century student of American communitarianism, speculated on Keil's personality and the causes contributing to the Missouri community's success. According to Hinds, Keil was:

doubtless fanatical, as his defamers assert, but it is none the less marvelous that, with limited education, without reputation, without new or well-defined religious or social principles, he should, after a residence in this country of only six years, gather about him a thousand souls ready to risk their all in a communistic experiment. I can only account for this by recalling, that when Dr. Keil began his independent career the people of the Eastern and Middle States had just passed through a series of religious and other excitements that made them eager for new social conditions, and so quick to follow those who offered to lead them where such new conditions would prevail, and by supposing that Dr. Keil, however foolish his fanaticism and preposterous his claims, had yet wonderful powers of gaining and holding the attention and hearts of men.[7]

A similar explanation could be given for other nineteenth-century communal groups treated in this book. A charismatic leader combined with a widespread religious excitement led to new and unique religious experiments.

All of the Bethelites were German. Agriculture was the primary occupation of the colony, which owned 4,700 acres. In addition, the colonists raised cattle and sheep and operated a tannery, distillery, gristmill, sawmill, woolen mill, general store, and post office. They wove cloth, made shoes and plows, and were well known for their corn and rye whiskey sold under the "Golden Rule" label. Gloves made in the colony won first prize at the New York World's Fair in 1858.

Unlike most other contemporaneous communal groups, the Bethelites shared the traditional views of society regarding sexuality and marriage. Members married, had children, and lived in nuclear family units. Marriages could only occur between members of Bethel. Each family had their own house and a plot of land for a vegetable garden and raising pigs and chickens.

Colony principles encompassed obedience, communalism, monogamous marriage, family life and care of children, love for each other according to the Golden Rule, labor for the common good, plain living, cleanliness, and economy. Colonists did not adopt any costume but wore the same clothes as other contemporary farm families.

Community structures were built of handmade brick. *Das grosse Haus* was a large structure used as a hotel, restaurant, boardinghouse for unmarried members, and a warehouse. Keil and his wife and five children lived in a massive two-and-a-half- story brick and stone house called Elim located one mile east of the village.

The colony church, surrounded by a grove of trees, was on a hill on the northeast side of the village. Built in 1848, the brick and stone structure was 60 by 100 feet with an eighty-foot tower with a balustrade, belfry, and steeple. An interior gallery ran around three sides, and there was a railed-off area for the band. Men and women entered separately and sat separately.

Services were held every other Sunday and were well attended but not mandatory. Keil, known for his dynamic speaking ability, usually preached. He also announced the transgressions of the members, who were exhorted to confess and repent. Baptism and confirmation were not practiced. Communion was not a formal sacrament but a common meal at the home of a believer. Special observances occurred on Easter and Pentecost. Christmas was celebrated with decorated trees, gifts for the children from Kris Kringle, and a church service with a band concert and congregational singing.

The children attended school, which was conducted in English. A small number of young men attended college if there was a need for their specialty in the colony. Music was important. A band and choir directed by Conrad Finck performed at church services and gave weekly concerts in the colony and in other Missouri towns. Holidays and festivals were celebrated with music and dancing.

Despite their prosperity and success, eventually the Bethel community experienced internal dissension, including questioning of Keil's authority. His position as leader was heavily based on his strong ego and charismatic personality. Needing to take a dramatic step to reaffirm his position, Keil decided to establish a second community in Oregon.

In May 1855, Keil led a caravan of twenty-five wagons and seventy-five communitarians 2,000 miles over the Oregon Trail. The trip was not uneventful. Keil's nineteen-year-old son, Willie, who had longed to go to Oregon, died shortly before the journey commenced. The first wagon in the Keil caravan contained Willie's body in a lead-lined coffin filled with alcohol. Willie was buried in Oregon.

After Keil befriended hostile Indians on the trail, he was arrested and tried by the U.S. Army on charges that he had disparaged Americans to curry favor with the Indians. Keil was not convicted, and the charges were dropped.

An advance party for the Oregon community selected a site at Willapa Bay in Washington. Keil rejected it and personally chose several hundred acres on the banks of the Pudding River in the Willamette Valley, south of Portland. In the following decade, approximately half the residents of Bethel relocated to Aurora while the others maintained the original settlement. Keil remained the undisputed leader of both colonies.

In Aurora, named after Keil's favorite daughter, houses, a sawmill, a gristmill, a general store, a drugstore, a tannery, barns, a cabinetmaker's shop, a blacksmith's shop, a wagon-maker's shop, a tailor's shop, a shoemaker's shop, a carpenter's shop and a tin shop, a church, and a hotel were built. The hotel, used as a summer resort by people from Portland, was especially successful. They planted extensive orchards. By 1872, the colony of 1,000 members owned 23,000 acres of land.

Charles Nordhoff visited Aurora in June 1873 and commented on its utilitarian look and lack of aesthetics. He said that the colony focused only on the necessities of life; nothing was beautiful. Everything looked well scrubbed, and food was plain and plentiful.[8]

Nordhoff described Keil, who was then sixty-one years old, as "a short, burly man, with blue eyes, whitish hair and white beard. . . . He seemed excitable and somewhat suspicious; gave no tokens whatever of having studied any book but the Bible, and that only as it helped him to enforce his own philosophy . . . and evidently laid much stress on the parental character of God. As he discussed, his eyes lighted up with a somewhat fierce fire; and I thought I could perceive a fanatic, certainly a person of a very determined, imperious will, united to a narrow creed."[9]

Wilhelm and Luise Keil had five children. In addition to their son Willie, who died in Missouri, three daughters and another son died in a smallpox epidemic in November and December 1862. Ten years later, he showed Nordhoff where his children, all of whom died between the ages of eighteen and twenty-one, were buried. Keil said, "Here . . . lie my children—all I had, five. . . . One after the other I laid them here. It was hard to bear. . . . He gave them, and I thanked him; he took them, and now I can thank God for that too."[10]

Wilhelm Keil died December 30, 1877. In June 1879, the two colonies severed their connections and divided their common holdings. Bethel's 200 residents dissolved the community in 1879. Members received their original contribution. In addition, men received $7.76 for every year of membership, while women received half that amount. How traditional! Bethel was incorporated as a town in 1883. Aurora was formally dissolved in Oregon in 1883.

At the time of dissolution, there were between 175 and 200 Bethel Colony members and about 250 Aurora Colony members. The two societies' real and personal property was valued at approximately $175,000.[11]

The concept of creating a museum at Aurora grew out of a centennial celebration that was organized in 1956 by descendants of the Aurora colonists. In 1966, the museum was dedicated and has functioned to preserve the history of the Keilite colony at Aurora.

Tour

Although Bethel, Missouri, and Aurora, Oregon, are separated by thousands of miles of the trans- Mississippi American west, we include tours of both sites in this section on the Keilites, who, because of their leader, shared much of a common history.

Bethel, Missouri

The Keilite site at Bethel, Missouri, is more in a state of suspended history rather than active restoration. Bethel, a small hamlet of 132 residents, is a living Missouri town that, through the efforts of the Bethel German Colony, is trying to preserve its unique history. While there is no official visitors' center, one can visit the **general store** to pick up a map for a self- guided tour and rent an audiotape program that describes the buildings from the Keilite era. Most of the historic buildings can be viewed from the outside only, unless one is on a prearranged guided tour.

Der Schneider Laden, the **Tailor Shop**, was the location where clothes were made for the colony's men and boys; it was supervised by Nicholas Will, the colony tailor, whose family lived on the first floor.

The **Ziegler House**, located in **Colony Park**, is used for tours and demonstrations. The lower level of **Fest Hall** is a small restaurant, while the upper story is a museum. The **Gross House** is now used as a Senior Citizens Center. During the era of Keil's colony, the upstairs was used as a dormitory for single men. The **Bair House** was the home of Reuben Bair, the colony wheelwright. The **Miller House** was the last building to be erected by the communal group; it was home to one of the community's teachers.

The **Bauer House** was the home of J. G. Bauer, druggist and jeweler.

The **Elim Mansion House**, home of Wilhelm Keil, located one and one-half miles from town, can be toured only by appointment.

Special events include the Harvest Fest held the first weekend of October.

Aurora, Oregon

Aurora was designated a National Historic District in 1974. The **Old Aurora Colony Museum** buildings may be visited on a self-guided tour. Before your tour, see the orientation slide presentation in the **Ox Barn Museum**.

The Ox Barn Museum, one of the original big colony barns, was completed in 1862–63. Before being converted to its present use as a museum, it had been used variously as an ox barn, horse barn, state and trucking depot, a store, and a home. It became the property of Mrs. A. Hurst, who sold the building to the Aurora Colony Historical Society in 1963. Serving as the main building in the museum complex, it now contains exhibits related to the colony period. Among the exhibits are photographs of the Aurora Colony Church, which was torn down in 1912, and the Keil family, an exhibit on the Keilites' trek on the Oregon Trail, and maps and illustrations of the early colony. In addition, there are exhibits on music, crafts, education, furniture, tools, and other items related to the colony's history.

The **George Kraus House**, in the up and down board and batten style, is a two-story frame house built in 1863–64. It was the home of Elizabeth Giesy before her marriage to George Kraus in 1879. Presented to the historical center by John Kraus, the son of George Kraus, it is furnished with Aurora handmade furniture and other period pieces. Of special interest is the pioneer kitchen, which contains a wood-burning stove and baking oven. Pieces made in the colony are the corner cupboard and the dry sink.

The three-room **Steinbach Log Cabin**, built by George and Catherine Steinbach in 1876, was presented to the museum complex by their grandson, Ernest Becke, and his wife, Marian. Constructed of peeled and hand-hewn logs, chinked with mud, it illustrates early colony building techniques. Among its colony furnishings are tables, chairs, dishes, a spinning wheel, a spool bed, a handwoven tablecloth, and a colorful pieced quilt.

The **Colony Washhouse** a general utility building, was shared by a number of families. Community women gathered in this out-kitchen to make soap, stuff sausages, boil clothes, and can fruit.

The **Stauffer-Will Farm**, complete with farmhouse, barn, and outbuildings, is used for living history programs for school children. During the colony era, the farm, as a functioning part of the commune, provided flour, milk, cheese, vegetables, and fruit.

Additional buildings are a **farm machinery building** and the **William Keil and Company Gift Shop**, located in the old colony store annex.

Special events presented by the Aurora Colony Historical Society include a Candlelight Tour in January, Oregon Pottery and Baskets Show in February, Antique Spinning Wheel Show in March, Annual Spring Auction in May, a Strawberry Social in June, Coverlets from Oregon Show in July, Harvest Fest in October, a Quilt Show in October, and Christmas in Old Aurora in December.

Erik Jansson's Janssonists

Big Brick, a large communal building where many residents of Bishop Hill lived and dined. Built in 1851, it burned down in 1928. Photograph courtesy of the Illinois State Historical Society.

BISHOP HILL
1846–1861, Bishop Hill, Illinois
STATE HISTORIC SITE, NR, NHL

ADDRESS: Bishop Hill Heritage Association, P.O. Box 1853, Bishop Hill, IL 61419; and/or Site Superintendent, P.O. Box D, Bishop Hill, IL 61419
TELEPHONE: (309) 927-3899, (309) 927-3345
LOCATION: In western Illinois, 157 miles west of Chicago; 17 miles east of I-74; 20 miles south of I-80; 2 miles north of US 34.
OPEN: The Heritage Museum is open daily, 10:00 a.m.–4:00 p.m., April–December. The Colony Church, Colony Hotel, and Bishop Hill Museum are open daily, 9:00 a.m.–5:00 p.m., closed Thanksgiving, Christmas, and New Year's Day; hours may vary in winter.
ADMISSION: Heritage Museum: adults, $1.00; children, $.50. Colony Church, Colony Hotel, and Bishop Hill Museum: free.
RESTAURANTS: Red Oak; P. L. Johnson's Dining Room.
SHOPS: Colony Woodshed; Prairie Workshop; Red Oak; Bishop Hill Colony Store; Antik Affar Village Smithy Gift Shop; Hintze Pottery; Friends Weave; Prairie Paperworks; Clothier in Colony Blacksmith Shop.
FACILITIES: Visitors' Center with orientation film; special events.

OVERVIEW

A gem of a town, Bishop Hill is a restored Swedish religious communal site as well as a living community of approximately 140 people. Nestled among the small farming towns of western Illinois, travelers to Bishop Hill will find within driving distance from Chicago a bit of nineteenth-century Sweden transplanted to the prairies of western Illinois. Large classical structures built to accommodate a communal lifestyle make this mid-nineteenth-century town appear like an apparition in western Illinois farm country.

Bishop Hill was founded in 1846 by Swedish immigrants under the leadership of Erik Jansson (1808–50), a highly charismatic man who attracted many followers. Jansson was a religious leader, farmer, and traveling wheat flour salesman who preached a doctrine of perfectionism considered heretical by the Swedish Lutheran Church. Originally members of the Swedish Reader, or *Lasare*, movement, Janssonists came to believe that the Bible was the sole guide to religious belief and practice. Jansson condemned the religious literature of the Lutheran Church, and he and his followers publicly burned those books. This put them into direct conflict with both Sweden's religious and civil authorities; Jansson was arrested and imprisoned.

The freedom of worship guaranteed by the U.S. Constitution appealed to the Janssonists. Olof Olsson, dispatched by Jansson to find suitable land for a colony in the United States, selected a site on the Illinois prairie. In 1846, Jansson led hundreds of followers from Sweden to Henry County, Illinois. Adopting a communal lifestyle, the Janssonists sold their property in Sweden and

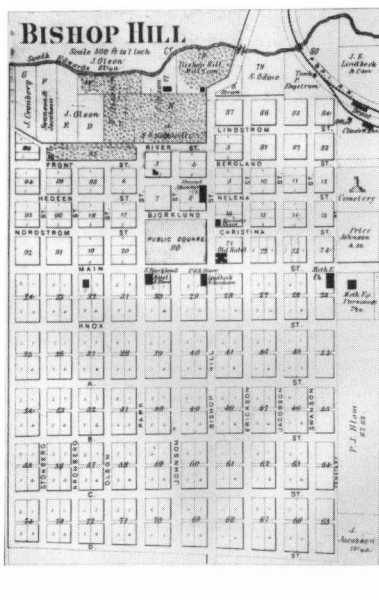

Map of the community of Bishop Hill. Photograph courtesy of the Illinois State Historical Society.

pooled their resources. Between 1846 and 1854, 1,500 followers of Jansson sailed from Sweden to the United States to form the religious commune in Bishop Hill, Illinois. The colony followed Jansson's strict religious prescriptions and continued after his death in 1850. From initial hardship, they achieved economic success through farming, orchards, a tannery, and mills.

The religious colony lasted fifteen years, until 1861 when it was dissolved because of dissension among the members. Thirteen original buildings built by the colonists remain. Some are restored and open to the public, some are used as shops, and others are privately owned and not open to the public. A remarkable collection of paintings by the folk artist, Olof Krans, who lived in the colony as a child, is displayed at Bishop Hill.

HISTORY

Wheat Flour Messiah is the intriguing title of Paul Elmen's biography of Erik Jansson, an uneducated Swedish farmer from Sweden's Uppland region who led a religious communal group to the Illinois prairie.

Jansson as well as other farmers in his native region of Sweden grew wheat, which was necessary to produce white flour. Further north, where rye, not wheat, was grown, white bread was highly prized by women who tired of rye bread. The desire of Halsingland farm wives for wheat flour to bake pure white bread created a market for the enterprising farmer and salesman Erik Jansson.

While on extended sales trips, Jansson sought out opportunities to preach to local *lasare* groups, lay people who gathered in homes to read the Bible, discuss religious literature, and pray. In written accounts by persons who heard Jansson preach, he is often referred to as a traveling wheat flour salesman.

Erik Jansson's Janssonists

Erik Jansson, the son of Johannes Mattson was born December 19, 1808, on a farm in the parish of Biskopskulla, the village of Landsberga, in Uppsala, Sweden. When Erik was one or two years old and being cared for by his seven-year-old brother Jan, the first and second fingers of Erik's left hand were accidentally cut off by Jan, who was playing with a knife or axe.

Jansson, in his autobiographical account, described his conversion experience, the "first summons," that called him to his life's mission at age twenty-two. While working in his father's fields, he suffered an acute attack of rheumatism. After much thought about Jesus Christ's mission on earth, he was "struck" that he was to "do the same great works today." At that moment, he was completely cured of his pain. Further, he now knew that he had been deceived by the teachings of the evangelical Lutheran Church that he had received from his parents, teachers, and clergy. He felt that he had no one to turn to because all the ministers were spiritually blind.[1]

Rejecting the authority of the Lutheran Church, Sweden's official church, Jansson concluded that the Bible was the only true source of the word of Jesus Christ. One could gain salvation without clerical intervention.

Jansson now joined the *Lasare* movement, which he saw as an alternative to institutionalized religion, which he considered formal and stagnant. Lay readers were part of the Pietist movement, which believed that one's personal sense of faith and devotion to God was more important than the church's authority. Following a simple Pietism, they did not approve of drinking, card playing, swearing, and dancing.

Although Sweden's Conventicle Edict of 1726 forbade the holding of religious meetings by the laity without the presence of clergy, the *lasare* persisted in meeting in groups to read and discuss the Bible. At first, the Lutheran clergy saw them to be devout but simple lay people who did no harm. While traveling in Halsingland to sell wheat flour in early 1843, Erik Jansson met Jonas Olsson, a farmer and local leader of the *lasare* in the area. Jansson, who preached to the group, made a profound impression on his listeners, who either saw him as God's messenger or the devil's agent. As was his style, he garnered both followers and enemies.

In 1835, when he was twenty-seven, Erik married Maria Kristina Larsdotter, a twenty-year-old young woman who had been a servant in the Jansson farmhouse for the previous six years. "Maja Stina," as she was called, was pregnant at the time of the marriage. Believing that their son had married beneath his status, Jansson's parents disapproved of the marriage. He left home without his father's blessing.

Erik and Maja's first child, a son, Johannes, died at age six months, and their second child, born in 1837, died at three months of whooping cough. Two other children, Eric and Mathilda, survived.

In 1838, Erik purchased a small farm property, Lotorp, Sankarby, and five years later, he sold it and moved his family to northern Halsingland, where most of his followers lived. He bought Lumnas at Stenbo, four miles south of

Forsa, from Jon Olsson, whose son Olof had become an ardent Janssonist. With Stenbo as his base of operations, he held meetings in farmhouses at Trogsta, Akre, and Hamre.

Although no pictures of Jansson survive, he was described in court records in October 1845, at age thirty-seven, as being "of ordinary build, decently dressed in a blue broadcloth coat, with short, light brown hair, thin pale features with prominent cheekbones, straight, pointed nose, deep-set blue eyes, thin compressed lips, uncommonly long and broad teeth in the upper jaw."[2]

Women followers occasionally accompanied Jansson on his combination evangelical and wheat flour sales trips to Halsingland. This led to a scandal. On May 6, 1844, six members of the Delsbo church signed a statement alleging that Jansson had confessed in their presence that he had tried to seduce Karin Ersdotter, a twenty-seven-year-old Nyaker servant girl who had rejected his advances. Tried on these charges on November 18, 1845, Jansson denied any wrongdoing. Karin testified that Jansson made verbal sexual remarks to her, including wanting to get rid of his wife so he could marry her and give Karin a baby. In his autobiography, Jansson explained that although he was aware of Bos-Karin's desire for him, he had not been sexually tempted for the preceding "fourteen years," so "whatever was happening between us was her fault." Although feeling "natural desires," Jansson claimed that he "did not do what David did." Following the Scripture's admonitions, he killed his "fleshly desires. Bos-Karin, like Potiphar's wife, was frustrated in her lust for me and then she said it was my fault."[3]

The central doctrine of Erik Jansson's theology was the Perfectionist belief that it was possible for believers to lead sinless lives. Supporting his doctrine, Jansson cited 1 John 1:7, "If we walk in the light, as he is in the light, we have fellowship one with another and the blood of Jesus, his son, cleanseth us from all sin."

Jansson's major differences with the Swedish Lutheran Church were his condemnation of religious literature approved by the church including the writings of Luther and Arndt, and his teaching that believing Christians were without sin, or Perfect, and were incapable of sin. He felt his mission was to shatter the traditional distinction between forgiveness of sins and the achievement of holiness, which he saw as inseparable and simultaneous. The elect would not be striving for sinlessness, but would have achieved it. He foresaw a blessed community of those elect who had achieved perfection. This was an extremely controversial idea that led to a head-on collision with the established Lutheran Church's teachings on Justification by Faith and human sinfulness.

By 1845, the increase in the number of Jansson's followers now concerned the Reverend Mr. Hans Norborg, interim pastor of the Alfta church in Halsingland. In a letter to a county administrator published in the Stockholm newspaper *Aftonbladet* Pastor Norborg claimed that 250 of his parishioners had become Janssonists. The clergy of the Church of Sweden were blamed in a follow-up article for not countering the Janssonist threat. More moderate observers, however, commented that Janssonism was but one of other small religious groups such as Pietism and Herrnhutism that were deviating from Sweden's established Lutheran Church. Church officials adopted an attitude of passive tolerance toward these groups, which they assumed would be short lived.

Jansson, however, did not passively practice his religious beliefs. He and his disciples staged a well-attended dramatic book burning in Alfta in which the works of Luther, Arndt, and Norborg, an obscure assistant pastor in the Finnish church in Stockholm whose sermons had been published, were put to flames.

The book burning reflected the strong anti-intellectual streak that infused Janssonism. Rejecting all theological writing, Jansson urged his followers to read only the Bible. He was uneducated and had no respect for educated people, especially the Lutheran clergy who were university graduates. He said they did nothing but perform empty rituals and mouth theology by rote, whereas he was infused with the Holy Spirit and the wisdom of God.

In Sweden, Lutheranism was the state religion; offenses against the church were considered civil cases and were dealt with by local civil authorities. On April 15, 1844, in Langhedsby, Sheriff Holmdahl and a posse of forty men arrested Jansson, even though many followers protected him. Gunshots, fighting, and shouting ensued while Jansson hid in an attic. The sheriff's men broke through a chimney to find Jansson, who was imprisoned in Gävle.

At Jansson's preliminary trial, examinations by a medical doctor and a court chaplain were ordered. The physician's report described the thirty-five-year-old Jansson as "lean and of good stature, gifted with a lively imagination and infatuated by religious speculation, is in an ecstatic state of mind, bordering on partial insanity, with otherwise unimpaired mental faculties and without signs of physical defects." His ability to memorize, combine, and interpret Bible passages revealed to the examiner "more than ordinary powers of apprehension in an otherwise crude and uneducated person."[4] The clergyman's report found Jansson, with an inflated "sense of self-righteousness," deluded by his "doctrine of sinlessness and alleged call to preach the Gospel." [5]

The court dismissed Jansson, warning him to never return to Gävleborg. Ignoring the court, Jansson held meetings in Gävleborg that attracted larger crowds than ever. On October 28, at Lynas, he presided over a second book burning of catechisms and psalmbooks. A hostile crowd threw stones at the worshipers. The sheriff arrived, and Jansson was arrested, released, then rearrested.

Near Jansson's home at Stenbo, his followers held a third book burning on December 7, 1844. On December 22, he and fifteen followers, charged with resisting arrest and breaking the Sabbath, were imprisoned in Gävle until April 1845.

Throughout 1845, hostility grew to the Janssonists, whose meetings were routinely attacked by mobs of local people. Erik Jansson went into hiding after a price of thirty crowns had been put on his head. Despite many unprovoked violent assaults on the Janssonists, no charges were brought against their at-tackers because when the Janssonists left the Lutheran Church they also lost their citizenship and legal protection under the law.

In October 1845, Jansson submitted himself voluntarily for trial at Delsbo on charges that he had violated the Conventicle Edict, which forbade religious meetings without clergy. The court remanded Jansson to the custody of Gävle prison pending further investigation. While traveling to Gävle, a sympathetic guard, Sven Jacob Pira, warned Jansson that the authorities planned to have him killed in prison by another inmate. Jansson got word of this plot to Pehr Pehrsson, who with three other Janssonists ambushed the guards and kidnapped the prisoner. Other sympathizers spilled goat's blood on a nearby road and claimed that Jansson had been killed. Maja Stina Jansson claimed to be a widow and wore mourning clothes. Erik went into hiding.

The repeated official and unofficial harassment led to Jansson's decision that he and his followers should relocate in the United States. Olof Olsson and his wife were dispatched to America to find a safe haven for the religious group. They arrived in New York harbor in late December 1845 and spent that winter with Olof Gustaf Hedstrom, who had established a ministry on the Bethel ship *John Wesley*. In the spring, when the canals opened, Olsson traveled to Victoria, Illinois, where Jonas J. Hedstrom, Olof Hedstrom's brother, lived and farmed. With Jonas's help, Olsson selected land in Henry County for the Janssonists to purchase. The prairie property had rich fertile soil, running water, and a grove of trees.

Meanwhile, Jansson's belief that he was God's appointed messenger on earth turned the farmer and traveling salesman into a self-proclaimed Messiah with an inflated sense of mission. On the eve of his departure for the United States, Jansson wrote that he spoke for Christ, who "shall judge you on the last day, since he who despises me has despised God himself."[6]

Dressed in disguises, Jansson went to his followers and asked them to sell their possessions and come with him to the United States. In preparation for the trip to America, Maja Stina Jansson and their two children, Eric seven, and Mathilda three, traveled to Christiania, Norway, where, reunited with Erik, they boarded the first outgoing vessel bound for Copenhagen. The Janssons traveled under the passports of Mr. and Mrs. Eric Larson. From Copenhagen, they took a train to Hamburg and boarded a ship for Hull, England. They proceeded to Liverpool by rail and then sailed for New York. After their long journey, they reached New York in late March or early April 1846.

Jansson made converts while in New York, including the woman who would be his second wife, Sophia Pollock. When the Jansson family commenced their journey westward, Sophia and her husband traveled with them, as did two other women. Serving as translator, Sophia tutored the family in English. The Jansson party took a steamer to Albany, a canal boat to Buffalo, a propeller-driven boat through the Great Lakes to Chicago, a canal boat to Peru, and a horse and wagon to Victoria, Illinois. Arriving in July, they reunited with Olof

Olsson and stayed in Jonas Hedstrom's log cabin.

Of the estimated 1,500 to 4,000 Janssonists in Sweden, approximately 1,200 men, women, and children immigrated to Illinois. This first mass emigration from Sweden caused consternation among Swedish government officials. The immigrants sold all their property and put the funds in a common treasury.

The Swedish Janssonists were utopians whose dream was to purchase land with the money in their common treasury and build a city of God in which they could live and practice their religion without fear. Used to hard work and difficulty, they were not afraid to face the Illinois frontier. Adopting communalism in their American settlement was a practical step to ease their economic difficulties. Without communal resources, they would have been unable to pay their passage to America, buy land and animals, and build a settlement. Communalism resulted in a mutual sharing and dependency.

The Janssonists who joined the exodus to the United States were primarily agriculturists in the middle to lower ranges of the Swedish socioeconomic strata. According to an analysis of Swedish tax records done by Charles Nelson, 31 percent were peasants who owned their own farms, 8 percent were crofters who leased land, and over 12 percent were cottars, or farm laborers, who worked for others. Nearly 8 percent were tradesmen, 10 percent were nonagricultural workers, and 9 percent were commissioned and noncommissioned officers. Twenty percent of the immigrants were males over fifteen years of age in service[7]

Some Janssonist immigrants, discouraged by the difficult transatlantic journey in which several passengers died, chose to settle in New York or Chicago. Among those who stayed in Chicago was Erik Jansson's brother, Jan. Arriving in Henry County, Illinois in late fall 1846, the colonists were too late to plant crops. Jansson named the community Bishop Hill after his birthplace in Sweden, Biskopskulla. By the end of the year, there were 400 people at Bishop Hill. Housing consisted of log cabins erected by previous owners, along with twelve dugouts on both sides of the ravine, which had log sides and earthen backs with two windows in the front. The church was a log structure in the form of a cross covered with canvas and skins. In addition to being the site of morning and evening services and three services on Sunday, new arrivals often slept there. There were three adobe kitchens and eating halls.

During the first winter on the Illinois prairie, 1846–47, ninety-six people died. Because of the extreme difficulties they faced, the immigrants adopted celibacy. The residents of Bishop Hill were struggling to feed themselves; they did not wish to burden themselves with babies. In Sweden, the Janssonists had no prohibition against sex and marriage.

Bishop Hill's communalism and policy on celibacy was reflected in the living arrangements. Men and women sat in separate sections in church and at separate tables for meals. There were separate living quarters for men and women. Clothing was drawn from a common storeroom, and everyone dressed alike. Everyone participated in work assignments.

Bishop Hill

Jansson lifted the ban on marriage in June 1848, saying that marriage was in fact pleasing to God. How pleasing it was to women is another question, as Bishop Hill men were free to marry any women, and women had no voice in the matter. Over the next two months, fifty-nine couples were wed in simple ceremonies.

The Janssonist colony had a policy of voluntary entrance. Those who expressed a sincere wish to be holy and adhere to the communal lifestyle could join. Jansson was a charismatic leader, an inspiring preacher, and the undisputed ruler of the Bishop Hill colony. Under his rule, religious regulations were strictly enforced. Those who wished to leave the community were free to go, though they would first be denounced by Jansson. The other condition of withdrawal was forfeiture of the assets originally deposited in the colony. Disgruntled former colonists left with nothing. The justification was that the economic stability of the community was of primary importance.

Education consisted primarily of English language study. Although Jansson had promised that they would be able to speak English when they set foot on American soil, they learned, to their disappointment, that would not be the case. Half of the colony was illiterate. English classes were given for both children and adults. Colonists were eager to learn English and become Americans. A year and a half after his arrival, Jansson preached in English. Minutes of meetings were in both Swedish and English. Jansson's funeral service was conducted in English. In addition, men who were preparing to be missionaries received theological training. However, little Janssonist missionary activity actually occurred.

One of the first permanent buildings erected at Bishop Hill was the large white frame church that also contained living quarters on its lower floors. A building spurt ensued after a local man, Philip Mauk, taught the colonists in the summer of 1848 how to make kiln-dried brick using local clay. A brick bakery, brewery, and flour mill on Edwards Creeks were soon constructed. Bishop Hill grew into an attractive town plotted around a park with large, impressive dwellings and workshops built around it. Storehouses were built farther away. Trees lined the streets.

Meals, eaten in silence, began with grace by Erik Jansson and closed with prayers and hymns. Their diet was simple, consisting of soup, thin crispbread, and cornmeal mush, with occasional meat, poultry, and butter. Colonists drank a nonfermented drink called "svagdricka," a near beer, and on special occasions an alcoholic drink called "Number 6." They drank coffee and used tobacco. To feed hundreds of people, they frequently fasted on Sunday, more out of necessity than as a penitential expression.

Within five years, the town, with a population of 800, had become prosperous. The colonists were hardworking people as well as experienced farmers and skilled craftsmen. By 1850, the community included many carpenters, smiths, shoemakers, wheelwrights, tailors, a carriage builder, a miller, and a harness maker.

Farming was the community's major occupation. In the central Illinois rich soil, the Swedes grew Indian corn, broomcorn, and flax. They raised hogs, cattle, sheep, chickens, turkeys, and geese and had oxen and horses. They also ran a hotel for stagecoach travelers. The women of Bishop Hill used skills learned in Sweden to weave thousands of yards of linen cloth. The Janssonist settlement had a church, school, hotel, hospital, bakery, brewery, flour mill, dairy, tannery, brick kiln, hundreds of head of livestock, and 12,000 acres of fertile farmland. Hard work and a simple lifestyle led to economic prosperity.

Cholera, which had broken out sporadically in the Illinois and St. Louis, Missouri, areas since 1832, reached epidemic proportions in the spring of 1849. Norwegian converts, many of whom were ill when they arrived, carried the disease to Bishop Hill in July 1849. Jansson held strong beliefs on illness, which he said manifested a lack of faith. A holy person's body would not exhibit symptoms of disease. This belief resulted in sick individuals being exhorted to become holy rather than being treated medically. Cholera raged through the community until mid-September. Despite his beliefs, Jansson ordered colonists who were well to a colony farm. This did nothing to spare them. Jansson moved his own family to the colony fishing shacks on Arsenal Island near Davenport, but his wife succumbed to the disease.

After 200 Bishop Hill colonists died of cholera, Jansson yielded to their American neighbors' insistence that he get medical help. Dr. Robert D. Foster arrived, full of promises, but did little good for the patients. Gaining Jansson's confidence, he persuaded him to buy land and make investments with him. He also charged outrageous medical fees. For payment, Jansson signed a mortgage on the colony's inventories. When Foster demanded payment, Jansson had to forfeit, and the colony lost almost all of its possessions. Foster held a public auction in the fall of 1849, which included thirty pairs of oxen, eight pairs of horses, ninety-four calves, hogs, wagons, farm tools, grain, and food supplies.

The cholera epidemic exacted a devastating human and economic toll. In an effort to raise cash, two colonists were dispatched to Sweden in the spring of 1849 to collect money from the estates of sixty Janssonists who had drowned on the shipwrecked *Betty Catharina* the previous year. Olof Jonsson and Nils Hedin returned with $6,000. While they were gone, many discouraged colonists defected, settling in other parts of Illinois. In 1850, 550 people—100 men, 250 women, and 200 children—remained at Bishop Hill.

The death toll at Bishop Hill, which included the leader's wife, Maja Stina Jansson, struck a heavy blow at Jansson's credibility. Jansson attributed the epidemic to the satanic unbelief of the people, and, in a curious twist of logic, declared that the colony would be forgiven if he, Jansson, married again, thus restoring the spiritual mother of the colony. He married Anna Sophia Pollock Gabrielsson on September 16, 1849. It was Sophia's fourth marriage.

Jansson's paternal aunt, Anna Mattsdotter, a widow, and her three daughters were on one of the boatloads of Swedish Janssonists. One daughter stayed in Chicago, while Anna and her other two daughters, Charlotta and Sabina, settled in Bishop Hill. Anna died soon afterward. According to Swedish tradition, which assigned the responsibility of women and children to the eldest male family member, Erik assumed responsibility for Charlotta and Sabina.

In November 1849, Charlotta married John Root, who had arrived at Bishop Hill in 1848 by way of New Orleans and was said to be looking for a wife. Root was described as a handsome man with a military bearing and cultivated manner.

Charlotta would later claim that her husband signed a statement at the time of the marriage that if he were to lose his faith and want to leave the colony, she could remain behind. Root claimed there was no such document. In any case, Root never performed his share of colony work, and spent most of his time hunting.

After an extended absence, Root returned home and learned that his wife had borne him a son. Cholera was sweeping the colony, so Root decided to take his wife and son away, but Charlotta refused to leave. Root decided to force her and brought a friend, Daniel Stanley, to help him on March 2, 1850. When Charlotta again refused, the men grabbed the baby, and Charlotta followed. They hurriedly left the village.

When word of Root's action got out, twelve Bishop Hill men pursued the Root party on horseback. When they caught up with them, Charlotta was asked if she had left willingly. When she replied negatively, they brought mother and child back to the colony.

The next day Root swore out a writ for the arrest of Jansson and others, charging them with riot. Charlotta Root was subpoenaed as a witness and traveled to the court in Cambridge, Illinois. The case was dismissed because Root failed to appear in court. However, he was in Cambridge and took Charlotta and their son to Rock Island, then on to Chicago to the home of Charlotta's sister, Caroline, and her husband Pehr Ersson. Caroline notified her cousin, Jan Jansson, Erik's brother, about the arrival of the Roots. When Root was away from the house, Jan whisked Charlotta and her child back to Bishop Hill.

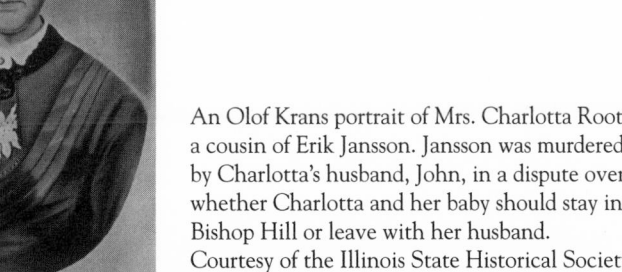

An Olof Krans portrait of Mrs. Charlotta Root, a cousin of Erik Jansson. Jansson was murdered by Charlotta's husband, John, in a dispute over whether Charlotta and her baby should stay in Bishop Hill or leave with her husband.
Courtesy of the Illinois State Historical Society.

169

The furious Root considered Erik Jansson an enemy who had his wife under his spell. He felt thoroughly justified in taking his wife wherever he wanted without Jansson's interference. He gathered a crowd of sympathetic, unruly friends who accompanied him to Bishop Hill on March 26 to get Charlotta. When they couldn't find her, they returned the next night, threatening to burn the town. They forced all the men into the church basement and the women and children into the hospital. When no resistance was offered, they let the people return to their homes. The following night some haystacks and outlying buildings were burned.

Meanwhile, Erik Jansson was hiding under the floor of a farming outpost near the village called Sor Stuga. He, his wife Sophia, Charlotta and her son, and six men decided to avoid the life-threatening mob by fleeing to St. Louis. There Charlotta swore out an affidavit attesting that she had not been kidnapped by the colonists, that she had returned to Bishop Hill of her own free will, and that she did not want to return to her husband because of his violent temper and her fear for her life. The affidavit was sent to the Illinois governor, Augustus C. French, in an attempt to secure protection from the mob that repeatedly threatened the colony. After three weeks in St. Louis, mob activities subsided, and Jansson and his party returned home. Jansson was notified that he must appear in Henry County Circuit Court in relation to several court cases.

Anticipating trouble, Jansson preached on May 12 on a scriptural passage that seemed to relate to his death. "[T]he time of my departure is come. I have fought the good fight, I have finished my course. I have kept the faith; henceforth there is laid up for me the crown of righteousness."[8] During Communion, he announced, "I shall not drink henceforth of this Fruit of the vine until that day when I drink with you in my Father's kingdom."[9]

When Richard Mascall arrived on Monday, May 13, with a horse and buggy to drive Jansson to the courthouse at Cambridge, Jansson said to him, "Well, Mr. Mascall, will you stop the bullet for me today?"[10]

Mascall did not stop any bullets, as the attack came not on the road but in the courthouse during the noon recess. Only Jansson and the clerk of the court, S. P. Brainard, remained in the second-floor courtroom when John Root rushed in shouting Jansson's name. Verbal exchanges in Swedish followed. Then the clerk heard Jansson exclaim, "A sow should be good enough for John Root!" With that, Root drew a pistol, firing twice at Jansson striking him in the shoulder and heart. He fell and died some five minutes later. Jansson was forty-one years old.

Root was arrested, and that afternoon the grand jury indicted him for Erik Jansson's murder. The next day, May 14, Root was arraigned on the murder charge and pleaded not guilty, alleging self-defense. He claimed that Jansson had threatened to kill him on several occasions. His attorney, Julius Manning, indicated that the defense would prove that Jansson's intense and prolonged provocation had caused Root to yield to a sudden and violent impulse, but with no malice aforethought. Root was jailed at Toulon, Illinois.

Root not only struck a deathblow at Jansson but at the entire Bishop Hill community, which believed that the prophet would not die. Jansson's body was brought back to the colony. The colonists waited for the body to rise again on the third day, but that did not happen. A funeral was held in the colony church. At it, Sophia Jansson rose and placed her hands on the head of Andrew Berglund whom she declared would be the head of the colony until Erik Jansson's twelve-year-old son reached maturity. Berglund conducted the funeral service in English.

Because of the sensation in Henry County caused by Jansson's murder, John Root was granted a change of venue. He was transferred to the prison at Rock Island, and his trial began in September 1852 in the Knox County Circuit Court. Root's attorney, Julius Manning, argued that the shooting was a natural response of a husband whose wife's affections had been alienated by Erik Jansson. The jury agreed, finding Root guilty of manslaughter. He was given a two-year prison sentence. In May 1853, with her husband in prison at Alton, Illinois, Charlotta Root sued for divorce and custody of her two-year-old son, John, both of which she won.

Meanwhile, Root's friends were agitating for his release. Six hundred citizens of Rock Island signed a petition for Root's release, which was sent to Governor Matteson. Initially, the governor agreed to commute Root's sentence on the condition that he never return to Illinois. Lydia Matteson, the governor's daughter, delivered the good news to Root in the Alton prison. She found him in poor health and extremely distraught about being banished from Illinois. She begged her father to drop that condition, which he did. On March 7, 1854, Governor Matteson signed a pardon for Root. He moved to Rock Island, then Chicago, and died in 1856.

Jansson, who claimed to govern with Divine authority, was the personal force that held the Bishop Hill community together. His rule was autocratic. His untimely death only four years after founding the Illinois settlement was devastating to the believers, yet the colony did not end then. In fact, the following years were ones of financial success.

Jonas Olsson and other men had been in California prospecting for gold for the colony when they learned of Jansson's death. Olsson asserted his leadership on his return. Under Olsson, the colony reached its height of economic prosperity. Highly profitable markets for broomcorn were found in Peoria and Chicago. The added income enabled the colony to increase its farm holdings from 1,420 acres in 1850, to 8,028 acres by 1855, and to 12,000 acres by 1860.

The colony also embarked on several major construction projects, including Big Brick, then the largest structure in the United States west of Chicago. The three-story building was 45 feet wide and 200 feet long, with ninety-six rooms and a basement. It burned down in 1928. Because Bishop Hill was a communal society, property was owned by the group, and people lived and ate together in large units rather than in small family homes. Each room in Big Brick housed a family, although larger families might have more than one room.

Big Brick had two large dining rooms, in which several hundred people could eat at one time, as well as a kitchen in the cellar. One dining room was for adults, with separate tables for men and women, the other for children.

Other buildings included a carpenter and wagon shop constructed in 1852, a bakery and brewery and a meat storage house in 1853, the Steeple Building and the colony store in 1854, a dairy building in 1855, an administration building in 1856, a blacksmith shop in 1857, and a school building in 1860.

In January 1853, the colony incorporated under the leadership of an elected seven-member board of trustees. According to its regulations, the Corporation's business was to be "manufacturing, milling," and "mechanical business, agriculture and merchanting."[11] The regulations of incorporation also set forth the colony's aims and mode of operations. Its property and proceeds were to be a common fund that, under the board of trustees, would provide for the needs of its members. It would be used to care for the aged, infirm, and sick members of the community. It would provide for the burial of the deceased and for education of its children. The trustees were commissioned to transact any business necessary for the colony's "prosperity, happiness and usefulness."[12]

Although the trustees enacted no regulations governing the colony's religious affairs, they banned marriage and introduced celibacy in 1854. This action generated substantial dissent. They also enacted a policy of expulsion without compensation for violators of the community rules.

The trustees, guided by Olof Jonsson, began investing in railway stock, bonds, land, and real estate in nearby Galva and in Chicago. The Crimean War created great demand for grain, which strengthened their economy. The war-generated boom, however, was followed by bust. In the 1857 depression that followed the Crimean War, at least $98,000 in railroad and bank shares, notes, and personal accounts became worthless. These large economic losses led to lack of confidence in the trustees. One vocal critic, E. U. Norberg, was expelled from the colony. Norberg applied to the Illinois state legislature to get the bylaws of the community cancelled and the property divided among its members. Norberg's attempt failed. Norberg was reinstated in 1860, when many colonists, increasingly critical of the trustees' economic policies, called for ending communalism.

By February 1860, a decision had been reached to divide the property. Gradually, the colonists learned that the trustees had not fully disclosed the amount of the debt and losses. In 1861, Bishop Hill ceased to be communal. Land and property were divided among the men, with those thirty-five or older receiving a full share and those under thirty-five a half share. In 1868, Norberg sued the colony trustees. The suit did not end until 1879 and substantially increased the society's debt, resulting in more animosity among the people.

After the colony's dissolution, Bishop Hill's settlers went their own way. Many colonists joined the local Methodist Church, while others joined the Second Adventist Church. Sophia Jansson moved with her son to the Shaker colony in Pleasant Hill, Kentucky, where she resided briefly. Returning to Illinois, she operated a boardinghouse in Galva. She died in the county poorhouse in 1888 and was buried near Erik Jansson's grave.

Many former colonists remained at Bishop Hill, where their descendants still reside, engaged in farming or in business.

Tour

In the century after communal dissolution, the buildings in Bishop Hill gradually fell into disrepair. A movement to restore the Swedish settlement began in the 1940s. Of the twenty major colony buildings erected in the 1840s and 1850s, thirteen remain, some of which surround the city park. Restoration by the state of Illinois and the Bishop Hill Heritage Association has returned several buildings to their 1861 appearance. Other buildings are used as shops, which sell antiques, crafts, and Scandinavian imports.

In 1947, Bishop Hill became an Illinois State Memorial and is now a National Historic Landmark and a State Historic Site. The Illinois Historic Preservation Agency owns and maintains the Colony Church, Colony Hotel, Village Park, and the Bishop Hill Museum. The Bishop Hill Heritage Association, a nonprofit corporation interested in preservation, owns six of the original colony buildings and two postcolony buildings.

The 1848 **Colony Church**, a State Historic Site, was the community's first permanent building and was used for worship and as a residence. The church is a three-story white frame gambrel-roofed building with two sets of outside stairs. The unheated sanctuary on the second floor, which could seat 1,000 people, is simply designed. Pale blue walls contrast with pews made of native black walnut and turned maple rungs. The pulpit panels were painted to resemble marble. A center divider separates the men's pews on the west side and the women's and children's pews on the east. Reproduction wood and wrought-iron chandeliers are reminiscent of brass chandeliers in Swedish cathedrals. Services, which often lasted two hours, were held twice each weekday, and three times on Sunday.

The first floor and basement contained ten one-room apartments on each floor. Each apartment was home to a family who used it primarily for sleeping. Cooking, eating, laundry, and bathing facilities were in other buildings.

The Colony Church was restored to its 1848 appearance in the 1960s, and the sleeping rooms contain exhibits related to the early settlers. **The Sweden They Left** depicts life in Sweden around 1850. Another room focuses on **The Immigration** and the route taken from Sweden to Illinois. Items brought from Sweden to Bishop Hill are displayed, including shoes, baskets, wooden and metal boxes, pots, Bibles, coins, and photographs of their homes. There are displays of the tools used by the colonists, as well as the construction process used in building the Colony Church. Many Bishop Hill men served in the Civil War and were in Company D Fifty-seventh Illinois Infantry. Their uniforms, weapons, and drums are exhibited.

If Bishop Hill offered nothing more than its collection of Olof Krans paintings, it would still be well worth a visit. Over a hundred paintings of early settlers, buildings, landscapes, and pioneer farming practices painted by Krans vividly portray the colonists' lifestyle. Certainly an outstanding feature of Bishop Hill, Krans has been called one of America's finest folk artists. Krans's paintings are displayed in the **Bishop Hill Museum**, built in 1988.

Krans's mesmerizing portraits of the colonists were probably done from photographs. The subjects' pale blue eyes, which seem to follow viewers as they move through the room, are a distinctive though unsettling feature of Krans's portraits. The bearded, unsmiling men are typically dressed in black suits and white shirts, and the women wear dark dresses.

Krans was the son of Eric and Beata Olsson, who came from the parish of Nora, Uppland. He was born in Sweden on November 2, 1838, and was twelve when his family settled in Bishop Hill. In his youth, he worked as an ox-boy, a painter in the church and hotel, and a blacksmith's assistant. He fought in the Civil War, reaching the rank of sergeant. After the war, he adopted the name Krans. He worked in Galesburg and Galva as a painter, decorator, and painter of advertisements and theater scenery. His remarkable collection of Bishop Hill scenes and portraits was done in his sixties and seventies, from memory.

The 1854 **Steeple Building** is a three-story Greek Revival stucco-covered brick structure that was built as a hotel but used as a residence for colonists. A two-story octagonal wooden cupola houses a clock, built by Sven Bjorklund, Lars Soderquist, and P. O. Blomberg, with four faces, each of which has one hand that marks the hours only.

The Steeple Building houses the **Bishop Hill Heritage Museum**, which has exhibits on the immigration of Swedish people to America, lighting, textiles, clocks and watches, furniture, wood stoves, and brooms, as well as the **Archives and Research Library** for the Bishop Hill Heritage Association. It also serves as the **Visitors' Center** and an orientation film is shown.

The **Bjorklund Hotel**, a State Historic Site, was built in 1852 as a two-story brick residence but was converted to a hotel when Bishop Hill became the overnight stop on the stage route between Peoria and Rock Island. A series of additions began in 1857 with a barroom on the first floor and the hotelkeeper's quarters on the second. Next, a kitchen and second-story quarters were added, making the building U-shaped. A third floor that included a ballroom and a large tower was the last addition.

The hotel was owned by the colony and managed by a noted clock maker, Sven Bjorklund. After the communal period of Bishop Hill ended, Bjorklund became the owner of the hotel, which he operated until his death. The Bjorklund family ran the hotel until the 1920s, when it was converted to a private residence.

The first floor of the hotel and a bedroom on the second floor are open to the public. A clock made by Bjorklund still keeps time in the men's sitting room. Other furnishings include an original cherry table, beds, and a bureau. The kitchen has a bake oven with a forty-loaf capacity, a dry sink, a cupboard with dishes, cooking utensils, and coffee bean roasters. Baskets, pottery, jars, and wooden boxes are on display in the pantry.

Some original buildings are privately owned and are now well-stocked craft and antique shops. The **Colony Store** was the center of the colony's commerce with its neighbors. It sold shoes, clothes, cloth, liquor, medicine, lumber, wagons, and harnesses and provided millwork, grain grinding, and blacksmithing. Today the store sells Swedish imports, Bishop Hill craft items, and books about the colony.

At the **Blacksmith Shop**, built in 1857, hardware for wagons was made. A ramp at the back of the building led to the area where the wagons were assembled. The wagons were then lowered down the ramp and taken to the carpentry and paint shops.

The blacksmith shop is now a craft center with handmade items for sale, including handwoven shawls, blankets, and coverlets. Hand-thrown pottery and brooms are available in the 1882 **Poppy Barn** owned by the Heritage Association, while baskets and wooden objects are found in the **Cobbler Shop**. The **carpenter and paint shop**, built in 1852, is now a small grocery store and post office.

In the **Bishop Hill Cemetery**, a white marble monument marks Erik Jansson's grave. The ninety-six colonists who died during the first winter are buried in **Red Oak Cemetery** three miles west of town. The site of the dugouts is along the upper edge of the ravine that extends northwest at the north end of Park Street.

Several restaurants are open for lunch only and serve Swedish-American food.

Special events at Bishop Hill include *Valpurgis* and Spring Premier in April; Counted Cross-Stitch and Quilt Shows in May; Midsummer Festival and Sundays in the Park Concerts in June; an Antique Show in July; *Sommarmarknad* (Summer Market) in August; Old Settlers Day, *Jordbruksdagarna* (Agricultural Days), and Art Show in September; *Julmarknad* (Christmas Market) in late November and early December Lucia Nights (Festival of Lights) in mid- December; and *Julotta* (nondenominational candlelight service) on Christmas Day.

Lauer Meeting House in 1934. Courtesy of the Library of Congress.

AMANA COLONIES
1855–1932, Amana, Iowa
NR

ADDRESS: Amana Heritage Society, P.O. Box 81, Amana, IA 52203; and/or Amana Colonies Convention and Visitors Bureau, P.O. Box 303, Amana, IA 52203

TELEPHONE: Heritage Society, (319) 622-3567; Visitors Bureau, (319) 622-3828, (800) 245- 5465

LOCATION: In southeast Iowa, 100 miles east of Des Moines; 21 miles southwest of Cedar Rapids; 15 miles northwest of Iowa City; I- 80 Exit 225, then north on US 151 to US 6; five colonies are on Highway 220, and two colonies are on US 6.

OPEN: Village shops, restaurants, and accommodations are open year-round. The Museum of Amana History is open Monday–Saturday, 10:00 a.m.–5:00 p.m., and Sunday, noon–5:00 p.m., from mid-April to mid-November. The Communal Kitchen and Cooper Shop Museum are open Monday–Saturday, 9:00 a.m.–5:00 p.m., and Sunday, noon–5:00 p.m., May–October. The Communal Agricultural Exhibit is open Monday–Saturday, 10:00 a.m.–5:00 p.m., May–September.

ADMISSION: Museum of Amana History: adults, $2.50; children, $1.00. Communal Kitchen and Cooper Shop Museum adults, $1.50; children, $.75. Communal Agricultural Exhibit: adults, $1.00; children, $.50. Combination tickets and group rates available.

RESTAURANTS: Amana: Ronneburg Restaurant; Ox Yoke Inn; Amana Barn Restaurant; Brick Haus Restaurant; Colony Inn; Colony Cone. South Amana: Colony Market Place Restaurant. Homestead: Homestead Kitchen; Bill Zuber's Restaurant. Middle Amana: Pizza Factory and Grill. Little Amana: Little Amana Bratwurst Haus; Seven Villages Restaurant.

SHOPS: Antique, craft, wool, furniture, meat, and wine and cheese stores throughout the Amana colonies.

FACILITIES: Seven related villages with museums, shops, and restaurants.

OVERVIEW

Seven Amana colonies were established in 1855 by over a thousand German immigrants who were members of a Pietist Protestant Church or denomination called the Community of True Inspiration. Leaving Germany in the 1840s to escape religious persecution, they initially settled in Ebenezer, New York. Needing more land, they looked west and selected an 18,000-acre site in Iowa's Iowa River valley.

Amana, selected from a biblical reference, means remaining faithful. The Inspirationists are a distinct religious group and should not be confused with other denominations such as the Amish or the Shakers.

Amana originally functioned as a communal theocracy; the administration of economic and religious affairs was intertwined. Christian Metz (1793–1867), the leader of the Inspirationists, was a *Werkzeuge* or inspired one, a human instrument, like the ancient prophets, through whom God spoke. Their belief in continuing revelation, through divine inspiration, was a tenet that separated the Community of True Inspiration from other Pietist sects.

The German-speaking residents of Amana dressed plainly and attended church services eleven times a week. They married and lived in nuclear families though children were placed in day care at age two so mothers could return to the work force. Communal houses, which resembled large single-family dwellings, usually accommodated four families or individuals. They contained no kitchens or dining rooms as cooking was done in communal kitchens, which each served about forty people who ate their hearty meals together. The community prospered through agriculture and industry, including the woolen mills whose flannel and blankets became well known.

In 1932, the residents at Amana voted to end communalism. Descendants of the original settlers who remain in the Amana villages continue to practice the same religion.

The seven Amana Colonies constitute a very unique outdoor museum village, with fine collections of original furnishings and artifacts displayed in the restored museum buildings. The layout of the towns remains unchanged with the possible exception of Amana, which is the most heavily visited by tourists. The Amana Heritage Society has restored buildings in three of the original seven colonies. Crafts, architecture, and institutions reflect their German heritage. Although many original Amana buildings are private residences, others are used as bed-and- breakfasts, craft shops, restaurants, and food stores.

HISTORY

Amana, Iowa, was founded in 1855 by a communal group of German immigrants who were members of a Christian pietistic sect called Inspirationists. The sect, known as the Community of True Inspiration, had its roots in German Radical Pietism, a branch of Christian Pietism, which was a religious reform movement in mid-seventeenth century Europe. Pietists, who were opposed to the strict dogmatism of both the Protestant and Catholic Churches, advocated a simpler, primitive, apostolic form of Christianity.

German Pietism represented a return to a personalized religion emphasizing a sincere, heartfelt attitude of piety and humility aided by an earnest study of, and belief in, the Holy Scriptures. The Pietist movement was primarily composed of lay people of the working classes, especially craftspeople, domestic servants, and peasants.

Many pietistic ideas derived from the writings of Philipp Spener and August Herman Francke, who are considered the founders of Pietism. Radical Pietism, based heavily on the writings of Jakob Boehme, added elements of mysticism, including divine inspiration. In this phenomenon, the Holy Spirit delivered the word of God either verbally or in writing through human instruments, called *Werkzeuge,* who received messages in a trance-like state.

In 1714, August Friedrich Pott, a native of Halberstadt, Saxony, received the power of inspiration. Pott's preaching and that of his two brothers strongly affected Johann Frederick Rock and Eberhard Ludwig Gruber, who were both

Christian Metz's Community of True Inspiration

from Württenberg. The Community of True Inspiration was founded by a small group including Rock, Gruber and his son, Johanna Melchior, Gottfried Neumann, and Johann Tobias Pott at Himbach, near Marienborn, in November 1714. With the exception of the elder Gruber, all of these individuals possessed the gift of inspiration.

Strange, violent bodily movements often preceded a revelation by a *Werkzeuge*. During the revelation, the instrument, whose eyes were closed, frequently changed position, going from walking to kneeling to shaking or laying prone on the floor. Written revelations were called *Einsprachen*, while spoken revelations were *Aussprachen*. A person called a recorder documented these revelations in writing. The style and tone of the revelations were biblical.

A revelation was a spontaneous, involuntary phenomenon. The utterances given to the spiritual head while in a trance-like state were believed to be the word of God given through a human voice, and had the moral weight of Bible passages. All affairs of any importance to the community were governed by revelations, and it was the duty of the membership to obey the commands thus delivered to them.

The creed of the Inspirationists was based on the Bible, the inspired statements of the *Werkzeuge*, and two sets of rules drafted by the Grubers. Eberhard Ludwig Gruber (1665–1728), a Lutheran pastor and Protestant scholar with a doctorate of theology, wrote the "Twenty-one Rules for the Examination of Daily Life," a fundamental ethical code.

In July 1716, his son, Johann Adam Gruber received a revelation known as the "Twenty-Four Rules of True Godliness," which dealt with the spiritual devotion of the Inspirationists. These rules condemned idolatry, lying, hypocrisy, greed, prejudice, impudence, boisterousness, and contact with sinners of the world, and they encouraged harmony with fellow members, obedience to the elders, and a well-kept covenant with God.

Johann Friedrich Rock, a saddler born in 1678 in Oberwelder, Württemberg, was an early *Werkzeuge* in the Community of True Inspiration. The son of a Lutheran pastor, he became active in Pietist groups in Halle, Prussia, around 1701, after recovering from a serious illness. He converted to the Inspirationists and became one of the community's original founders.

Inspirationist membership declined after Rock's death in 1749 as no *Werkzeuge* replaced him for the next sixty years. The small groups of Inspirationists who remained in northern France, Switzerland, and Germany were finally reinvigorated by a revival, which began in 1817, led by Christian Metz and Barbara Heinemann, the principal leaders in a new generation of inspired ones. That year, Michael Krausert, a tailor journeyman from Strasbourg, reported his mystical experience to Inspirationist elders at Bischweiler, in Alsace, and was declared truly inspired.

Christian Metz was one of the young people who attended prayer meetings in Ronneburg and heard Krausert speak. Metz was born at Neuwied on December 30, 1793, the fifth of seven children. Soon after his birth, the Metz family moved to Ronneburg. Christian was from an Inspirationist family. His great-grandfather Johann Georg Metz was visited by Johann Gruber in April 1716. His grandfather Jakob Metz, a stocking weaver, was an elder. Christian's father, Wilhelm Metz, a tanner, and his mother, Johannette Catherine Cassell, were Inspirationists. Johannette and her two brothers were disinherited by their parents for joining the movement.[1] When he was fifteen, Christian Metz was apprenticed to a cabinetmaker who was an Inspirationist elder.

Metz recounted that though he was guilty of sin, influenced by Krausert's revelations, he had experienced "*Busskampf*" to such a degree that, overcome with weeping, he had repented. This repentance (*Reue* and *Busse*) was followed by a sense of inner peace.[2] Subsequently, Krausert received a revelation directing Christian Metz to accompany him to Homburgshausen to strengthen the faithful there.

In 1818, Barbara Heinemann, an illiterate servant girl from Hermersweiler, Alsace, became inspired. Twenty-three-year- old Barbara received her first spoken inspiration in Bergzabern, in the Palatinate, on Christmas 1818. She joined the Inspirationists, and in the spring of 1819, prophesied that Metz would receive the power of revelation.[3] In May 1819, Metz's first revelation occurred.

Leadership problems developed between the three inspired ones. Krausert and Heinemann received revelations that led to their charging each other with false inspiration. Metz emerged as the leader when Krausert, admitting that he no longer was inspired, was ordered to leave the community in the summer of 1819. Metz then lost his gift of revelation, which he interpreted as a punishment for his participation in the quarrels.[4] He regained it January 20, 1823, in Strasbourg.

Just prior to her marriage to George Landmann in 1823, Barbara Heinemann lost her gift of inspiration. She too was banished from the congregation for her worldly actions—that is, getting married. She regained her gift of prophecy in 1849 when she was fifty-four years old and remained inspired until her death in 1883 at age eighty-eight.

Metz and his followers preached and attracted converts in the years after Heinemann and Krausert's departures. Inspirationist theology directly opposed the state Lutheran Church in that members refused to serve in the military or send their children to state schools. During the 1820s, religious persecution of the sect intensified so that in the early 1830s, Metz directed his widely scattered followers to live together on several rented estates in Hesse, a province known for its political tolerance. By 1840, 350 to 400 members lived on these estates, while another 600 were spread throughout Germany, Alsace, and Switzerland.[5]

Persecution of the Inspirationists by the German states continued, particularly in regard to their schools, which were not under state control, and their refusal to take oaths. Metz received a revelation on July 21, 1842, that instructed him that the Lord's people "could no longer abide in a land" whose rulers "were so indifferent to the welfare of those who were performing His work." The Lord would lead them to a "free land," which would be "their future residence."[6] Subsequent revelations informed the Inspirationists that they were to go "over deep waters" to *"eine neue Heimat,"* a new home in America, "a land free from persecution."[7] Further, Wilhelm Noe, G. A. Weber, Gottlieb Ackermann, and Christian Metz were to undertake a preliminary journey to find a location for the community.

The Inspirationists' advance party sailed from Bremerhaven on the *New York* on September 18, 1842, arriving in New York harbor October 26. They intended to purchase government land that was selling for $1.25 per acre. A New York land agent recommended property in Chatauqua County, New York, but when the party arrived in Buffalo, they learned of the possibility of acquiring acreage on the Seneca Indian Reservation which was about to be vacated.

After looking at both the Seneca and Chatauqua properties, the Inspirationists selected the reservation property. They purchased 5,000 acres from the Ogden Company, which had acquired the Seneca land, at $10 an acre. This was a much higher price than they had originally calculated and caused genuine concern about the community's ability to raise so high a sum.

The establishment of a communal economy by the Inspirationists was clearly related to their need to pool assets to pay for their American property. In February 1843, Metz wrote a thirty-five-point document introducing communalism and detailing the organization of the community in America. The land and buildings were to be owned by all members, though four members were listed as titleholders. Members would surrender their property and money to provide a capital fund. They would work for wages and would buy food from the society. Kitchens, gardens, and houses would be provided. This plan was to be effective for a trial period of two years. If a member left within that period, he was to receive his investment with interest.

Metz received approval of this document through a revelation. The communal arrangement marked a definite change from the economic arrangements in the *Gemeinde* in Germany. There a private enterprise economy functioned with each member earning his own income, resulting in wide financial variations.

Negotiations with the Ogden Company and the Seneca Indians dragged on so long that the Inspirationists began looking at land in Ohio. During their Ohio trip, Metz and Ackermann visited the religious community at Zoar, Ohio, where communalism had resulted in economic success. Carl Ludwig Mayer, Zoar's representative in business affairs, was converted to Inspirationism by the visitors and joined them in August 1843. (See the chapter on Zoar.)

In April 1843, as the Seneca Indians finally began leaving the reservation, the advance party and the first fifty Inspirationists from Germany settled on the land. Because the Ogden Company had not dealt honestly with the Native Americans nor obtained clear title from them, the Inspirationists had title problems until 1846 when the government forced the Seneca Indians to move to another reservation.

Despite the confused situation, 350 Inspirationists immigrated to the western New York settlement, named Ebenezer, in 1843. Two years later, a community of 800, which constituted approximately one-half to three-fourths of the Inspirationists, owned 9,000 acres of land. By 1850, the population reached 1,200.

At Ebenezer, religious and economic interests were intertwined in a communal theocracy. Although communalism was originally a pragmatic solution to the problem of obtaining enough land to support an 800-member community, it soon assumed the force of a religious tenet. By 1854, Christian Metz, in an inspired sermon, stated that "eternal disgrace, shame, and disfavor" would befall any who sought to dissolve the communitarian compact.[8] At the end of the two-year trial period, a constitution that permanently continued the communal system was approved by the membership in January 1846. Under this constitution, workers would not receive wages nor have to buy food but would receive an annual allowance to use in making purchases from the village store.

In 1874, on a visit to Amana, Charles Nordhoff commented that the Inspirationists "had evidently thought pretty thoroughly upon the subject of communal living; and knew how to display to me what appeared to them its advantages in their society: the absolute equality of all men—as God made us; the security for their families; the abundance of food; and the independence of a master."[9]

In April 1846, the community was incorporated under New York law as the Village of Ebenezer. A second act incorporated the land as a road and school district under the name The Trustees of the Village of Ebenezer. All community business was to be transacted by these trustees.

Four villages with their own craft shops, kitchens, bakery, meetinghouse, farm, houses, meat market, school, and store were founded in New York. They were named Mittel (Middle) Ebenezer, Ober (Upper) Ebenezer, Nieder (Lower) Ebenezer, and Neue (New) Ebenezer. There were two other settlements across the Canadian border. These German immigrants engaged in both agriculture and industry, operating a sawmill, woolen mill, soap works, and vinegar mill. The large number of weavers who became Inspirationists brought to the community the skills to operate woolen mills in New York and in Iowa. Amana woolen goods would become well known and highly regarded commodities throughout the country.

The governing structure of the Community of True Inspiration that Metz devised consisted of the *Werkzeuge* at the top, a position Metz later shared with Barbara Heinemann Landmann when her gift of inspiration returned in July 1849. Next came a thirteen-member board of trustees, or the Great Council, which consisted of elders who represented each village and who were elected annually. The trustees were responsible for the general economic affairs of their entire church-state, while elders in each village were responsible for its religious affairs and day-to-day operations. The elders managed larger businesses and hired workers.

Christian Metz's Community of True Inspiration

By the 1840s, central and western New York were no longer a part of the American frontier but had well-established towns, including Rochester, Albany, Syracuse, and nearby Buffalo. From 1825 to 1850, a period of intense religious revivalism swept upstate New York, which sparked so many religious fires that it was dubbed the "burned-over district." Charles Finney, a revivalist preacher, influenced John Humphrey Noyes, founder of the Oneida community. Joseph Smith, founder of the Mormons, discovered the prophetic golden plates in this region. The Inspirationists were one of many religious sects, including Shakers, Mormons, and Oneidans, living in that region of New York.

In 1854, Metz, guided by revelations, decided that he and his followers should leave Ebenezer because the 1,200-member sect required more land for agriculture. Land prices were prohibitive in New York. Although the Inspirationist community had no criminal activity, the proximity of Buffalo with its vices and materialism presented a temptation about which the leaders constantly warned their members, especially the younger ones.

In June 1855, a party of Inspirationists purchased 3,300 acres of congressional land in Iowa for $1.25 per acre and an additional 4,000 acres from homesteaders for prices ranging from $3.00 to $17.00 per acre. Metz, who was in his early sixties and in poor health, was not a member of the Iowa advance party. He came to Iowa for the first time in April 1856. The timberland and pastureland on the Iowa River in Iowa County, Iowa, was more distant from the corrupting influence of the city than Ebenezer.

The Iowa acquisition put a great financial strain on the Ebenezer community, which was having trouble selling that property. The capital from New York was needed to finance the Iowa community. Metz, in chronic poor health, had to shuttle back and forth between the two communities to resolve myriad problems.

The Civil War caused Metz much anxiety. Inspirationists were pacifists, and Metz worried about the possibility of conscription. As with many of Metz's other worries, he received revelations concerning the Civil War.

On December 9, 1860, Metz received a revelation, addressed to the president of the United States, to the Senate and House of Representatives and the governors of the states of the Union. Metz was also directed to have the message translated into English by Carl Mayer and forward it to the country's leaders. The revelatory message implored the national leaders to abandon their prejudices and offer "the hand of peace and of union" to each other. Unless the nation's leaders conceded "justice to each State" and allowed the people to enjoy their rights and deal with each other peacefully, "the destroyer" would "drench the land with blood."[10]

The message was sent to President James Buchanan who replied in a letter to Carl Mayer that a day of fasting and prayer had been arranged for January 4, 1861. Unsatisfied with Buchanan's response and hoping for issuance of the revelation as a public proclamation, Mayer went to Washington and showed it to many senators and representatives without success.

Amana Colonies

Metz's fears about conscription were well founded. The Amana Inspirationists wrote to federal authorities in August 1862 explaining their pacifism and requesting exemption as conscientious objectors. The request was ignored. In the winter of 1862, sixteen Amana men were drafted a short time after Congress passed a bill allowing conscientious objectors to pay $300 in lieu of serving in the army. The community paid $4,800 to the U.S. government for its members to avoid conscription in the U.S. Army.

By December 1864, the New York property had been sold and the last group from Ebenezer had joined Amana. Over a thousand members moved from Ebenezer to Amana.

Metz's health continued to deteriorate; he died July 24, 1867, and was buried in the cemetery on the western edge of the village of Amana.

The new home of the Community of True Inspiration in Iowa was named Amana, which meant remaining faithful and was taken from the Song of Solomon, "Go forth, from the heights, the hills of Amana." The move began in 1855, with small parties resettling in Iowa over the next decade. Six villages were established named Amana, West Amana, Sud (South) Amana, Amana vor der Hohe (High Amana), Ost (East) Amana, and Mittel (Middle) Amana. A seventh village, Homestead, was purchased because of its railroad terminal. Soon Amana's land holdings increased to 26,000 acres.

Following a European village pattern, houses, craft shops, and barns were clustered together surrounded by agricultural fields and pastureland. Villages typically had a blacksmith shop, cabinetmaker's shop, general store, post office, school, church, kitchen houses, bakery, dairy, and wine cellar. Each village had a farm manager responsible for cultivating that village's land. Corn, oats, wheat, hay, and potatoes were grown. A canal dug in the 1860s provided waterpower to the sawmills, gristmills and woolen mills.

Amana houses resembled large one-family dwellings rather than communal structures. Three or four families occupied each communal house, which was typically a two-story building of unpainted wood, brick, or sandstone. Built without kitchens or dining rooms, these houses usually had two two-room suites on each floor with a family or individual in each suite. Extended families of relatives often shared a house. Vegetable and flower gardens were near each house, and trellises for grapevines were attached to the sides of most homes.

Interior walls were whitewashed light blue. Rooms were heated with iron stoves. Furnishings belonged to the occupants and consisted of heirlooms as well as new furniture purchased from Amana cabinetmakers. Acceptable decorations were religious images and mottoes in illuminated script.

Houses were grouped in neighborhoods served by communal kitchens and dining rooms. Groups of thirty to forty people were assigned to each kitchen to eat their five daily meals. Breakfast was at 6:00 a.m. followed by a small lunch of cheese, bread, and coffee at 8:30 a.m. An 11:30 a.m. dinner was followed by lunch at 2:30 p.m. and supper at 6:30 p.m. Meals were eaten in silence. There were separate tables for men, for women and children, for the elders, and for the hired help. Both boys and girls ate with their mothers until age fourteen when the boys moved to the men's table. Food was delivered in baskets to those who were ill or aged.[11]

Members of the Inspirationist Church were organized into three orders, with the first or highest rank populated by church elders, many unmarried adults, and married adults who abstained from sexual relations. The second order contained celibate adults who were less spiritually advanced than those in the first order, while the lowest order was comprised of children and married adults who bore children.

The three orders indicate Inspirationist attitudes toward marriage and sexuality. Although marriage was permitted, celibacy was viewed as a special gift from God. Unmarried males who were elders or teachers lost their positions if they married unless a divine inspiration came to their rescue. Marriages had to be approved by the elders, who usually prescribed a one- to two-year engagement while the young man and woman lived in different villages. A woman could marry at twenty and a man at twenty-four.

Nordhoff, quoting the early theologian, Eberhard Gruber, portrays a rather amusing picture of the Inspirationist view of sexuality:

> The sex, I believe, is not highly esteemed by these people, who think it dangerous to the Christian's peace of mind. One of their most esteemed writers advises men to "fly from intercourse with women, as a very highly dangerous magnet and magical fire." Their women work hard and dress soberly; all ornaments are forbidden. To wear the hair loose is prohibited. Great care is used to keep the sexes apart. In their evening and other meetings, women not only sit apart from men, but they leave the room before the men break ranks. Boys are allowed to play only with boys, and girls with girls. . . . At meals and in their labors they are also separated. With all this care to hide the charms of the young women, to make them, as far as dress can do so, look old and ugly, and to keep the young men away from them, love, courtship, and marriage go on at Amana as elsewhere in the world.[12]

Christian Metz, the Inspirationist prophet who led his people to America, never married. However, in 1818, when he was twenty-five, he and Charlotte Bussinger had one daughter, Anne Marie. She married Heinrich Kramer, Metz's assistant in his cabinet shop in Armenburg, in Ebenezer on December 8, 1844. The couple had two daughters. When her husband died in 1850, Anne Marie and her children moved into Metz's home, much to his delight.

Amanans lived in traditional nuclear families, though day care allowed women to be productive community workers. On giving birth, a mother was excused from communal labor and cared for her child until he or she was two years old. Then the child was placed in the Kinderschule, or village nursery, while the mother resumed her work assignments. Several older women were assigned to care for children under five in the nurseries. These children returned to their home and parents each night.

At age five, children in Amana began school. The curriculum included arithmetic, geography, grammar, and religious training. School was in session six days a week throughout the year, except when students were needed to help with the harvest or apple picking in the fall. Each school day was divided into three parts. First, the *Lehrschule* focused on reading, writing, and numbers. Next came the play hour, called the *Spielstunde*, followed by the *Arbeitschule*, which emphasized manual training, trades, and crafts. Younger boys and girls were taught to knit and crochet, while older boys were sent to the factories and craft shops for training. Schoolmasters were male and were accorded high esteem in their village. Women usually taught the knitting and needlework.[13]

Students also studied the catechism at the end of which was the code of "Sixty-six Rules for the Conduct of Children." Boys and girls were expected to learn and follow these rules, which ranged from the sublime to the mundane. Examples include: "Be polite and friendly towards everybody, and let this be from genuine love of God and your fellow men, not from mere habit"; and "In the winter-time do not go on the ice, do not throw snow balls at others, and do not go sliding with wicked boys."[14]

Children finished school at fourteen. Elders then made work assignments with input from the young person involved. Boys were either sent away to prepare for a career needed in the community, such as a doctor or teacher, or given a job in the mills or the fields or trained in a trade. Girls were usually assigned to the communal kitchens, while married women usually tended the gardens.

Following his 1874 visit, Nordhoff described the Amanans as quiet, industrious, honest, kindly, religious, and frugal people who appreciated comfort but not beauty. Most came from Germany's peasant class and were farmers, weavers, or mechanics. Commenting on their plain dress, Nordhoff wrote:

> The men wear in the winter a vest which buttons close up the throat, coat and trousers being of the common cut. The women and young girls wear dingy colored stuffs, mostly of the society's own make, cut in the plainest style, and often short gowns, in the German peasant way. All, even to the very small girls, wear their hair in a kind of black cowl or cap, which covers only the back of the head, and is tied under the chin by a black ribbon. Also all, young as well as old, wear a small dark-colored shawl or handkerchief over the shoulders, and pinned very plainly across the breast. This peculiar uniform adroitly conceals the marks of sex, and gives a singularly monotonous appearance to the women.[15]

Religion, the foundation of the Inspirationists who founded Amana's villages, was the center of their lives and society. Church services were held eleven times weekly, including prayer meetings every evening, a meeting of each order on Wednesday and Sunday mornings, and general meetings on Saturday morning and Sunday afternoon. Children began attending services at age seven.

Christian Metz's Community of True Inspiration

Simplicity and plainness characterize the architecture of Inspirationist churches, which were large buildings of red bricks made at Amana and brown sandstone quarried nearby. The church in each village had a central rectangular room, or *Saal*, with a small room or hallway on each side. Interiors featured pale blue whitewashed walls, lamps hanging from the ceiling, plain, bare wooden floors with a strip of carpeting on the center aisle, and rows of pine benches; a table covered with a green cloth served as a pulpit. There were no statues, altars, paintings, or stained glass. The elders sat together on a bench facing the faithful.

An early account, written by Eberhard Gruber, described an Inspirationist service. After singing a hymn, the congregation observed silence and then joined in prayer led by anyone who was moved. After another period of silence, a chapter from the Bible was read, followed by a psalm, and then a final hymn. Should an Inspired One be present and receive a revelation, the service would be halted until they concluded.[16] Most of the inspired messages received by *Werkzeuge* occurred at church meetings and were always carefully recorded.

The belief in divine inspiration and human instruments serving as God's messengers was central to the community's belief system. In this church society, *a Werkzeuge* held the highest spiritual position and represented the highest degree of authority. Only two figures were *Werkzeuge* in America, Christian Metz and Barbara Heinemann Landmann, both of whom received their gift in Germany. Of the two, Metz was the more powerful figure, serving as the community's inspired leader until his death in 1867. Barbara Landmann lost her gift for twenty- six years but regained it in 1849, retaining it until her death in 1883.

Metz was a highly respected figure in his community. Like other leaders of utopian groups, he was a charismatic person as well as a wise and humane leader known for his humility, pity, and forgiveness. Metz's personality has been described as tolerant, kind, and understanding.

In addition to regular meetings, the Inspirationists held *Liebesmahls*, which included mutual foot washing and Holy Communion. There was no baptism. Confession was held yearly. There was no professional clergy, and elders conducted the services.

Unlike the Shakers, the Inspirationists did not send preachers to recruit additional members. New members were either born into the community or were Germans or Americans whose application to join was accepted.

When they died, the bodies of the Inspirationists were dressed in white for burial. Women wore a white gown, shawl, cap, and stockings, while men wore a white gown, tie, and socks. Bodies were kept in the family home for two days before the funeral, which was conducted by an elder. After the church service, a procession of mourners dressed in black followed the pallbearers carrying the coffin to the village cemetery. There were no family plots. The deceased was buried in the grave next to the last person who died. Identical headstones were placed on all of the graves, indicating the name, date of death, and age or date of birth.

188

Amana Colonies

Amana's communal system provided for the material needs of its members. Families or individuals were provided with a book designating an annual amount of credit, decided by the trustees on the basis of family size, which could be used to make purchases in the community. Amanans brought their books to the community tradespeople, who recorded each purchase.

Economically, the Amana community did not exist in isolation and was neither totally insular nor self-sufficient. At Ebenezer, products from the woolen mills were sold to customers from other regions. Amana sales of farm produce, calico prints, and woolens to outside markets were important factors in their economic prosperity. The society also acquired products from external sources. A store in each village handled purchases of needed goods like coffee, sugar, hardware, boots, coal, and oil, as well as raw materials like wool, grain, and cotton goods.

Amana was economically tied to national markets through its sales of farm products and woolen goods. By the 1930s, growing industrialization, urbanization, and a national transportation system had weakened Amana's craft-centered handicraft economy. The woolen mills, which had generated high profits during World War I due to war contracts, declined after the war. On August 12, 1923, ten colony buildings that housed the flour and woolen mills were destroyed by fire. Because they were uninsured, the loss to the community was hundreds of thousands of dollars. The hiring of outside workers in Amana's industries and farms caused another economic strain. The salaries paid to these employees along with having to provide accommodations for them put a heavy financial burden on the society. The depression of the 1930s further strained the village-based economy of small craft shops and farms.

In addition to strains caused by economic change, Amana faced the problem of the succession of leaders and challenges to its religious orthodoxy. After Metz's death in 1867 and Barbara Heinemann Landmann's death in 1883, the Amanan Church was without an inspired one. Between 1900 and 1920, Christian Science, a denomination founded by Mary Baker Eddy, spread throughout the country. Its claim to heal through prayer was particularly appealing. In 1906, a former Amanan who had converted to Christian Science convinced some village residents of its value. Amana's board of trustees denounced Christian Science, but apparently some villagers concealed their allegiance to the creed for the next ten years, when it reappeared. Despite being condemned again, some Amanans continued to call in Christian Scientists if a member of their family was ill. Cracks in Amana's religious solidarity appeared, which lessened the authority and control of community leaders who no longer could rely on the authority of divine inspiration.

Culturally, young people were attracted by automobiles, fashionable clothes, motion pictures, and earning their own money. Consumerism, which appealed to adults as well, had repeatedly forced the trustees to ban worldly products and practices. Among the items condemned were greeting cards, outside newspapers, tricycles, baby carriages, and bicycles. Practices they found offensive were birthday, wedding, and Christmas celebrations, music in church, card playing, drinking parties, wearing hair down, and open vests.[17]

When the communal theocracy ended in 1932, secular and religious matters were separated. Referred to as "the Great Change," 90 percent of the members voted to end the communal economy and form a corporation in which they would be shareholders. The adoption of a capitalist economy was indeed a great change as the Inspirationists had lived communally for nearly ninety years.

The plan adopted in 1932 established the Amana Church Society, responsible for the religious, benevolent, and charitable activities, and the Amana Society, a profit-based stock company that owned the farmland, orchards, and factories. Each member received shares of stock that carried voting rights, with the number of shares based on years lived in the community. Members could sell some of their stock to buy the houses they lived in, which had formerly been communal property.[18] Communal kitchens and dining rooms were abandoned. The corporation provided employment for everyone who wanted to work.

There was no mass exodus from the Amana colonies. Cultural and religious ties remained. Church services were conducted only on Sundays and included the traditional German service as well as English services added in 1960.

TOUR

As you tour the Amana Colonies, try to visualize them both as a whole and as separate communities. The seven colonies together form a way of life that originally was organized according to Inspirationist religious beliefs and the transplanted traditions of nineteenth-century rural Germany.

The **Museum of Amana History**, located in the village of Amana, is maintained by the Amana Heritage Society, a nonprofit organization dedicated to maintaining Amana's cultural heritage. Three nineteenth-century buildings constitute the Museum of Amana History: the 1864 **Noe House**, the 1870 **Schoolhouse**, and the **Washhouse/Woodshed**. The Noe House, which has been restored to the communal period, was originally a communal kitchen and later a doctor's residence. Artifacts, tools, utensils, and lithographs that belonged to Amana families are used to trace the history and development of Amana. The Amana Schoolhouse was an active school from 1870 to 1955. It contains the Christmas Room, a *Kinderschule*, a *Strickschule*, and a toy exhibit. A film on the history of Amana is shown in the schoolhouse auditorium, and the **Museum Store** is located here. Audio programs in the Washhouse/Woodshed give background information on exhibits of tools and garden implements.

Amana, the busiest of the seven colonies, has many bakeries, meat shops, wine and cheese stores, and antique and craft stores. Don't miss the **Amana Furniture and Clock Shop**, a workshop and display room of handcrafted walnut, cherry, and oak furniture; the **Amana Woolen Mill,** featuring famous

190

Amana woolen goods including clothes, blankets, and fabrics; **Amana General Store**, an original store built in 1858; the **Millstream Brewing Company**, Iowa's oldest brewery and four wineries; and **Amana Meat Shop and Smokehouse**, an old-fashioned butcher shop featuring ham, bacon, and sausages.

The Amana Heritage Society's **Communal Agriculture Exhibit** is in South Amana. Housed in an 1860 oxen barn are agricultural implements including equipment for planting, plowing, harvesting, haymaking, and livestock management. An exhibit focuses on the system of communal farming in the villages, each of which had its own cropland, pasture, timber, farm boss, and farm labor crew. Trades related to agriculture including blacksmithing, harness making, and wagon making are highlighted. Also in South Amana is the **Barn Museum**, which has a large collection of miniatures built by Henry Moore.

The **Communal Kitchen** and the **Cooper Shop** in Middle Amana are also maintained by the Amana Heritage Society. Homes in the colonies did not have kitchens. Amana had as many as sixty communal kitchens, where meals were prepared for thirty to forty people three times a day. Amana's only intact communal kitchen, the 1863 **Ruedy Kitchen**, with its large brick hearth, dry sink with wooden tubs, cooking implements, and dining room with long tables, has been preserved as it appeared in 1932, the year the society dissolved. The Cooper Shop, built around 1863, is the only one remaining in the colonies. Original coopering tools as well as buckets, tubs, and barrels are displayed. Also in Middle Amana is **Hahn's Hearth Oven Bakery**, where breads and pastries are still baked in an original wood-burning oven, and the appliance company **Amana Refrigeration, Inc.**, which began as a colony industry.

In High Amana, visit the **Amana Arts Guild Center,** which is an art gallery and museum shop featuring early Amana art, folk art, and crafts. There is also an **Old Fashioned High Amana Store**, a gift store whose interior has not changed in 100 years.

Homestead has the **Ehrle Brothers Winery**, the oldest, original winery in the Amana Colonies. There are also one- and three-mile nature trails.

Thomas Hughes's Christian Cooperatives

Portrait of Thomas Hughes (1822–1896), author of *Tom Brown's School Days* and founder of the community at Rugby, Tennessee. Courtesy of the Library of Congress.

HISTORIC RUGBY
1880–1887, Rugby, Tennessee
NR

ADDRESS: P.O. Box 8, Highway 52, Rugby, TN 37733
TELEPHONE: (615) 628-2441, (615) 628-2430
LOCATION: In northeastern Tennessee, about 125 miles northeast of Nashville and about 70 miles northwest of Knoxville; 35 miles from both I-75 Exit 141 and I-40 Exit 300; on TN 52.
OPEN: Monday–Saturday, 9:30 a.m.–5:00 p.m., and Sunday, noon–5:00 p.m., February–December; tours by appointment only in January.
ADMISSION: Adults, $4.00; senior citizens, $3.50; students, $2.00.
RESTAURANTS: Harrow Road Café.
SHOPS: Rugby Craft Commissary; Board of Aid Bookshop.
FACILITIES: Visitor Centre; guided tours; craft workshops; special events. Bed-and-breakfasts: Newbury House, 1880 Pioneer Cottage, and Percy Cottage.

OVERVIEW

Thomas Hughes (1822–96), a nineteenth-century British visionary imbued with Christian principles, envisioned the American West as the ideal location to settle talented young Englishmen who were unable to realize their career potential in England. He was reacting against a restrictive social system and primogeniture wherein only the eldest son inherited his father's title and property. Thomas Hughes was an energetic lawyer, member of Parliament, Christian socialist, champion of the working man, advocate of trade unions, and author. In England and the United States, Hughes was best known for his book *Tom Brown's Schooldays*, a semiautobiographical story of a boy's life at Rugby, the English public school that he attended.

After visiting the United States, Hughes established a planned experimental community in eastern Tennessee where educated younger sons of England's landed gentry could initiate a new life, own land, and work at their chosen careers in the United States' open social environment. Hughes envisioned the community as an Anglo-American project featuring the best of each tradition, and citizens of both countries were welcome.

Rugby survived from 1880 to 1887 with various successes and setbacks. At its peak about 1884, there were over 400 residents, sixty-five buildings, and a variety of commercial enterprises. From 1887 on, Rugby gradually declined. Among its problems were the settlers' inexperience with agriculture and manual skills, typhoid, and heavily forested lands unsuited for farming. The community's ultimate failure left its founders, including Hughes, heavily in debt.

Today, nestled among the lush vegetation of Tennessee's Cumberland Plateau is a restored Victorian English village of more than twenty original or reconstructed buildings, about half of which are privately owned. They are vestiges of Hughes's planned experimental community.

Historic Rugby

Rugby's wooded setting is isolated; make sure you have enough toothpaste, aspirin and batteries for your camera. Overnight accommodations are available in restored buildings, the Newbury House, 1880 Pioneer Cottage, and the reconstructed Percy Cottage.

The village is adjacent to the southern portion of the 105,000-acre Big South Fork National River and Recreation Area. A winding road from the interstate passes through scenic but sparsely populated rural and mining hamlets so remote that they only received electricity in the 1950s.

HISTORY

Thomas Hughes described his plan for Rugby: "Our aim and hope are to plant on these highlands a community of gentlemen and ladies; not that artificial class which goes by those grand names, both in Europe and here, the joint product of feudalism and wealth, but a society in which the humblest members, who live by the labour of their own hands, will be of such strain and culture that they will be able to meet princes in the gate, should any such strange persons ever present themselves before the gate tower of rugby in the New World."[1]

With a strong sense of Christianity fostered both by family background and education, Thomas Hughes devoted much of his life to fighting social injustice. In industrial England, he believed that Christian principles should be applied to factory workers, who carried much of the burden of industrialization but reaped few of the benefits.

Hughes was not alone in his ideas; he was known as a follower rather than a leader. However, those who believed in workers' rights and Christian socialism in mid-nineteenth-century England were condemned as radicals by the upper-class establishment. Hughes, a likeable man, successfully worked with a wide range of personalities, including many fairly eccentric colleagues.

Thomas Hughes was an internationally known author, member of Parliament, lawyer, Christian socialist, and utopian community founder. He was born October 20, 1822, at Uffington in Berkshire, England, near the Vale of the White Horse, the second son of John Hughes and Margaret Wilkinson. Several of his ancestors were clergymen, including his grandfather who was the rector at Uffington. All his life, Hughes was attracted to the ministry, though he never took clerical orders. Thomas's father was an editor and writer.

In the first half of the nineteenth century, it was customary among the gentry for their sons to be educated at boarding schools. As members of that class, Tom, at age eight, and his brother George, who was thirteen months older, attended a private school at Twyford, near Winchester. In 1833, when the Hughes family moved to Donnington Priory, a mansion near Newbury, Tom and George left for Rugby, a prestigious English public school founded in 1567. English public schools are really private schools that are open to a tuition-paying public.

Thomas Hughes's Christian Cooperatives

At Rugby, which he attended until 1841, Thomas came under the influence of its headmaster, the educational reformer Thomas Arnold, who had been an Oxford classmate of John Hughes. Arnold's open-mindedness, tolerance, social liberalism, and sense of Christian responsibility made a strong impression on young Tom Hughes.

Thomas Arnold was born June 13, 1795, on the Isle of Wight. He was educated at Winchester, a public school founded in 1382, and at Oxford, where he was a scholar of Corpus Christi and won first class honors. From 1815 to 1818, he was a fellow of Oriel College, Oxford. He was ordained a deacon and then became a master of a small private school at Laleham, where he began developing his educational theory.

In 1828, Arnold was ordained a priest in the Church of England, took his Doctor of Divinity degree, and became the headmaster of Rugby. Arnold made only slight curricular changes at Rugby, as he placed great value on classical education. The curriculum emphasized Latin and Greek, although younger boys received instruction in writing and arithmetic and older boys studied some geometry, algebra, and classical geography. Arnold introduced French and German.

In ruminating about his schooling in later life, Hughes praised England's public schools and particularly Arnold for instilling the virtues of "reticence, hardiness, independence, a high sense of honour, especially in all money matters, and good fellowship, manifesting itself in readiness to stand by and help one another."[2]

Despite the prestige of English public schools, which served sons of the upper classes, brutality and immorality characterized student life. Bigger boys bullied and intimidated younger ones. Fighting was commonplace, and homosexuality was rampant. School disciplinary measures included the stick and flogging.

Thomas Arnold, headmaster of Rugby, deplored these conditions and resolved to make Christianity the foundation of education and to imbue Rugby's pupils with the Christian spirit. He initiated reforms of student living arrangements, disciplinary methods, teaching conditions, and student behavior. He encouraged gentlemanly conduct, moral behavior, intellectual achievement, and an awareness of social justice in his students.

After leaving Rugby, Hughes studied law at Oxford and was admitted to the bar in January 1848. The previous August he had married Frances Ford after a five-year engagement during most of which Fanny's parents forbade the young people to see each other or to correspond. The Hughes had nine children, and lived in London's Mayfair region for the majority of their lives.

At Oxford, Hughes became acquainted with a new movement in the Church of England called Christian socialism. A social reform movement initiated in the late 1840s, its founders were J. M. Ludlow, Frederick Denison Maurice, and Charles Kingsley. Christian socialists believed that organized Christianity should address the social problems of the age, particularly those related to industrialization. Supporting social justice and Christian brother-hood, they rejected laissez faire economics. They promoted cooperative work-shops, distributive societies, and social and educational reforms. After hearing Frederick Denison Maurice preach, Hughes became a disciple of Maurice and an advocate of Christian socialism.

Hughes, a lifelong champion of working-class people, sought to reform both laws and customs that negatively impacted them. Supporting the coop-erative and the trade-union movements, he helped found the London Work-ing Men's College in 1854 and served as its principal for eleven years.

The college's mission was to educate factory workers. Only evening classes were conducted. Its rather unfocused curriculum included classes in the gospel, politics, English literature, Shakespeare, grammar, drawing, and law. Hughes, known for his physical prowess, had trouble identifying a class to teach that attracted students. He finally settled on boxing and engaged his students per-sonally. He also organized a cricket and rowing club.

In 1856, Thomas Hughes began writing a novel based on his own school experiences at Rugby during Arnold's tenure. His literary project was stimu-lated by his concern to prepare Maurice, his eight-year-old son, for entering school. Although written fifteen years after leaving Rugby, Hughes vividly re-captured the world of English public schools.

Encouraged to publish his work, Hughes approached Macmillan and Com-pany Publishers, whose list included books on religious liberalism and social reform, as well as works by Maurice, Kingsley, Arnold, and Samuel Taylor Coleridge. In September 1856, Alexander Macmillan, who had read several chapters, enthusiastically agreed to publish Hughes's book.

Hughes put aside the unfinished manuscript in November when four of his children and his wife contracted scarlet fever. His eldest daughter, Evie, died in his arms on December 3. Despite his grief, Hughes completed the manu-script, and *Tom Brown's Schooldays* was published anonymously under the pseud-onym "An Old Boy" in April. It enjoyed such wide acclaim that the publishers soon revealed the author's identity. A second edition of *Tom Brown's Schooldays* was published in July, and four more printings occurred in its first year of pub-lication.

In the preface to the sixth edition, Hughes spoke about his sons and neph-ews who were preparing to go away to school and his motive for writing this book. This "makes one ask one's self, whether there isn't something one would like to say to them before they take their first plunge in the stream of life, away from their own homes, or while they are yet shivering after the first plunge." Hughes continued by extolling the virtues of Rugby's alumni: "the mark by which you may know them, is, their genial and hearty freshness and youthful-ness of character. They lose nothing of the boy that is worth keeping, but build up the man upon it." Hughes then asked, "And what gave Rugby boys this character, and has enabled the School, I believe, to keep it to this day?" An-swering his own question, he proclaimed, "I say fearlessly,—Arnold's teaching and example . . . his unwearied zeal in creating 'moral thoughtfulness' in every boy with whom he came into personal contact."[3]

Tom Brown's Schooldays brought Hughes fame. He was one of the most well-known Englishmen of his time, even in the United States. Tragically, the son that *Tom Brown's Schooldays* was written for, Maurice Hughes, died in 1859, just two years after the novel was published.

Hughes also wrote several biographies and religious works including *The Scouring of the White Horse* (1859), *Tom Brown at Oxford* (1868), *Alfred the Great* (1869), *Memoir of a Brother* (1873), *Rugby, Tennessee* (1881), *Life of Daniel Macmillan* (1881), and *Gone to Texas* (1884). His religious works include *A Layman's Faith* (1881), *The Old Church* (1878) and *The Manliness of Christ* (1877).

In the 1860s, Hughes, involved in the labor cause, became a legal advisor to the leaders of the trade-union movement. Hughes was elected to the House of Commons from Labeth in 1865, then Frome in 1868 and served until 1874. He was appointed as queen's counsel to Victoria in 1869.

Hughes was an admirer of the American poet James Russell Lowell. In 1859, the two authors began a thirty-year correspondence. An invitation to Boston from Lowell in 1870 resulted in Hughes's first visit to the United States, where he enjoyed a warm reception. Describing Hughes "as charming," "simple, hearty, and affectionate," Lowell wrote that parting with him was like "saying good-bye to sunshine."[4]

On a two-month whirlwind tour, Hughes visited Boston, New York, Niagara Falls, Chicago, Sioux City, Council Bluffs, Omaha, St. Louis, Cincinnati, Philadelphia, Gettysburg, Baltimore, and Washington. He met prominent American literary, political, and business people, including Ralph Waldo Emerson, Henry Wadsworth Longfellow, Oliver Wendell Holmes, and Robert Todd Lincoln.

Although Hughes condemned slavery and strongly championed the Union during the American Civil War, he found himself having to defend England's foreign policy of neutrality and covert support of the South. In a speech in the Boston Music Hall to an audience of what he called "3,000 of the brainiest men in Massachusetts," Hughes emphasized the deep divisions in England over the American Civil War that had separated the aristocracy from the majority of Englishmen. He defended England's conduct over neutrality, recognition of the South, and rebel cruisers as a policy above reproach. Hughes's Boston speech was printed in the newspapers. The *New York Tribune* on October 13, 1870, editorialized that America trusted Hughes as an Englishman with whom she could speak freely.[5]

Returning to England, Hughes lectured at the Working Men's College on the great opportunities to immigrants offered by America's West, with its caste-free system and high wages. Pointing out the advantages that the United States offered to would-be purchasers of land, Hughes referred to the America's western states as an indispensable location for Europe's surplus population. He depicted an attractive future awaiting potential immigrants: their own farm, common schools for their children, and a higher living standard.[6]

Hughes conceived of a project for establishing an American colony for younger sons of the British upper classes who had received a classical education but because of primogeniture received no inheritance and were limited to the overcrowded professions of law, medicine, the military, and the ministry. According to primogeniture, the traditional inheritance pattern in nineteenth-century England, upper-class first-born sons received their fathers' titles and estates. Younger sons, who were not heirs, were educated at elite public schools, really prestigious private schools, like their older brothers, yet they would never own their own land. Their classical public school education left them unprepared for business, particularly the economic impact of the Industrial Revolution. Considered gentlemen, they were encouraged to earn their living by entering the professions of ministry, law, medicine, public service, or the military. In fact, many younger sons did not enter these overcrowded professions and were left unemployed, living on an inadequate allowance as their only income.

On his tour of the United States, Hughes met Franklin W. Smith, a financier who headed the Board of Aid to Land Ownership, a Boston company with an option on 100,000 acres of East Tennessee land intended as a relocation site for unemployed workers. Because of an economic upturn, the Tennessee property was no longer needed for that purpose, and Smith offered it to Hughes. After obtaining financial backing from Henry Kimber and John Boyle of London, Hughes became the president of the land company, which retained its original name. The property was beautifully situated on a heavily wooded high plain between two deep river gorges.

Because the Board of Aid to Land Ownership was a commercial venture, purchasing land in the new community was not restricted to residents of England, though the project was heavily publicized in the United Kingdom. According to Hughes, participants would lead a peasant's life during working hours but find themselves in a cultivated society when their work was done. He named the community Rugby after the school he had attended, and the town officially opened in October 1880.

The board reserved common areas and parklands, developing bridle paths and trails. Settlers would be able to purchase town lots and farm lands from the board at reasonable prices. Unfortunately, the first manager was dishonest and overcharged buyers. The board also built a schoolhouse/town hall, land office, commissary, hotel, sawmill, stable, and a barracks for single men.

Three weeks after its official opening, Rugby's population was 120, and by January 1881, it had grown to 200 people from England and Scotland, plus a good percentage of Americans, some of whom were natives of the Tennessee mountains. Despite the emphasis on second sons, the population was almost evenly divided between men and women.

Hughes was not a radical social reformer with an overall plan to reform society according to his personal philosophy. His goal was to provide social freedom and economic opportunity for gentlemen who were denied it in England. Immigrants to Rugby, Tennessee, shared a similarity with earlier immigrants to America who sought religious freedom and economic opportunity denied them in their native lands.

Although Hughes's vision was somewhat utopian, it was not communal. In his opening address at Rugby, he stated: "Certainly we can all agree at once that we have no sympathy whatever with the state communism of Europe, represented by Lasalle and Karl Marx. . . . [W]hile respecting the motives and lives of many of those who have founded or are carrying on communistic experiments here and in Europe, we have no desire or intention to follow in their steps. We are content with the laws relating to private property and family life as we find them."[7]

Hughes strongly believed in developing a sense of community—of having something in common and sharing common values: "We shall be all of one mind, I think, as to the preservation of all natural beauty here in the treatment of grounds and buildings; and the sense of a common interest and life which an ample provision of public buildings and grounds will secure to our community."[8]

In England, Hughes favored industrial partnerships in which employees owned a share of the business and received a percentage of the profits as a Christian method of reconciling labor and business classes. He advocated similar arrangements in the fledgling Tennessee community.

> We have all of us a number of imperative wants which must be provided for and satisfied day by day. We want food, clothes, furniture, and a great variety of things besides, which our nurture and culture have made all but essential to us. These must all be provided here, either by each of us for himself, or by some common machinery. Well, we believe that it can be done best by a common machinery, in which we should like to see every one take a hand. We have a "commissary" already established, and have used that word rather than "store" to indicate our own wishes and intentions, as a "commissary" is especially a public institution. Our wish is to make this commissary a centre of supply, and that every settler, or, at any rate, every householder here, should become a member and part owner of it.[9]

By the summer of 1881, Rugby had a café, a boardinghouse, a three-story hotel, and private homes, in addition to the cooperative commissary. Recreational and cultural facilities included tennis courts, bowling greens, bridle paths, a gentlemen's swimming hole, croquet, hunting, and musical events. A number of clubs were formed, including the Lawn Tennis Club, the Rugby Social Club, Rugby Musical and Dramatic Club, the Philharmonic Society, the Masonic Lodge, the Ladies Church Working Society, and the Cornet Band. A weekly newspaper, the *Rugbeian*, began publication in 1880. The Rugby schoolhouse was constructed in 1880, and in 1882, a public library was built. Religious services were held in the school until Christ Church Episcopal was built in 1887. Colonists dressed for afternoon tea at four o'clock. Because Hughes was a temperance advocate, liquor was prohibited in the village.

Despite its optimistic beginnings, Rugby encountered a series of problems. Although John Boyle, who had been sent by Hughes to survey the suitability of the Cumberland Plateau land, had raved about the climate, the first winter in Rugby was harsh and very cold, the worst winter in that part of Tennessee in twenty-five years. Typhoid broke out in August 1881; twenty cases were reported, and seven people died. The contamination was traced to one of the earliest buildings constructed in Rugby, a three-story hotel called the Tabard Inn. Though the inn was closed, frightened residents fled the community, and the population plunged from 300 to 60 by December.

Some purchasers were able to obtain clear title to their land only after months of litigation. The land was heavily timbered and could not be farmed until cleared, which was arduous work. The soil was less fertile than some colonists had expected.

One of the original assets of the location was the proximity of the Cincinnati and Southern Railroad, which by 1878 ran between Chattanooga and Cincinnati. It provided a means by which products could be shipped to market. However, the closest station, Sedgemoor, was seven miles from Rugby. The board built a graded dirt road, but traveling in the mountainous terrain often took hours. A promised railroad spur to Rugby never materialized.

The many difficulties encountered in Tennessee weighed heavily on its founder. In a letter to his friend Lord Ripon, Hughes stated that his American settlement had proved to be a "very troublesome and onerous business" in which all was "going wrong." He later wrote Ripon that, while the fever was nearly over, a drought had destroyed almost all the crops planted in the first year.[10]

Despite this inauspicious beginning, Hughes was determined that the colony would succeed. Though he remained a British subject, Hughes visited the community for a few months annually. His brother Hastings, and his daughter Emily, did live in Rugby, and in 1881, Thomas's mother, Margaret Hughes, moved to Rugby, where she lived until her death at eighty-nine in 1887. Margaret Hughes's presence had a steadying effect on the shaky community's morale. After her death, Thomas would never visit Tennessee again.

Gradually, Rugby's population increased. By 1884, there were between 400 and 450 residents and some sixty-five buildings. Commercial activities included farming, a canning company, a sawmill, boardinghouses, public stables, a drugstore, blacksmith shops, and summer tourism with guests accommodated at the reconditioned Tabard Inn. Unfortunately, the Tabard Inn was destroyed in a fire in October 1884. A new Tabard Inn was opened in the summer of 1887, the year Christ Church Episcopal was built.

Rugby survived from 1880 to 1887 with various successes and setbacks, but from 1887 on, it gradually declined. Many factors contributed to the community's decline. Very few of the English pioneers possessed manual skills, business ability, or agricultural knowledge. The canning factory closed. An English public school for young gentlemen, the Arnold School, operated only from 1885 to 1887. The newspaper, the *Rugbeian*, ceased publication.

Thomas Hughes knew that his optimistic experiment was unsuccessful. Financial losses to the founders of the community were heavy; his indebtedness was more than £7,000. His losses made him a "poor man" at a time when it would be hard to recover.[11]

Hughes's financial losses related to the Rugby colony had forced him to take a position as a county court judge in Chester in June 1882, traveling a circuit through this mining region. He and his wife, Fanny, rented their London home in 1885 and built a new home along the River Dee in Chester. His last visit to Rugby was in 1887, the year his mother died. Hughes died in England in March 1896.

In the early 1900s, the Board of Aid to Land Ownership sold its remaining 25,000 acres to American investors. Most original colonists had already left Rugby. Hastings Hughes, Thomas's brother, left and relocated in Massachusetts.

Rugby, Tennessee, overlooked and neglected for the following half century, existed as a small farming community. As with many historic sites, progress in terms of urban sprawl and highway construction destroys, while neglect preserves. Rugby's remote location helped much of the Victorian village remain intact. In 1966, a sixteen-year-old boy, Brian Stagg, led a Rugby restoration movement. Tours of historic buildings began in 1967, and in 1972, the village was placed on the National Register of Historic Places. Historic Rugby, Inc., has restored several buildings and reconstructed several others. A master plan for the historic site includes restoration and rebuilding of even more buildings.

TOUR

Rugby, set picturesquely in Tennessee's forested Cumberland Plateau, is a small village of Victorian cottages. A concern for appropriate structures at Rugby is evident in the Board of Aid to Land Ownership's determination to set "a good example in public building." The board approved "plans and models of houses of different sizes, such as we think will suit the site, and do us credit as a community."[12]

Tours begin at the **Schoolhouse Visitor Centre**, a two-story frame structure built in 1907 and used as a school until 1951. It replaced a three-story schoolhouse built in 1880 that was destroyed by fire in 1906. Photographs and documents on exhibit in the schoolhouse focus on Thomas Hughes, Rugby, cottage Victorian architecture, and the Cumberland Mountains. Guided tours leave from the schoolhouse.

Rugby's pièce de résistance is the **Thomas Hughes Free Public Library** housed in its original 1882 one-story frame building with a cupola. The collection of 7,000 rare books includes 2,000 volumes brought from England and

5,000 donated books. Gold lettering on the arched frosted glass panels on the front doors announces that the Hughes Public Library was opened October 5, 1882. One of the finest collections of Victorian literature in the United States, no volume published after 1899 is on the shelves, and the oldest book was printed in 1687. The books are in remarkably good condition. The building has no electricity and is unheated. Floor to ceiling bookshelves line the walls in addition to freestanding bookcases, wooden tables, and chairs.

Christ Church Episcopal, built in 1887, still holds Sunday services today. The carpenter Gothic church, designed by Cornelius Onderdonk, has board and batten siding with maroon and gray trim. Its interior is paneled with native yellow pine, which was not painted or stained but has darkened naturally. The stained glass window above the altar was dedicated to Margaret Hughes and Mary Blacklock. Other windows, which are original, are clear, although they had previously been covered with rice paper to give the illusion of stained glass. The original oil lamps were electrified in the 1950s. The rosewood harmonium reed organ, made in London in 1849, is still in use.

Kingstone Lisle is the house built in 1884 for Thomas Hughes, who made annual visits to Rugby. The wooden walls, ceilings, and floors of the interior are yellow pine. Furnishings were either made in Rugby or imported from England by Rugby colonists. The parlor has a Weber piano and a silver plate for calling cards. Windows have long puddling drapes. In the bedroom is Thomas Hughes's green felt-covered writing desk as well as his trunk.

The reconstructed **Harrow Road Café** is a flourishing restaurant. Another reconstruction is the **Rugby Craft Commissary**. This cooperative commissary originally supplied all the needs of the town's residents. Today it is a craft shop featuring Appalachian crafts such as quilts, baskets, and dulcimers. The **Board of Aid** land office is a bookshop.

Overnight accommodations are available in the simple one- story frame **Pioneer Cottage**. Built in 1880, it served as a temporary residence for early colonists until their houses were built. Thomas Hughes stayed at Pioneer Cottage during his first visit to Rugby. Another bed-and-breakfast, the **Newbury House**, 1880, was Rugby's first boardinghouse. The two-story, mansard- roofed inn has been restored, and its five bedrooms are furnished in the Victorian period. A third lodging facility is **Percy Cottage**. This Victorian cottage was reconstructed on its original foundation. The original Percy Cottage was built in 1884 for Sir Henry Kimber.

Many of the privately owned houses in Rugby have also been restored and can be seen from the outside. Once a year they are open for touring during the Rugby Pilgrimage held the first weekend in October. Another annual event is the Spring Music and Crafts Festival held in mid-May. The festival features craftspeople selling and demonstrating their crafts, as well as British and Appalachian music and dancing. Crafts are also available at the Thanksgiving Marketplace held Thanksgiving weekend. The Christmas at Rugby celebration, held in early December, features candlelight tours and a Victorian dinner.

Thomas Hughes's Christian Cooperatives

Workshops are offered in a variety of crafts such as cane seating, hand spinning, tatting, and basketry.

Colonists are buried in the **Laurel Dale Cemetery** on Donnington Road. From there, an 1880s trail leads to the **Gentlemen's Swimming Hole** a half mile away. This trail continues for one mile to the **Meeting of the Waters**, where Clear Fork River and White Oak Creek intersect.

A lecturer gives an introduction to Koreshan site in a room filled with photographs, paintings, and cellular cosmogony exhibits. Courtesy of the Florida Department of Commerce, Division of Tourism.

KORESHAN STATE HISTORIC SITE

1904, Estero, Florida

NR

ADDRESS: P.O. Box 7, Estero, FL 33928
TELEPHONE: (813) 992-0311
LOCATION: In southwestern Florida, on the Gulf Coast, south of Fort Myers, north of Naples; on Corkscrew Road at US 41, I-75 Exit 19.
OPEN: Daily,
ADMISSION: State Park: vehicles with maximum of eight adults and children over six, $3.25; pedestrians and bicyclists, $1.00. Ranger guided tours: $1.00, minimum four adults.
SHOPS: In park entrance station.
FACILITIES: Guided tours; orientation video; picnic area; nature trail; camping; canoe rental.

OVERVIEW

Koreshan State Historic Site is a Florida state park with eleven restored and preserved structures that belonged to the Koreshans, a late-nineteenth- and early-twentieth-century utopian community. It is the only Koreshan site in the country that still has physical remains.

Koreshanity was a religion founded by Cyrus Read Teed (1839–1908), a New York physician. Teed had a powerful religious vision in 1869 in which he was named the Messiah. Subsequently, he tried to attract converts to his religion, which included beliefs in communalism, celibacy, and an unusual theory of the universe called cellular cosmogony, which postulated that the earth was hollow and that the sun and all life existed inside the earth.

In 1894, a follower donated 320 acres in Florida to the group. Ten years later, the Koreshans left their Chicago headquarters to build a community on their Florida acreage. After Teed's death in 1908, the number of Koreshans declined so that by 1918, only 100 members remained. The sect donated their land to the state of Florida in 1961. Buildings have been restored to 1904, when the community's population peaked at 200.

HISTORY

Cyrus Read Teed and his followers established the Koreshan Unity Settlement in the Florida wilderness in 1894. Teed called himself Koresh, the biblical translation of his Christian name, and his religion Koreshanity. Cyrus was born in Teedsville in Delaware County, New York, on October 18, 1839, to Jesse Teed, a doctor, and Sarah Ann Tuttle. He was the second of their eight children. When he was eleven, Cyrus left school for a job on the Erie Canal.

Koreshan State Historic Site

At age twenty, young Teed began studying medicine with his uncle, Dr. Samuel Teed. During the Civil War, he joined the Union army medical service and was attached to a field hospital. He completed his medical studies at New York Eclectic College after the war, graduating in 1868. He then established his own practice in Utica, New York. He married Delia M. Row, and they had one son, Douglas Arthur Teed.

In addition to practicing medicine, Cyrus Teed studied alchemy, a pseudoscience seeking to change base metals to precious ones. Claiming amazing success in his perusal of alchemy, Teed said he had transformed matter into energy and reduced that energy to another kind of matter. He said he had discovered the elusive "philosopher's stone" for which so many had searched.

One night in 1869 when Teed was in what he referred to as his electroalchemical laboratory, he found himself mentally transported from earthly things. Teed described the experience as a "relaxation . . . of the brain, and a peculiar buzzing tension at the forehead or sinciput. . . . There gradually spread from the center of my brain to the extremities of my body, and, apparently to me, into the auric sphere of my being, miles outside of my body, a vibration so gentle, soft, and dulciferous that I was impressed to lay myself upon the bosom of this gently oscillating ocean of magnetic and spiritual ecstasy."[1]

Next Teed beheld a brilliant light that materialized into the apparition of a beautiful woman who proclaimed, "Offspring of my most potential desire, thou art chosen to redeem the race," and "I have brought thee to this birth to sacrifice thee upon the altar of all human hopes that through thy quickening of me, thy Mother and Bride, the Sons of God shall spring into visible creation."[2] Teed interpreted the woman's announcements to mean that he was to be the new Messiah.

Teed spent the years after what he termed his "illumination" in New York seeking converts. An inspiring preacher, he espoused communalism, celibacy, and the millennium. His preaching to his patients while treating them medically had a negative impact on his practice.

Success eluded Teed until 1886 when he received a warm reception while addressing the National Association for Mental Health in Chicago. Soon, he and a very small band of adherents moved to Chicago and established a communal society called Beth- Ophra in a large mansion that also housed the Guiding Star Publishing House and the College of Life, later renamed the Koreshan University. A number of Chicagoans were attracted to Koreshanity, and in the early 1890s, 126 members were living at Beth-Ophra. Koreshan literature generated by the Guiding Star Publishing House was widely distributed and led to the formation of several other small Koreshan groups throughout the country.

One of the tenets of Koreshanity was celibacy, though Teed himself had married and had a child, and there was a marital order in Koreshanity. Celibacy was regarded as a requisite to higher natural and mental states. According to Teed, "To become immortal one must cease to propagate life on the plane of mortality. The standard of Koreshan purity is the virgin life of Jesus the Messiah. The Central Order of the Koreshan Unity is celibate and communistic."[3]

Teed's interest in communalism led him to propose a merger with the Harmonists at Economy, Pennsylvania, to John Duss, the trustee of the Harmony Society, but that did not occur. Certain doctrines of Koreshanity, including communalism, abolition of private property, celibacy, and the coming of the millennium, paralleled the religious beliefs of communal groups like the Shakers and the Harmonists of Economy, Pennsylvania. However, a doctrine espoused by Teed called cellular cosmogony set the Koreshans apart. This theory of the universe stated that the earth was a hollow sphere with the sun in the center and with life existing on the inside. The central sun was always half-lit and half-dark, resulting in day and night. The earth's surface was concave rather than convex.

Teed was not the first person to postulate a hollow earth theory that contradicted the Copernican view of astronomy, and he may have been aware of earlier proponents. Captain John Cleves Symmes published a work in 1868 called *A Hollow Globe*, and Jules Verne published a fictionalized version of the hollow earth in 1864.

John Duss, in his autobiography, *The Harmonists, a Personal History*, provides an account of his correspondence with Teed. According to Duss, Teed interpreted the line in the Lord's Prayer, "Thy kingdom come *in earth* as it is in Heaven" literally. Duss went on to say that Teed believed "that the earth is a concave sphere, a gigantic electro-magnetic battery, a vast alchemic- organic cell in which we have our being." Teed, called Koresh, regarded acceptance of the doctrine of the earth's concavity as necessary to truly understanding God. Indeed, he regarded those who continued to believe in the earth's convexity to be rejecting God and his works.[4] Duss further explained Teed's doctrines as resting on "transmutation," a religio-alchemic law in which matter and spirit were interchangeable. For Teed, the perfection of the Creator and Universe "was illustrated in Jesus the Messiah, . . . a Microcosmic reflection of the perfect goodness and grandeur of the Creator, the perfect Seed and Archetype of the coming perfect race of men."[5]

John Duss's association with Teed was reported by the press in a sensationalist coverage that generated negative publicity for the Harmonists. The press alleged that Teed was trying to grasp millions of dollars from the Harmony Society whose large assets were well known. Teed received only a small donation of $100 from the Harmonists.[6]

Despite the sensational publicity generated by Teed, Duss was flattered by Teed's interest in the Harmonists and their communal organization. Duss viewed the charismatic Teed as sincere, friendly, spirited, and courageous. He was, in Duss's words, "a qualified scientist and scholar" who possessed "a vast fund of learning."[7]

In 1893, Gustav Damkohler, a German immigrant who was fascinated by Teed's teachings, invited the religious leader to his home in the Estero Bay area of Florida. Teed, who had been searching for a site for his New Jerusalem, which he projected would be a city of six million people, found it at Estero. The Chicago group moved to Florida, where they became pioneers hacking out habitable space in the wilderness. On land donated by Damkohler, they created a settlement that by 1906 had grown to more than thirty-five buildings on their nearly 7,000 acres of land.

In Florida, the Koreshans conducted scientific experiments to prove that the earth was concave. In 1897, they surveyed a line six miles long on Naples beach, using instruments that they called rectilineators. These instruments, which had been specially designed to project a perfectly straight line, consisted of three twelve-foot long flat mahogany sections with a cross arm with a brass double T square. By manipulating the rectilineator and placing a telescope along its axis, they extended a line to a point where the line met the water's surface four miles in the distance. Teed concluded that the earth curves upward and is therefore concave.

The population of the Koreshan Florida settlement did not reach Teed's projected six million and, in fact, never exceeded 200. Life for the men and women at Estero revolved around work, religion, study, and cultural pursuits. They built a prosperous colony with a band, an orchestra, and tropical gardens. Dredging the river, they drained the swampy land. Many of their buildings were located on the right bank of the Estero River. Businesses included a general store, bakery, boat works, water taxi, printing press, sawmill, machine shop, woodworking shop, concrete works, and plant nursery. Central light and water systems as well as a waste disposal system were installed.

The Koreshan school was open to those outside their community. The Guiding Star Publishing House remained in operation until it was destroyed by fire in 1949. A Koreshan newspaper, the *American Eagle*, and a religious magazine, the *Flaming Sword*, were published.

The Koreshans ate communal meals at long tables in a large dining hall with the brethren on one side and the sisters on the other side of the room. The sisters lived together in communal residences, as did the brothers. A visiting Shaker, Elder Ezra J. Stewart, favorably compared the devotion and love between Koresh and his disciples with that between Shaker families and their leaders. Elder Stewart, penning an idyllic picture of the setting at Estero, described a tropical landscape of "sunken gardens," and banana, paw-paw, palm, and eucalyptus trees, and bamboo and ornamental grasses. Interspersed among the garden-like setting were artistic footbridges and houses with verandas covered by flowering vines.[8]

Religious and governmental structures of the community were intertwined. Teed ruled jointly with Annie G. Ordway, known as Victoria Gratia, preeminent, who, according to Elder Stewart, was identified during Teed's illumination as his dual associate as well as the mother of the 144,000 sons of God. Stewart, who met Victoria Gratia while visiting Estero, described her as a beautiful, refined, and musically talented sixty-year-old woman. Stewart was informed that Victoria's greatest work would begin with Koresh's martyrdom, which Teed himself had predicted. Although he did not know how and when he would meet his death, Koresh predicted that his martyrdom would be followed by Victoria's exaltation into "divine motherhood and imperial pre-eminence, as the divine natural head of all the orders of church and State."[9]

The Koreshans were organized into several orders, patterned after the stars and planets. During religious services, members of the orders would occupy several platforms with the highest one reserved for the central duality of Koresh and Victoria. Other platforms held females from the Planetary Chamber, males from the Stellar Chamber, and males and females from the Signet Chamber.[10]

The Koreshans, who led a nontraditional communal celibate lifestyle, got along well with their neighbors with one exception—they felt that they were not getting their fair share of road taxes from the county commissioners. Consequently, Teed inaugurated his own political party, the Progressive Liberty Party. Politicians from Fort Myers and Lee County attempted to disenfranchise the Koreshans. Conflict ensued, resulting in an attack on Teed by the town marshal of Fort Myers on October 13, 1906. Teed's injuries were severe, and many Koreshans felt that they eventually led to his death on December 22, 1908.

Teed had said that he was immortal, and many of his people waited for him to rise again. After several days, the county health authorities ordered the body to be buried. Teed's remains were placed in a concrete mausoleum with the inscription "Cyrus, Shepherd Stone of Israel" and placed on Estero Island. In 1921, a hurricane blew his tomb into the Gulf of Mexico.

After Teed's death, power struggles over leadership ensued. Members drifted away, and the number of converts gradually declined. By the 1940s, only a dozen Koreshans remained. Hedwig Michel, the community's leader, was responsible for donating 305 acres of Koreshan property to the state of Florida as a historical site. In 1961, the state accepted this property along with the Koreshan-built structures to be designated as the Koreshan State Historic Site. The last surviving member of the Koreshan Unity, Hedwig Michel, died in 1982.

Tour

Although a small number of Koreshans lived at the Florida site until the 1970s, the Koreshan settlement has been restored to the 1904–7 period when the colony had reached its peak population of 200. At that time, the Chicago community had completed its move to Estero, and Cyrus Teed, the founder, was still alive.

The Koreshans constructed more than seventy-three buildings, some of which have been destroyed by fire. The **Art Hall**, also known as the Music and Art Building, was built of local pine in 1905. With a seating capacity of 150, it was used for music concerts and plays. An orientation video is shown here, and paintings by Cyrus Teed's son, Douglas, are exhibited.

Koreshan State Historic Site

The **Planetary Court**, built in 1903, is a two-story frame building with a second-story veranda. It housed seven women who were members of the governing council of the Koreshan unit. Teed's governmental structure consisted of Annie G. Ordway, whom he designated as Victoria Gratia, preeminent, as the central duality, a Planetary Chamber consisting of seven women, a Stellar Chamber of four men, a Signet Chamber of six men and six women, and himself.

The ovens in the **Bakery**, built in 1903–4, had a capacity of more than 500 loaves per day. In addition to supplying the settlement, surplus bread was sold to local people. On the second floor of the bakery were rooms for visitors.

The **Vesta Newcomb Cottage**, a frame double-pen house, and the **Members Cottage** were used as residences. They were moved to their present location in the 1930s.

The **Founder's House** was built in 1896 and repeatedly modified until Koresh's death in 1908. Part of the structure was probably used as a school, as it was also called the Children's House.

The **Damkohler House**, built in 1892 or 1893, was the home of Gustav Damkohler, the German immigrant who invited Teed to Florida. The original settler, Damkohler donated this house and 320 acres to Koreshanity. Originally located on the Estero River, the house was moved after the establishment of the Koreshan settlement.

The **Koreshan Unity General Store** was built during the early 1920s after the **Tamiami Trail** was opened between Tampa and Miami. The store was a flourishing business. It also was the local post office, a warehouse, and a restaurant. There were rooms for brothers upstairs. There is also a **Generator Building**, a **Small Machine Shop**, a **Large Machine Shop**, and **Bamboo Landing** on the Estero River. The river was the highway between communities in this wilderness area. Koreshans shipped excess agricultural products to Fort Myers's markets.

The **Koreshan Museum and Library**, on the east side of US 41, is owned and operated by the board of directors of the Koreshan Unity Foundation and includes the **World's College of Life** building. Koreshan archives are housed in the library. A short **nature trail** leads to the **Anna Lewis house**, a circa 1930 bungalow that was home to a Koreshan family for many years.

NOTES

Ephrata Cloister

1. E. G. Alderfer, *The Ephrata Commune: An Early American Counterculture* (Pittsburgh, Pa.: University of Pittsburgh Press, 1985), p. 43.

2. Russell P. Getz, "Music in the Ephrata Cloister," *Communal Societies* 2 (1982): 31.

3. Ibid., p. 28.

4. Alderfer, *Ephrata Commune*, p. 125.

Old Salem

1. Kenneth O. Gangel and Warren S. Benson, *Christian Education: Its History and Philosophy* (Chicago: Moody Press, 1993), p. 171.

2. Gillian Lindt Gollin, *Moravians in Two Worlds: A Study of Changing Communities* (New York: Columbia University Press, 1967), p. 4.

3. J. Taylor Hamilton and Kenneth G. Hamilton, *History of the Moravian Church: The Renewed Unitas Fratrum, 1722–1957* (Bethlehem, Pa.: Interprovincial Board of Christian Education, Moravian Church in America, 1967), p. 24.

4. Chester Davis, *Hidden Seed and Harvest: A History of the Moravians* (Winston-Salem, N.C.: Wachovia Historical Society, 1973), p. 13.

5. Ibid., p. 14.

6. Ibid., p. 38.

7. Gollin, *Moravians in Two Worlds*, p. 76.

8. Ibid., p. 69.

9. Thomas Mainwaring, "Communal Ideals, Worldly Concerns, and the Moravians of North Carolina, 1753–1722," *Communal Societies* 6 (1986): 138–62, 149.

Biographical Sketch of Mother Ann Lee

1. Nardi Reeder Campion, *Mother Ann Lee, Morning Star of the Shakers* (Hanover: University Press of New England, 1990), p. 35.

2. Ibid., p. 40.

3. Stephen J. Stein, *The Shaker Experience in America: A History of the United Society of Believers* (New Haven: Yale University Press, 1992), pp. 13–14.

4. Priscilla J. Brewer, *Shaker Communities, Shaker Lives* (Hanover: University Press of New England, 1986), p. 12.

5. Ibid., p. 40.

6. Stein, *Shaker Experience in America*, p. 174.

7. Ibid., p. 17.

Mount Lebanon Shaker Village

1. Charles Nordhoff, *The Communistic Societies of the United States* (New York: Harper and Brothers, 1875), p. 154.

2. Ibid., p. 172.

3. Priscilla J. Brewer, *Shaker Communities, Shaker Lives* (Hanover: University Press of New England, 1986), p. 228.

4. Stephen J. Stein, *The Shaker Experience in America: A History of the United Society of Believers* (New Haven: Yale University Press, 1992), p. 169.

5. Ibid., p. 201.

6. Nordhoff, *Communistic Societies*, pp. 152–53.

Notes

Hancock Shaker Village

1. Deborah E. Burns, *Shaker Cities of Peace, Love, and Union: A History of the Hancock Bishopric* (Hanover: University Press of New England, 1993).
2. Ibid., pp. 44–46.
3. Nathaniel Hawthorne, quoted in Burns, *Shaker Cities of Peace, Love, and Union*, pp. 121–22.
4. Burns, *Shaker Cities of Peace, Love, and Union*, pp. 150–51.
5. Ibid., p. 140.
6. Ibid., p. 173.

Canterbury Shaker Village

1. Charles Nordhoff, *The Communistic Societies of the United States* (New York: Harper and Brothers, 1875), p. 186.
2. Ibid., p. 184.

The Shaker Museum

1. Stephen J. Stein, *The Shaker Experience in America: A History of the United Society of Believers* (New Haven: Yale University Press, 1992), pp. 146–47.

Shaker Village of Pleasant Hill

1. From the *Richmond Enquirer*, April–May 1825, quoted in E. G. Swem, ed., *Letters on Kentucky, 1825* (New York: C. T. Heartman, 1916).
2. Elmer R. Pearson and Julia Neal, *The Shaker Image*, 2d ed. (Pittsfield: Hancock Shaker Village, Inc., 1994), p. 42.
3. Charles Nordhoff, *The Communistic Societies of the United States* (New York: Harper and Brothers, 1875), p. 212.
4. Ibid., p. 214.

Shakertown at South Union

1. Stephen J. Stein, *The Shaker Experience in America: A History of the United Society of Believers* (New Haven: Yale University Press, 1992), p. 57.

Old Economy

1. From the *Annals of the Congress of the United States, 1789–1824* (42 vols., Washington, D.C.: 1834–56), 9th Cong., 1st sess., 1805–6, quoted in William E. Wilson, *The Angel and the Serpent: The Story of New Harmony* (Bloomington: Indiana University Press, 1964), pp. 217–18.
2. George B. Lockwood, *The New Harmony Movement* (New York: D. Appleton and Company, 1905), pp. 9–10.
3. Richard D. Wetzel, *Frontier Musicians on the Connoquenessing, Wabash, and Ohio: A History of the Music and Musicians of George Rapp's Harmony Society (1805–1906)* (Athens: Ohio University Press, 1976), p. 17.
4. Karl J. R. Arndt, ed., *A Documentary History of the Indiana Decade of the Harmony Society, 1814–1824*, vol. 1, *1814–1819* (Indianapolis: Indiana Historical Society, 1975), p. 775.
5. Ibid., p. 10.
6. Wetzel, *Frontier Musicians*, p. 25.
7. Arndt, *1814–1819*, p. 613.

Notes

8. Ibid., p. xii.

9. John S. Duss, *The Harmonists, a Personal History* (Philadelphia: Porcupine Press, 1972), pp. 310–11.

10. Arndt, *1814–1819*, p. ix.

11. Karl J. R. Arndt, *George Rapp's Successors and Material Heirs, 1847–1916* (Rutherford: Fairleigh Dickinson University Press, 1971), pp. 190–91.

Zoar Village State Memorial

1. Charles Nordhoff, *The Communistic Societies of the United States* (New York: Harper and Brothers, 1875), p. 104.

2. Karl J. R. Arndt, *A Documentary History of the Indiana Decade of the Harmony Society, 1814–1824*, vol. 1, *1814–1819* (Indianapolis: Indiana Historical Society, 1975), p. 379.

3. Ibid., pp. 544–45.

4. Ibid.

5. Nordhoff, *Communistic Societies*, p. 106.

6. Karl J. R. Arndt, *A Documentary History of the Indiana Decade of the Harmony Society, 1814–1824*, vol. 2, *1820–1824* (Indianapolis: Indiana Historical Society, 1978), p. 152.

7. William A. Hinds, *American Communities* (Oneida, N.Y.: American Socialist, 1878), p. 130.

8. Ibid., p. 107.

9. Nordhoff, *Communistic Societies*, pp. 109–10.

10. Ibid., p. 109.

11. Victor Peters, "The German Pietists: Spiritual Mentors of the German Communal Settlements in America," *Communal Societies* 1 (1981): 61.

12. William A. Hinds, *American Communities and Co-Operative Colonies* (Chicago: C. H. Kerr, 1878), p. 104.

Historic New Harmony

1. Robert Owen, *The Life of Robert Owen; Written by Himself, with Selections from His Writings and Correspondence* (1857–58; reprint, New York: Augustus Kelley, 1967), 1:1–2.

2. Margaret Cole, "Robert Owen until New Lanark," in *Robert Owen: Industrialist, Reformer, Visionary, 1771–1858* (London: Robert Owen Bicentenary Association, 1971), pp. 4–14.

3. Owen, *Life of Robert Owen*, 1:34–38.

4. Harold Silver, "Owen's Reputation as an Educationist," in *Robert Owen: Prophet of the Poor*, ed. Sidney Pollard and John Salt (Lewisburg, Pa.: Bucknell University Press, 1971), p. 65.

5. J. Percy Moore, "William Maclure—Scientist and Humanitarian," *Proceedings of the American Philosophical Society* 91, no. 3 (August 1947): 234.

6. John C. Greene, *American Science in the Age of Jefferson* (Ames: Iowa State University Press, 1984), pp. 306–11.

7. E. T. Haney, *The Travels of the Naturalist Charles A. Lesueur in North America, 1815–1837*, ed. and trans. H. F. Raup (Kent, Ohio: Milton Haber, 1968), p. 31.

8. George B. Lockwood, *The New Harmony Movement* (New York: D. Appleton and Company, 1905), p. 84.

Notes

9. Ibid., pp. 105–8.

10. Ibid.

Oneida Community

1. Robert David Thomas, *The Man Who Would Be Perfect, John Humphrey Noyes and the Utopian Impulse* (Philadelphia: University of Pennsylvania Press, 1977), pp. 91–93.

2. John Humphrey Noyes, *Witness* 1 (January 23, 1839), quoted in Lawrence Foster, *Religion and Sexuality: The Shakers, the Mormons, and the Oneida Community* (Urbana: University of Illinois Press, 1984), p. 83.

3. Foster, *Religion and Sexuality*, p. 77.

4. Maren Lockwood Carden, *Oneida: Utopian Community to Modern Corporation* (Baltimore: Johns Hopkins Press, 1969), p. 6.

5. Foster, *Religion and Sexuality*, p. 81.

6. John Humphrey Noyes, *Male Continence* (Oneida, N.Y.: 1872), p. 12.

7. Constance Noyes Robertson, ed., *Oneida Community: An Autobiography, 1851–1876* (Syracuse, N.Y.: Syracuse University Press, 1970), pp. 9–10.

8. Ira L. Mandelker, *Religion, Society, and Utopia in Nineteenth-Century America* (Amherst: University of Massachusetts Press, 1984), p. 125.

9. Foster, *Religion and Sexuality*, p. 103.

10. Pierrepont Noyes, *My Father's House, an Oneida Boyhood* (New York: Farrar and Rinehart, 1937), pp. 132–33.

11. Robertson, *Oneida Community*, p. 54.

12. [John Humphrey Noyes?], *Mutual Criticism* (1876; reprint, with an introduction by Murray Levine and Barbara Benedict Bunker, Syracuse, N.Y.: Syracuse University Press, 1975).

13. [Noyes?], *Mutual Criticism*, p. 39.

14. Foster, *Religion and Sexuality*, p. 95.

15. Robert Allerton Parker, *A Yankee Saint: John Humphrey Noyes and the Oneida Community* (New York: G. P. Putnam's Sons, 1935), pp. 256–57.

16. Ibid., pp. 259–61.

17. *Circular* (April 3, 1965), quoted in Robertson, *Oneida Community*, pp. 343–44.

18. Robertson, *Oneida Community*, p. 337.

19. Ibid., p. 340.

20. Ibid.

21. Carden, *Oneida*, p. 102.

22. John Humphrey Noyes, "Proposal for a Modification of Our Social Platform," (August 20, 1879), quoted in Constance Noyes Robertson, *Oneida Community: The Breakup, 1876–1881* (Syracuse, N.Y.: Syracuse University Press, 1972), pp. 154–55.

23. Carden, *Oneida*, pp. 104, 123.

24. Ibid., p. 141.

25. Dolores Hayden, *Seven American Utopias: The Architecture of Communitarian Socialism, 1700–1975* (Cambridge, Mass.: MIT Press, 1976), p. 190.

26. John Humphrey Noyes, *History of American Socialisms* (Philadelphia: J. B. Lippincott and Company, 1870), pp. 641–43.

Fruitlands

1. Madelon Bedell, *The Alcotts: Biography of a Family* (New York: Clarkson N. Potter, 1980), p. 132.

2. Louisa May Alcott, *Transcendental Wild Oats* (Harvard, Mass: Harvard Common Press, 1981), pp. 84–86.

Notes

3. Ibid., p. 90.

4. Ibid.

5. Ibid., pp. 55–56.

6. Bedell, *Alcotts*, p. 258.

Historic Bethel German Colony and Old Aurora Colony Museum

1. Adolf E. Schroeder, *Bethel German Colony, 1844–1879, Religious Beliefs and Practices* (Bethel, Mo.: Historic Bethel German Colony, 1990), p. 13.

2. Mark Holloway, *Heavens on Earth: Utopian Communities in America, 1680–1880*, 2d ed. (New York: Dover Publications, 1966), p. 161.

3. Schroeder, *Bethel German Colony*, p. 3.

4. Ibid., pp. 4–5.

5. David Nelson Duke, "The Evolution of Religion in Wilhelm Keil's Community: A New Reading of Old Testimony," *Communal Societies* 13 (1993): 88.

6. Schroeder, *Bethel German Colony*, p. 4.

7. William A. Hinds, *American Communities* (Oneida, N.Y.: American Socialist, 1878), pp. 327–28.

8. Charles Nordhoff, *The Communistic Societies of the United States* (New York: Harper and Brothers, 1875), pp. 318–19.

9. Ibid., p. 318.

10. Ibid., p. 319.

11. William A. Hinds, *American Communities and Co-operative Colonies* (1908; reprint, Philadelphia: Porcupine Press, 1975), p. 338.

Bishop Hill

1. Paul Elmen, *Wheat Flour Messiah: Eric Jansson of Bishop Hill* (Carbondale: Southern Illinois University Press, 1976), p. 3.

2. Olov Isaksson, *Bishop Hill, Ill.: A Utopia on the Prairie* (Stockholm, Sweden: LT Publishing House, 1969), p. 32.

3. Ibid., pp. 47–48.

4. Elmen, *Wheat Flour Messiah*, p. 68.

5. Ibid., p. 100.

6. Ibid., p. 30.

7. Charles H. Nelson, "Toward a More Complete Approximation of the Class Composition of the Erik Janssonists," *Swedish Pioneer Historical Quarterly* 26, no. 1 (1975).

8. Elmen, *Wheat Flour Messiah*, p. 60.

9. Ibid., p. 160.

10. Ibid.

11. Isaksson, *Bishop Hill*, p. 132.

12. Ibid., p. 134.

Amana Colonies

1. Francis Alan Duval, "Christian Metz, German-American Religious Leader and Pioneer" (Ph.D. dissertation, University of Iowa, 1948), p. 50.

2. Ibid., p. 54.

3. Ibid., p. 58.

4. Ibid., p. 60.

5. Diane L. Barthel, *Amana: From Pietist Sect to American Community* (Lincoln: University of Nebraska Press, 1984), pp. 14–15.

6. Duval, "Christian Metz," p. 80.

Notes

7. Henry Schiff, "Before and after 1932: A Memoir," *Communal Societies* 4 (1984): 162.

8. Barthel, *Amana*, p. 23.

9. Charles Nordhoff, *The Communistic Societies of the United States* (New York: Harper and Brothers, 1875), pp. 40–41.

10. Duval, "Christian Metz," p. 271.

11. Johanthan G. Andelson, "Communalism and Change in the Amana Colonies" (Ph.D. dissertation, University of Michigan, 1974), p. 104.

12. Nordhoff, *Communistic Societies*, p. 35.

13. Barthel, *Amana*, pp. 46–47.

14. Bertha M. H. Shambaugh, *Amana That Was and Amana That Is* (Iowa City: State Historical Society of Iowa, 1932), pp. 184–86.

15. Nordhoff, *Communistic Societies*, p. 35.

16. Eberhard Ludwig Gruber, *Nothiges und nutzliches Gesprach, von der wahren und falshen Inspiration* (1716; reprint,1859), pp. 69–70, quoted in Walter Grossmann, "The European Origins of the True Inspired of Amana," *Communal Societies* 4 (1984): 142.

17. Barthel, *Amana*, pp. 88–89.

18. Ibid., pp. 102–3.

Historic Rugby

1. Thomas Hughes, *Rugby Tennessee, Being Some Account of the Settlement Founded on the Cumberland Plateau* (London: Macmillan, 1881), p. 106.

2. Ibid., p. 125.

3. Thomas Hughes, *Tom Brown's Schooldays* (London: Macmillan, 1857), preface.

4. James Russell Lowell, quoted in Edward C. Mack and W. H. G. Armytage, *Thomas Hughes: The Life of the Author of Tom Brown's Schooldays* (London: Ernest Benn, 1952), pp. 61–67.

5. Mack and Armytage, *Thomas Hughes*, pp. 184–85.

6. Ibid., pp. 188, 198.

7. Hughes, *Rugby Tennessee*, p. 96.

8. Ibid., p. 99.

9. Ibid., p. l00.

10. Mack and Armytage, *Thomas Hughes*, pp. 151–52.

11. Ibid., p. 252.

12. Hughes, *Rugby Tennessee*, p. 99.

Koreshan State Historic Site

1. Cyrus Teed, *The Illumination of Koresh: Marvelous Experiences of the Great Alchemist Thirty Years Ago, at Utica, N.Y.* (Chicago: Guiding Star Publishing House, n.d. [c. 1899]), pp. 7–8.

2. Ibid., pp. 12–17.

3. William A. Hinds, *American Communities and Co-operative Colonies* (Chicago: C. H. Kerr, 1908), pp. 483.

4. James E. Landing, "Cyrus R. Teed, Koreshanity, and Cellular Cosmogony," *Communal Societies* 1 (1981): 10.

5. John S. Duss, *The Harmonists, a Personal History* (Philadelphia: Porcupine Press, 1972), pp. 197–302.

6. Karl J. R. Arndt, *George Rapp's Successors and Material Heirs, 1847–1916* (Rutherford: Fairleigh Dickinson University Press, 1971), p. 172.

7. Duss, *Harmonists*, pp. 297–300.

Notes

8. Landing, "Cyrus R. Teed," p. 12.
9. Hinds, *American Communities and Co-operative Colonies*, pp. 480–81.
10. Ibid., p. 476.

INDEX

Index

Index

Index

Index

Index

Index

Index

Index

Index

Index